Cataloging Hebrew Materials
in the Online Environment

Cataloging Hebrew Materials in the Online Environment

A Comparative Study of American and Israeli Approaches

Susan S. Lazinger
School of Library, Archive & Information Studies
The Hebrew University of Jerusalem

Elhanan Adler
Coordinator, Israel Inter-University Library Network

Edited by Sheila S. Intner
Simmons College

With a Foreword by
Bella Hass Weinberg
St. John's University

1998
Libraries Unlimited, Inc.
Englewood, Colorado

LIBRARIES UNLIMITED, INC.
P.O. Box 6633
Englewood, CO 80155-6633
1-800-237-6124
www.lu.com

Production Editor: Kevin W. Perizzolo
Proofreader: Shannon Graff
Indexer: Jean Weihs
Typesetter: Judy Gay Matthews

Library of Congress Cataloging-in-Publication Data

Lazinger, Susan S. (Susan Smernoff)
    Cataloging Hebrew materials in the online environment : a
comparative study of American and Israeli approaches / by Susan S.
Lazinger, Elhanan Adler ; edited by Sheila S. Intner ; with a
foreword by Bella Hass Weinberg.
    xvi, 224 p. 22x28 cm.
    Includes bibliographical references and index.
    ISBN 1-56308-358-2
    1. Cataloging of Hebrew imprints--United States--Data processing.
2. Cataloging of Hebrew imprints--Israel--Data processing.
I. Adler, Elhanan. II. Intner, Sheila S. III. Title.
Z695.1.J48L39   1998
025.3--dc21   97-35508
                                                        CIP

To my children, Laura, Peter, and Shira,
who taught me how to spin straw into time.
Susan Lazinger

To my wife Chaya
רבות בנות עשו חיל ואת עלית על כלנה
Elhanan Adler

CONTENTS

5: Headings and Uniform Titles: American and Israeli Practices *(cont.)*

Part II: Hebraica Library Automation

FOREWORD

A number of years ago, Professor Sheila Intner invited me to write a manual of Hebraica cataloging for a series she was then editing. As I recall, I declined for three reasons: (1) I was swamped with other publication projects at the time (primarily the revision of the American National Standard for thesaurus construction), (2) it was my opinion that *manuals* of Hebraica cataloging should be produced by the Library of Congress (LC), whose practice, which cannot be predicted by anyone outside the Institution, most Judaica libraries follow; Paul Maher's *Hebraica Cataloging* had been published by LC shortly before Sheila's invitation, (3) at the invitation of Mohammad Aman, I had written a lengthy chapter surveying *issues* in Hebraica and Judaica cataloging, which appeared in *Cataloging and Classification of Non-Western Material* in 1980. Not all that much had changed since then, as the many quotations from that chapter in this book demonstrate.

I am pleased that Professor Intner subsequently succeeded in lining up two of Israels' leading librarians (with whom she no doubt became acquainted during the year of her Fulbright fellowship in Israel, 1992-1993) to write a book of much broader scope than a manual of Hebraica cataloging practice—a work that discusses the *why*, not just the *how*, of Hebraica and Judaica cataloging.

It is particularly meaningful to me that the focus of this book, a comparison of American and Israeli approaches, is based on the theme I suggested for the cataloging session of the First International Conference of Israeli and Judaica Librarians, held in Jerusalem in 1990. The letter inviting me to speak at that session was written by the late Amnon Zipin, the driving force behind that landmark conference. Volume 7 of *Judaica Librarianship*, containing the proceedings of the symposium of Jewish children's literature held in conjunction with the conference, was dedicated to his memory, and this book, which so frequently cites the research papers published in a special section of volume 6 of the journal, serves as further tribute to Amnon's memory.

My editorial accompanying the papers from the research sessions of the International Conference was entitled "Bringing Judaica Librarianship to Israel." In it I recorded the proposal for a Judaica librarian's organization in Israel (subsequently named the Judaica Librarians' Group), which was made by Ya'akov Arons at the Jerusalem conference, after the session on Hebrew subject headings. Gita Hoffman's paper on that subject, as well as the papers from the aforementioned cataloging session, are frequently cited in this work.

It is somewhat ironic that two Israeli librarians have codified current American Judaica cataloging practice. Both Susan Lazinger and Elhanan Adler were born in the United States, but the fact that they reside in Israel makes it possible for them to examine American Judaica cataloging policies critically and comparatively.

This work will surely be of interest to Hebraica and Judaica catalogers the world over, in research collections as well as in synagogue and religious school libraries. From a religious perspective, the work is of interest not only to Jewish librarians but also to those of other faiths. In teaching Information Sources in Religion at St. John's University it has been a source of satisfaction to me that Christian students have done studies of subject analysis for their denominations that were modeled on those done for Judaica cataloging.

Given the current emphasis on multiculturalism and multilingualism, the book is relevant to all librarians interested in providing access to their collections in the native languages of their readers. I hope that this book will also be read by catalogers in other nonroman script communities, including Arabic, Cyrillic, and Chinese-Japanese-Korean. As was noted in the conclusion of my lecture "Non-Roman Scripts in the Library of the Future" (presented by invitation at Brandeis University, March 11, 1996), catalogers working with one nonroman script rarely read the specialized journals or newsletters of those working with a different one, despite the commonality of issues. This has led to reinventing the wheel and to duplicating efforts in lobbying for change. The issuance of this book by a major library science publisher will, I hope, guarantee its wide distribution, as well as encourage readership outside the Hebraica cataloging community.

This book is relevant not just to catalogers but also to Judaica reference librarians, for it is not possible to provide effective reference without an understanding of the structure of catalogs, and Hebraica catalogs are particularly complex. I hope that library administrators will read this book as well, to understand the resources needed for the provision of thorough access to Hebraica collections. The extensive historical treatment of Hebrew spelling, romanization, and bibliography render the book of potential interest to scholars in many branches of Jewish studies and library science.

I thank Dr. Lazinger and Mr. Adler for producing a work that can serve as a text for my course on Hebraica and Judaica Cataloging (taught biennally at the Max Weinreich Center for Advanced Jewish Studies of the YIVO Institute for Jewish Research in New York). This is a book for experienced Hebraica catalogers as well as for students. The former are so often caught up with chasing the latest rule or heading that they forget *why* they are providing access in a certain way. As so many American Judaica librarians are currently planning for automation of their catalogs, the book is particularly timely—facilitating a review of principles and consideration of alternative approaches to input, indexing, and display of Hebrew bibliographic data, policies that can be determined locally, in contrast to cataloging standards.

As the Editor of *Judaica Librarianship*, I am proud of the many authors whose papers are cited in this work. I trust that those contributors whose manuscripts were returned for further amplification, clarification, illustration, and documentation will grant that better articles resulted from this time-consuming process. (Writing this Foreword gives me the opportunity to preserve for posterity Elhanan Adler's pronouncement at the Harvard conference on Judaica Librarianship: Facing the Future, held in 1988. Alluding to a forthcoming paper he said, "The next issue of *Judaica Librarianship* will appear whenever Bella gets it out!") I know that this book has also been long in the making, as the original proposal was submitted in 1993; I can appreciate the time and effort that went into it.

All those associated with the production of this book have been (and will, I hope, continue to be) important contributors to *Judaica Librarianship*. Elhanan Adler has published in *JL* seminal articles on the exchange of Hebraica cataloging data between Israel and the United States, as well as valued columns on library automation in Israel. Susan Lazinger for many years contributed an excellent column surveying developments in Judaica libraries in Israel. Her list of master's theses in Judaica librarianship produced in Israel (published in volume 6) provides evidence for her mastery of the research literature in this discipline. Susan Lazinger's and Elhanan Adler's important contribution to general library periodicals demonstrate their leadership in the field of catalog automation in Israel.

The chapters relating to the Hebrew capability of the Research Libraries Information Network (RLIN) and nonroman character sets have been reviewed by Joan Aliprand of the Research Libraries Group, who has contributed major articles on those subjects to *Judaica Librarianship*. It was a pleasure to work with Ms. Aliprand in the mid-1980s on the design of RLIN's Hebrew capability and to consult with her since then on the standardization of the Hebraic character set and related issues. The entire book has been edited by Professor Sheila Intner, well known for her books on general cataloging, and valued as a contributing editor (referee) for the Catalog Department of *Judaica Librarianship*. It has been fun to work with these friends and colleagues on this important book, which I hope will stimulate further research into and analysis of Hebraica and Judaica cataloging practice for many years to come.

To conclude with Gematria (Hebrew numerology) we may note that this overview of Hebraica cataloging is appearing 17 years after my chapter in the Aman book; that number is the value of the Hebrew word *tov* (good), and the publication of this work is unquestionably a good thing. My chapter was published at the dawn of the era of computerization of nonroman scripts; Lazinger and Adler's work is appearing during a time when Hebrew script is available on the network level but only in a few local library catalogs in the United States. It will be interesting to see how the field of Judaica librarianship will have changed in another 17 years—not just in terms of technology, but also from the perspective of cataloging principles.

Conferences are now being scheduled for the design of the third edition of Anglo-American Cataloging Rules (AACR3). The special characteristics of Hebraica and works in other nonroman scripts have, in my view, not been adequately addressed in AACR2 and its Library of Congress Rule Interpretations. I hope that this book will be studied by the members of the Joint Steering Committee on AACR for the purpose of creating a new cataloging code that is truly international in its scope and theoretical basis.

Bella Hass Weinberg
Professor
Division of Library and Information Science
St. John's University
Jamaica, NY
and
Consulting Librarian
YIVO Institute for Jewish Research
New York, NY

INTRODUCTION

When we started work on this book several years ago, we planned to write a comprehensive text for beginning and intermediate catalogers in English explaining the rules and traditions of descriptive and subject cataloging of Hebrew-alphabet materials, focusing on the two major languages in this alphabet, Hebrew and Yiddish. As often happens, the book took on a life of its own as we were gathering material, organizing chapters, and analyzing problems, and in the end turned into something different and, we hope, something more.

Throughout the years, the two centers of Hebrew cataloging—the Library of Congress and The Jewish National and University Library in Jerusalem—have followed very different traditions in their approach to the organization of this material, and these two major traditions must be traced both historically and in their contemporary manifestations, as exemplified in Hebraica cataloging in Israel's ALEPH-based academic library network and in America's RLIN system, in order to understand where Hebrew cataloging is today. Thus, in the first part of the book, "Traditions and Practices," we have explored and explained these two traditions back to their roots in the seventeenth century and summarized the various rules, customs and romanization systems that have sprung from these differing traditions.

In the second part of the book we discuss Hebraica library automation, again exploring the differences between the American and Israeli scene, with an emphasis on the two major bibliographic networks with vernacular Hebrew cataloging capability—America's RLIN and Israel's ALEPH-based academic library network. We close with an analysis of the potential for exchanging Hebrew bibliographic data and a forecast of the implications of automation for the future of Hebrew cataloging worldwide.

This book then is meant to be both a comprehensive text for catalogers and a historical-comparative chronicle of the major Hebrew cataloging and classification traditions in the two centers. In its role as basic textbook for English-speaking catalogers of Hebrew materials for determining how to approach this significant and growing body of bibliographic material, *Cataloging Hebrew Materials in the Online Environment* gives rules for formulating headings and uniform titles; analyzes and demonstrates systems for transliteration and transcription (we use ALA/LC romanization throughout); and traces classification systems for Judaica, Hebraica and Israelitica (material in or about Israel) historically and structurally. In its role as a historical and comparative work, it explores and compares the approaches of the two bibliographic networks with vernacular Hebrew cataloging capability—America's RLIN and Israel's ALEPH—and analyzes the potential and problems involved in the growing need for exchange of Hebrew bibliographic data between the practitioners of the two traditions. Synthesizing both its roles, it is meant to provide librarians with Internet access to Israeli systems with both the historical understanding and the specific tools they need to search and understand their catalogs.

Cataloging Hebrew Materials in the Online Environment is intended as a reference work for catalogers and database managers in all research libraries with Middle Eastern studies programs or Hebrew language or literature collections, both in America and throughout the world. We believe it will be useful not just for scholarly collections but for all libraries that deal with Hebrew language materials. Because we have attempted to be comprehensive in our coverage of the material, there will be sections that are of interest primarily to those seeking a historical explanation of the differing approaches, and sections of interest primarily to those seeking transliteration tables and specific rules—a step-by-step, "how to" approach. In the final analysis, however, we hope and expect that our book will provide everything you always wanted to know about Hebrew cataloging and didn't know where to find.

Acknowledgements

We would like to express our gratitude for the support, both financial and moral, of a number of both institutions and individuals.

First, a deep debt of gratitude is owed to Israel's Department of Libraries, Division of Arts and Culture, Ministry of Science and Arts for its generous financial support through a grant from the **Ruth Kahan Eber Fund For Research in Librarianship** (to the first author) to assist in the research and writing of this book.

Next, we would like to express our thanks to Professor Bluma C. Peritz, Director of the School of Library, Archive and Information Studies of The Hebrew University of Jerusalem, for giving generously of her advice (including advice on obtaining funding), of her encouragement, and of the use of the facilities of the school throughout the long process of researching and writing this book.

Finally, we would like to thank all the individuals with whom we consulted on various questions and problems during the writing process itself: Joan Aliprand of RLG, who read and contributed extensive advice and technical expertise on several chapters; John Eilts of RLG, who also answered questions and prevented our including inaccurate information on several issues involving RLIN; Paul Maher, of the Library of Congress; Aviva Shichor and Karniya Dan of Haifa Library; Rosalie Katchen of Brandeis University; Judith Levi of Ex-Libris, Inc., and many other colleagues in both Israel and the United States who answered our endless questions.

To all these people and organizations, we express our profound gratitude for their generous assistance. Much of what is correct in this book we owe to them; anything that is not is entirely ours.

Susan S. Lazinger
Elhanan Adler
Jerusalem
March 1997

Part I: Traditions and Practices

1 Traditional Hebraica Bibliography

Hebrew bibliography can be approached in two ways. The first, or chronological, approach is typified by Shimeon Brisman's organization in his chapter on General Hebraica Bibliographies in *A History and Guide to Judaica Bibliography*.[1] The second, or categorical, approach can be seen in the pair of articles by Elhanan Adler and Bella Hass Weinberg on the Hebrew bibliographic and Israeli traditions and Anglo-American traditions in Judaica cataloging published in 1992 in *Judaica Librarianship*.[2] This second approach divides bibliographic description of Hebrew books into two further approaches or categories: the "integrative" approach, which uses roman-character description as far as possible, entering only minimal data (if any) in Hebrew characters, and the "standalone," purely Hebrew approach. Since the segregated versus the integrated approach to Hebrew bibliography and Hebrew cataloging will be analyzed in depth in the next chapter, "Hebrew Descriptive Cataloging: Segregated or Integrated?", we will precede this categorical analysis with a brief chronological introduction to the major milestones in traditional Hebraica bibliography, a la (and heavily based on) Brisman, in this chapter.

Modern Jewish bibliography began in the seventeenth century with the publication of the first organized list of Hebrew books by a Swiss scholar, Johannes Buxtorf. Buxtorf became fascinated with Hebrew during his studies at the German universities of Marburg and Herborn, and later at the Swiss university of Basel, where he was subsequently appointed professor of Hebrew. He published a number of scholarly works on Jewish topics, such as Jewish laws and Hebrew grammar, and in 1613, he appended to his lexicographical work, *De abbreviaturis hebraicis*, a small volume listing 324 Hebrew works by title in alphabetical order, based on his own

---

[1]Shimeon Brisman, *A History and Guide to Judaic Bibliography* (New York: KTAV; Cincinnati: Hebrew Union College, 1977); (His Jewish Research Literature; vol. 1) (Bibliographica Judaica; 7), p. 2-35.

[2]Elhanan Adler, "Judaica Cataloging: The Hebrew Bibliographic and Israeli Traditions," *Judaica Librarianship* 6 (Spring 1991-Winter 1992): 8-12; Bella Hass Weinberg, "Judaica and Hebraica Cataloging: Anglo-American Traditions," *Judaica Librarianship* 6 (Spring 1991-Winter 1992): 13-23.

extensive Hebrew book collection. Entitled *Bibliotheca Rabbinica*,[3] it listed both printed and handwritten Hebrew works, with the entries (titles) in Hebrew characters and descriptive text, including transliterations and translations of the titles in Latin.[4]

Bibliotheca Rabbinica is significant in the history of Jewish bibliography for several reasons. First, it was the first list in a single volume of hundreds of printed and handwritten Hebrew works according to accepted rules of bibliography. Second, for centuries it determined the format of Hebrew bibliography by introducing the arrangement by title. Third, it generated an entire generation of bibliographers, both Christian and Jewish, who established Hebraica bibliography as an independent branch of universal bibliography.[5]

Although Buxtorf's *Bibliotheca Rabbinica* was the first bibliography devoted exclusively to Jewish literature, it covered only a small part of the overall titles in existence at the time. The first bibliographer to attempt to register in one work everything written by and about Jews was an Italian priest named Giulio Bartolocci. Born in Celleno, Italy, in 1613, the year that Buxtorf published *Bibliotheca Rabbinica*, Bartolocci spent decades of intensive planning and research of his project before the first volume of his bibliography of Hebrew works, *Bibliotheca magna rabbinica*, was published in Rome in 1675.[6] It was bilingual with two titles, one in Hebrew and the other in Latin. The Hebrew title, *Kiryat Sefer* (based on Joshua 15:15) would later be adopted for several other Hebrew bibliographies including, eventually, the national bibliography of Israel. Bartolocci died in 1687 before completing his monumental work, and the fourth and final volume of *Bibliotheca magna rabbinica* was edited and prepared by his student, Carlo Giuseppi Imbonati, and published in Rome in 1693, six years after Bartolocci's death. The massive four-volume *Bibliotheca magna rabbinica*—with nearly 3500 pages; 1,960 entries; and Hebrew and Latin indexes of titles, cross-references, subjects, and authors' and place names—was the first comprehensive Hebrew bibliography.[7]

At the same time that Bartolocci was working on the third volume of his *Bibliotheca*, a scholar in Amsterdam was working on what turned out to be the first Jewish bibliography compiled by a Jew. Shabbetai ben Joseph, the first significant Jewish bibliographer, was born in Poland in 1641 and educated in Prague, where he took the surname Bass. A clerk in a bookstore, he learned Latin and some Greek and acquired an interest in bibliography. Aware of the need for an all-inclusive Jewish bibliography, he began accumulating information for this project. Around 1670, when the government of Prague closed down all Jewish printing shops, he set out on travels

---

[3] Johannes Buxtorf, *Bibliotheca Rabbinica* (Basileae: Typis C. Waldkirchi, impensis L. Koenig, 1613).

[4] Shimeon Brisman, *A History and Guide to Judaic Bibliography,* p. 4-5.

[5] Shimeon Brisman, *A History and Guide to Judaic Bibliography*, p. 5.

[6] Giulio Bartolocci, *Kiryat sefer. Bibliotheca magna rabbinica de scriptoribus, et scriptis hebraicis, ordine alphabetico Hebraice et Latine digestis* (Romae: ex typographia Sacrae congregationis de propaganda fide, 1675-1693), 4 vols.

[7] Shimeon Brisman, *A History and Guide to Judaic Bibliography,* 7-8.

to Poland, Germany and Holland, where he compiled material for his bibliography. In 1679 Bass settled in Amsterdam and accepted a job as proofreader in a Jewish printing house. There he made friends with rabbis, scholars and wealthy book collectors and utilized their libraries of Hebrew books for his bibliography. In 1680 he published the first Hebraica bibliography compiled by a Jewish scholar and written entirely in Hebrew, including about 2,200 printed and handwritten titles (of which about 265 were duplications).[8]

Sifte yeshenim,[9] as Bass called his work, was divided into four sections:

  a. a two-part subject index;
  b. a list of titles (the body of the book);
  c. an author index; and
  d. a list of Judaica by non-Jewish writers.

In the author index Bass listed alphabetically all the authors referred to in the list of titles, Ashenazic authors by their second names and Italian and Sephardic authors by their first names. In the final section of the book, in which he listed about 150 Judaica works by non-Jewish scholars, he includes the bibliographies of Buxtorf and Bartolocci, giving us a glimpse of some of the sources he used.[10]

While Buxtorf and Bartolocci designed their Hebraica bibliographies primarily for the use of Christian Hebraists, what is most significant about Bass's bibliography is that it was compiled exclusively for the Jewish reader. Furthermore, as Adler points out, it set the pattern of entry approach for the Jewish bibliographers who followed him:

> Bass's work, while of no practical use today, was the first attempt to create a Hebrew bibliography for the Jewish public. It records books by title, with an index by author (forename entry) and a rudimentary subject index. This title-entry approach was followed by both Ben-Yaakov and Friedberg.[11]

Once Bass had laid the groundwork for Jewish bibliography in the seventeenth century, it began to flourish. During the eighteenth century at least two biblio-graphical works were published that can be traced directly to the earlier work of Bass. The author of the first bibliography, Johann Christoph Wolf, can be considered the last of the great Christian bibliographers of Jewish literature. His *Bibliotheca hebraea*[12] was published in three volumes over a period of 18 years, with the first volume appearing in Hamburg in 1715, three years before Bass's death. The publication of Wolf's *Bibliotheca hebraea*, according to Brisman, ushered in a new era in Jewish

---

[8] Shimeon Brisman, *A History and Guide to Judaic Bibliography,* 9-10, 30.

[9] Shabbetai Bass, *Sifte yeshenim* (Amsterdam: David Tartas, 1680).

[10] Shimeon Brisman, *A History and Guide to Judaic Bibliography,* 9-12.

[11] Elhanan Adler, "Judaica Cataloging: The Hebrew Bibliographic and Israeli Traditions": 8.

[12] Johann Christophe Wolf, *Bibliotheca hebraea...*(Hamburgi: Christian Liebezeit, 1715-1733).

bibliography. While acknowledging his indebtedness to Bass as well as Bertolocci, he did not rely blindly on their information, but rather investigated every fact and detail in their works, critically reexamined all entries in the light of new sources and incorporated them into his work. The *Bibliotheca hebraea* (*hebraea* rather than merely *rabbinica*) attempted to include everything written in Hebrew up to the year 1700. It was the only work of such magnitude started and completed by a single author and became the basis for the greatest Jewish bibliography of the nineteenth century, Moritz Steinschneider's *Catalogus* of the Hebraica collection in Oxford's Bodleian Library.[13]

Bass's other contemporary, Rabbi Jehiel ben Solomon Heilprin (1660-1746), contributed in fact far less to Hebraica bibliography than his Christian contemporary, Wolff. His major work of Jewish chronology entitled *Seder ha-dorot* included a section on Jewish authors and their Hebrew works[14] copied verbatim from Shabbetai Bass's *Sifte yeshenim*, except for some minor additions of authors and titles Bass overlooked and some omissions of data Bass included in his bibliography, such as biographical data and places of publication. The real significance of Heilprin's work was that by including a bibliography section in his great work of Jewish chronology, he gave Jewish bibliography status among Jewish scholars.[15]

Only one effort toward compiling a complete Jewish bibliography, including both Hebraica and Judaica, is know to exist, the *Bibliotheca Judaica: Bibliographisches Handbuch der gesammten Judischen Literatur* by Julius Fürst.[16] Born in Poland in 1805, Fürst studied at the yeshiva of the renowned Rabbi Akiba Eger in Poznan, then attended the universities of Breslau and Halle, receiving his doctorate at the latter in 1832. He later settled in Leipzig, where he was eventually appointed professor of Semitic languages at the university there. His greatest achievement among his many literary activities was his three-volume bibliography of Hebraica and Judaica. Written in German, the *Bibliotheca Judaica* has been estimated to include some 40,000 titles, of which between 13,500 and 18,000 (depending on various estimates) are Hebraica. Unlike the bibliographies described above, the entries were arranged alphabetically by author, with an index of Hebrew titles appended to volume three. In spite of gaps in what was intended to be a listing of all the Hebraica and Judaica printed up to and including the year 1840, as well as a number of works attributed to the wrong authors, the *Bibliotheca Judaica* was the only attempt ever made at compiling an all-inclusive bibliography of Hebraica and Judaica together. In spite of its faults, it remains a useful tool of Judaica research, particularly of German Judaica, even today.[17]

---

[13] Shimeon Brisman, *A History and Guide to Judaic Bibliography,* 12-15.

[14] Jehiel Heilprin, *Seder meḥabrim ve-seder sefarim* (Karlsruhe: Johann Friedrich Cornelius Stern, 1769 (third part of his *Seder ha-dorot*).

[15] Shimeon Brisman, *A History and Guide to Judaic Bibliography,* 16-17.

[16] Julius Fürst, *Bibliotheca Judaica: Bibliographisches Handbuch der gesammten Judischen Literatur,* Theil 1-3 (Leipzig: Verlag von Wilhelm Engelmann, 1849-1863).

[17] Shimeon Brisman, *A History and Guide to Judaic Bibliography:* 17-19.

Two centuries after the publication of Bass's *Sifte yeshenim* the second all-inclusive, all-Hebrew bibliography appeared. Born in 1858 in Vilna, Lithuania, Jacob Ben-Yaakov was, in fact, the inheritor of the bibliography his father Isaac Ben-Yaakov had spent his life compiling. The elder Ben-Yaakov spent several years in Leipzig, then the center of the book trade, during which time he became acquainted with most of the well-known Jewish German scholars, including the great Hebraica bibliographer Moritz Steinschneider, whose *Catalogus Librorum Hebraeorum in Bibliotheca Bodleiana*[18] (Catalog of the Hebrew Books in the Bodleian Library), published in three volumes between 1852 and 1860, will be discussed in the next chapter in the section on published Hebraica catalogs. It was probably during his Leipzig period that he began planning what he intended to be the definitive bibliography of Hebrew literature. Utilizing every source of information available, editing it three times, and sending the third revision to his friend Steinschneider for verification and annotation, Isaac Ben-Yaakov had managed to prepare the fourth revision of only the first eight letters of the alphabet after receiving Steinschneider's remarks, before he succumbed to a fatal illness in 1853, when his son Jacob was only five years old.

Jacob Ben-Yaakov grew up to become a successful businessman, a participant in the early Zionist congresses, and Theodor Herzl's host when the latter visited Vilna in 1903. But the major passion of his life was improving and publishing his father's bibliographical work. Working with various scholars and bibliographers, but most of all with Steinschneider, Jacob Ben-Yaakov finally published his father's bibliography in 1880 under the title of *Otsar ha-sefarim*.[19] It lists about 15,000 Hebrew (and a selection of Yiddish) works published up to the year 1863 in alphabetical order by title, as well as an estimated 3,000 manuscripts. While Ben-Yaakov's work shows a kinship to Shabbetai Bass's work of two hundred years earlier, it is distinguished from the earlier work by fuller entries, better scholarly quality, and a critical examination of the sources lacking in Bass's work. A sad and interesting postscript to the Ben-Yaakov bibliographical project, which spanned two complete generations, is the never-to-be published second edition of the *Otsar,* which Jacob Ben-Yaakov spent forty-five years preparing. Rejected by the Polish Academy of Sciences, which had earlier agreed to support the project, Ben-Yaakov's manuscript was offered to the Jewish National and University Library in Jerusalem in 1932, six years after his death, but rejected when it was learned that several years would be required to prepare the manuscript for print. During World War II, the holocaust that destroyed Poland's Jewry destroyed Ben-Yaakov's manuscript for the new edition of the *Otsar* as well.[20]

---

[18]Oxford University. Bodleian Library, *A Concise Catalogue of the Hebrew Printed Books in the Bodleian Library*, by A. E. Cowley (Oxford: The Clarendon Press, 1929).

[19]Jacob Ben-Yaakov, *Otsar ha-sefarim* (Vilna: Romm, 1880).

[20] Shimeon Brisman, *A History and Guide to Judaic Bibliography,* 19-23.

Brisman relates that "while Jacob Benjacob, with the help of Moritz Steinschneider, was preparing the supplement volume to his father's Hebrew bibliography, a young man of seventeen became so excited by the *Otsar Hasefarim* that he decided to follow its example."[21] Bernhard (Chaim) Friedberg was born in Cracow, Poland, in 1876, and spent his life as a business man, first dealing in books, then in diamonds. In his travels for business reasons, he visited most of the important libraries of Europe, where he discovered thousands of books that Ben-Yaakov missed. His finds led him to decide to collect the bibliographical information and use it to build what he called the *Bet 'eked sefarim*.[22] Printing of the *Bet 'eked sefarim* began in Antwerp in 1928 and ended in 1931. It listed about 26,000 works in Hebrew, Yiddish and various Jewish dialects, printed up to the year 1900, in alphabetical order by title. It also included a separate list of incunabula and limited edition works, three indexes and a list of several hundred duplicate entries in Ben-Yaakov's *Otsar*. Friedberg's bibliography received mixed reviews from Jewish scholars: on the one hand, his contribution to Jewish bibliography in updating the register of printed Hebraica to the year 1900 was applauded; on the other hand, they compared his scholarship unfavorably to that of Ben-Yaakov, who had mastered the entire field of Jewish literature and utilized all available sources. Friedberg survived the Holocaust and arrived in Israel in 1946, at the age of seventy. There he started preparing a new edition of his *Bet 'eked sefarim,* which was published in four volumes between the years 1950 and 1956 (he died 5 years later, in 1961).[23] The new edition listed about 50,000 various editions of Hebraica, printed up to the year 1950, making it the only all-inclusive Hebraica bibliography to include works printed from the beginning of printing through the first half of the twentieth century,[24] a distinction it retained until the publication on CD-ROM of the *Bibliography of the Hebrew Book 1473-1960* of the Institute for Hebrew Bibliography (Mif 'al ha-bibliyografyah ha-'ivrit) nearly forty years later, in 1994.

The Mif 'al ha-bibliyografyah ha-'ivrit (officially translated as the Institute for Hebrew Bibliography) was founded in 1959 as a direct reaction to the destruction of Hebrew works during the Holocaust, resulting in the real possibility that titles now available in only a few copies would disappear from the world in the next generation, and to the diminished number of Hebrew bibliographers, which left Jewish scholars concerned with the additional worry that within a generation there would be no scholars competent to compile a complete and accurate register of Hebraica. In the early 1950s an Israeli scholar, Dr. Israel Mehlmann, proposed to the Bialik Institute in Jerusalem that it sponsor a plan for compiling an all-inclusive Hebrew bibliography. The Bialik Institute agreed, invited several other Israeli institutions to participate in the project, and in 1959, the Bialik Institute, the Rabbi Kook Institute, the Ministry of Education and Culture of the State of Israel and the Hebrew University of Jerusalem

---

[21] Shimeon Brisman, *A History and Guide to Judaic Bibliography,* 24-25.

[22] Chaim D. Friedberg, *Bet 'eked sefarim* (Antwerp, 1928-1931).

[23] Chaim D. Friedberg, *Bet 'eked sefarim,* 2d ed. (Tel Aviv: 1950-56).

[24] Shimeon Brisman, *A History and Guide to Judaic Bibliography,* 24-26.

signed an agreement to jointly sponsor a project for preparing a complete register of printed Hebraica.

The Mif 'al ha-bibliyografyah ha-'ivrit began its work in 1960 on the premises of the Jewish National and University Library, with a staff of academicians, bibliographers and members of the book trade. A year later, the Rabbi Kook Institute withdrew from the project, but the other three sponsoring institutions continued their support. The estimated time for completing the project was eight to ten years to compile the material, with five years more to print it, and the estimated number of volumes that the bibliography would occupy was twelve to thirteen, listing between 80,000 and 150,000 works.[25] In actuality, the project has still not been completed 37 years after it began, and when the bulk of the bibliography did appear in 1994, it was not in printed volumes, but rather on a CD-ROM.

The Mif 'al established three principles for its bibliography:

1. It would register all books printed in the Hebrew language or in Hebrew characters to 1960.

2. It would register books from actual copies in hand, and not on the basis of other bibliographies, unless not a single copy was known to be extant.

3. It would compile a series of detailed indexes (title, subject, etc.) to supply the user with full access to the information in the bibliography.

The most crucial of the rules for entry were:

1. Arrangement was to be alphabetical by author, with an Anglicized transcription, except for anonymous works.

2. Title and all additional information was to be copied directly from the title page.[26]

In 1963 the Mif 'al published a mimeographed volume (116 leaves) entitled *Ḥoveret le-dugmah*,[27] consisting of five main-entry samples from the letter *alef*. An enlarged, printed edition of the *Ḥoveret* was published a year later, with an added title in English, *Specimen Brochure*.[28] Other additions were an introduction by the chairman of the editorial board, Professor Gershom Scholem, and the "rules of compilation" established by the Mif 'al, both in Hebrew and English.[29]

---

[25] Shimeon Brisman, *A History and Guide to Judaic Bibliography*, 27.

[26] Shimeon Brisman, *A History and Guide to Judaic Bibliography*, p. 28.

[27] Mif 'al ha-bibliyografyah ha-'ivrit, *Ḥoveret le-dugmah* (Jerusalem, 1963). (mimeographed)

[28] Mif 'al ha-bibliyografyah ha-'ivrit, *Ḥoveret le-dugmah* [*Specimen Brochure*] (Jerusalem, 1964).

[29] Shimeon Brisman, *A History and Guide to Judaic Bibliography*, 28.

The world had to wait 30 years for the next publication of the Mif 'al, a CD-ROM edition issued in 1994[30] which included everything printed in Hebrew and Hebrew characters *up* to 1960 except for items entered under the letter *taf.* Since the letter *taf* includes the Hebrew headings for "Bible" [תנ״ך] , "Prayers" [תפילות], and "Talmud" [תלמוד], there is still a significant amount of work to complete.

In describing the "integrative" versus the "standalone" approach to Hebraica bibliography, Adler names Buxtorf's *Bibliotheca* as the prototype of the first, or "American," approach which, by using roman-character description as far as possible and entering only minmal data in Hebrew, allows Hebrew data to be integrated into general catalogs and bibliographies, rendering it useable to some extent even by non-Hebrew readers. The "standalone," or Israeli, approach, which assumes full knowledge of Hebrew and segregates this data from general (roman character) bibliographic data, he traces back to Shabbetai Bass's *Sifte yeshenim.*[31] In the next chapter we shall discuss the complete history of these two traditions, their implementation in the two centers of Hebraica cataloging, and their implications for cataloging Hebrew materials in the online environment.

---

[30] *Bibliography of the Hebrew Book 1473-1960* [CD-ROM] (Jerusalem: EPI/Electronic Pubs. Intl. and the Institute for Hebrew Bibliography, 1994).

[31]Elhanan Adler, "Judaica Cataloging: The Hebrew Bibliographic and Israeli Traditions": 8.

2 Hebraica Descriptive Cataloging: Segregated or Integrated?

The first issue that must be decided in cataloging Hebrew materials—whether to retain or to romanize Hebrew characters—predates the advent of the computer by many years, dating in fact from the 17th century. What is involved here, in addition to problems and decisions with regard to *how* to romanize, if that approach is chosen, and *how much* to catalog in the vernacular if that approach is favored, is the issue of segregated or integrated catalogs or, in computerized catalogs, segregated or integrated access files or indexes. The "integrative" approach uses primarily roman-character access points as far as possible, entering only minimal data (if any) in the Hebrew alphabet, and the "standalone" approach uses primarily Hebrew access points. Romanizing Hebrew characters in cataloging allows Hebrew records to be integrated into roman-character catalogs; cataloging Hebrew publications in the vernacular means separate Hebrew- and roman-character catalogs. In general, and with notable exceptions, the Anglo-Saxon tradition has favored the integrated catalog while Israeli libraries have always maintained separate Hebrew-character catalogs in which all data was retained in Hebrew.

Historically, the "integrative" approach began with the first Hebrew bibliographic work, Johannes Buxtorf's *Bibliotheca Rabbinica* (1613), and continues to this day in cataloging of Hebrew materials outside of Israel.[1] Many American academic libraries have always cataloged nonroman materials in romanized form. The advantage to this approach was that it allowed them to maintain a single catalog in which all entries could be easily read and processed, even if not understood, by all readers and staff. At the same time, the major Judaica libraries in America (both Jewish and non-Jewish) rejected this approach for Hebrew alphabet materials, preferring a mixed cataloging entry in which some elements were entered in

---

[1]Elhanan Adler, "Judaica Cataloging: The Hebrew Bibliographic and Israeli Traditions," *Judaica Librarianship* 6 (Spring 1991-Winter 1992): 8.

romanized (or sometimes anglicized) form while others were retained in the original Hebrew.[2] Thus, there developed two approaches to integration of Hebrew records: full romanization of all Hebrew data and access points, and romanization of access points only. The latter approach was favored by the Library of Congress and most major Judaica libraries outside of Israel.

The "standalone" approach began with the first Hebrew bibliography by a Jew, Shabbetai Bass's *Sifte yeshenim* (1680), and continues to be used in Israeli cataloging practice today.[3] Romanization is used in Israeli libraries only for Israeli and Judaic headings for non-Hebrew materials (primarily Israeli corporate entries and Judaica uniform title entries). Possibly because romanization has never been used for cataloging Hebrew materials in Israel, the countrys' libraries have never bothered to agree on a single method of romanization for what *is* romanized in Israel, making cataloging and searching of romanized headings complicated. Most Israeli libraries, like most American libraries, use the American LC tables, but some, including the Jewish National and University Library, use the Academy of the Hebrew Language scheme. There are significant differences between the two (see Chapter 3: Romanization and Transliteration Systems).

Before launching into a more detailed discussion of the "integrative" versus the "standalone" approaches, a definition of some of the terms involved in Hebrew cataloging is in order. The words *transliteration*, *transcription* and *romanization* are bandied about in the literature of Hebrew cataloging with great frequency and nearly as great inconsistency. The following definitions, from Bella Hass Weinberg's 1974 article on transliteration, are succinct, clear and workable and will serve as our definitions throughout this book:

---

[2]Elhanan Adler, "The State of the Art in Hebrew Library Automation: American and Israeli Standards and Practices," in *Hebrew Studies: Papers Presented at a Colloquium on Resources for Hebraica in Europe Held at the School of Oriental and African Studies, University of London, 11-13 September 1989/11-13 Elul 5749*, edited by Diana Rowlands Smith and Peter Shmuel Salinger. *British Library Occasional Papers* 13, (London: The British Library, 1991), p. 213.

[3]Elhanan Adler, "Judaica Cataloging": 8.

Transliteration consists of assigning some letter of a given alphabet (or some group of letters of some artificial symbol) to each character of another alphabet, thus reproducing the *orthography* of the first alphabet in terms of the second...*Transcription* uses a given alphabet to represent the *pronunciation* of another alphabet or language...*Romanization* is a specific term meaning the conversion of names or text not written in the Roman alphabet into Roman alphabet form...*Reversibility* is a feature of exact transliteration only, becase each letter of the foreign alphabet is assigned a distinct corresponding symbol in the Roman alphabet, and conversion in either direction is a simple matter of table look-up.[4]

According to these definitions one can transcribe Chinese but never transliterate it. Further, one can either transcribe or transliterate Yiddish, but each process would yield a different result. With reversibility, ease of conversion is often bought at the price of pronounceability (as with Hebrew). These considerations explain why there are so many different schemes for transliterating and transcribing nonroman languages. Some schemes aim at giving an idea how a language is spoken, while others strive to represent its orthography. Ideally, transliteration and transcription would be identical and reversible, but in fact, that does not always occur. Russian, for example, *does* permit identical transliteration and transcription; Hebrew, with which we are concerned here, does not.

THE ANGLO-SAXON TRADITION:
The Integrated Catalog

As mentioned above, nearly all libraries in the United States follow the practice of romanizing at least some of the major access points of Hebrew cataloging records. Even today, with the capability of vernacular Hebrew cataloging available in RLIN, vernacular fields are an *additional* means of access to the entries, not a replacement for romanized access points (see Chapter 9: The American Scene: Hebrew in RLIN). The "integrative" or romanizing approach prevalent in the Anglo-Saxon tradition varies not in its essential belief in the need to romanize headings in order to integrate them into the roman-character catalog (or online file), but rather in the *extent* of romanization within the integrative tradition: partial romanization, used during most of its history by the Library of Congress and traditional bibliographies, and full romanization.

---

[4]Bella Hass Weinberg, "Transliteration in Documentation," *Journal of Documentation* 21 (March 1974): 18.

PARTIAL ROMANIZATION VERSUS FULL ROMANIZATION

Many American libraries with significant collections of Hebrew-alphabet materials have, in fact, always maintained separate Hebrew-Yiddish *title* catalogs. At the same time, nearly all American libraries follow the practice of transcribing *author* headings printed in nonroman form into roman form. The primary reason usually given for this practice is "to keep works by and about a person together in one catalog in a form that can be read by the overwhelming majority of American readers."[5] Another reason cited is to save the library the trouble and expense of hiring staff who can input Hebrew characters and of buying equipment that can input and display Hebrew characters: "Most libraries which organize all headings (author and title headings) in roman catalogs do so for the sake of convenience and economy."[6]

Not all authorities on Hebrew cataloging in the United States, however, accept these rationalizations for the "integrative" approach. Weinberg, one of the foremost American critics of romanization of Hebrew headings, has long held that none of the frequently-heard arguments for romanizing hold up under examination. In an early article on the subject, Weinberg claims that while the *how* of transliteration has been extensively examined, the *why* has been far less thoroughly explored. With regard to the first reason for romanizing—to keep all the works by and about an author together in the catalog—she admits some grudging justification, although she feels the case can only be made for authors who have been *translated* from languages in one alphabet to languages in another.[7] But she disagrees entirely with the second reason—that it is more economical—and denies that there is any benefit derived from romanizing *title* entries:

> But why do librarians transliterate *title* entries? My impression is that this allows the typing and filing of these entries to be done by the regular clerical staff. I daresay that the money saved by not hiring clerical staff with knowledge of foreign alphabets is completely spent on the Romanization process, cross-referencing from alternate forms, and teaching filers to recognize foreign articles.[8]

In fact, practices do differ within the Anglo-Saxon tradition with regard to title headings. Most libraries with small, superficial collections of Hebrew books have maintained a practice of transcribing title headings and interfiling them into the roman

---

[5]Bernard Hugo Rabenstein, "A Survey on the Use of Alphabetical Forms in Author and/or Title Headings in the Catalogs of Israeli Libraries," Master's Thesis, Catholic University of America, 1970, p. 27.

[6]Bernard Hugo Rabenstein, "A Survey on the Use of Alphabetical Forms in Author and/or Title Headings in the Catalogs of Israeli Libraries," p. 27.

[7]Bella Hass Weinberg, "Transliteration in Documentation": 21-22.

[8] Bella Hass Weinberg, "Transliteration in Documentation" : 22.

catalogs. Because most of these libraries have always used Library of Congress cards and, later, machine-readable records that contained the romanized entry forms, processing Hebrew books was rendered effortless and inexpensive for them. Bernard Rabenstein claims that some libraries with sizable collections transcribe the Hebrew titles into English, i.e., anglicize them, or even do away with the titles altogether for the sake of convenience and economy, justifying their practice by supporting one or more of three points of view: (1) that a Hebraist can find a Hebrew title in English letters once he familiarizes himself with the transcription system, (2) that a large collection of Hebrew books used primarily for research purposes will be used by a limited number of scholars, (3) that the author and short title approach to a Hebrew book is sufficient in some libraries at institutions where a book is referred to by its author primarily and its short title only when there is no author or editor to which to refer.[9] There are several problems with Rabensteins' statements concerning the "anglicized title/no-title" entry libraries, however. First, he doesn't give examples of libraries that cataloged their Hebrew-alphabet materials this way, and these authors have not seen this approach in any libraries with which they are familiar. Second, the jusification following does not seem to match: it seems to be jusification for *romanized* headings, not for anglicized. Point #3 is also not clear: it starts by citing an author *and short-title* approach, but the end implies that the short title is given only when there is no author.

In American libraries that have large collections of Hebraica, the practice has usually been to establish and maintain separate Hebrew-Yiddish title catalogs. One reason may be that whereas libraries that follow the practice of *full* romanization of all headings subscribe to the theory that most readers in the United States who read Hebrew know English and are capable of using roman catalogs with some proficiency, libraries that maintain separate Hebrew-Yiddish *title* catalogs do so from a concern to serve everybody who can read Hebrew whether or not he can read any other language. In addition (and perhaps even primarily), Hebrew title catalogs were established in these American libraries to avoid the problems of romanization from the reader's standpoint: the bilingual reader forced to search titles in romanized form would surely have had an extremely difficult time (and would probably have been shocked by many of the results). Romanized authors are easier to "swallow" since they usually follow the original pronunciation of the name—as opposed to titles, which would have caused the reader to run headfirst into the question of whether they were romanized according to sefardi (modern Israeli) or ashkenazi pronunciation. Obviously, it would be helpful to readers who know only Hebrew to be able to search author headings in Hebrew as well, but title headings are considered an adequate means for Hebraists to find books in most cases.

---

[9]Bernard Hugo Rabenstein, "A Survey on the Use of Alphabetical Forms in Author and/or Title Headings in the Catalogs of Israeli Libraries," p. 28.

LIBRARY OF CONGRESS TRANSCRIPTION PRACTICES

Since published catalogs of several of America's great Judaica libraries—The New York Public Library,[10] Hebrew Union College,[11] and Harvard[12]—incorporate a great many LC cards and therefore reflect to a great extent the title-page transcription practices of the Library of Congress, a historical review of LC Hebrew transcription practices is useful at this point.

Early twentieth-century Library of Congress practice was to transcribe the Hebrew title page completely, copying every diacritic and vowel point.[13] Presumably this was based on an interpretation of rule 136 in ALA' s 1908 *Cataloging Rules*: "The title is usually to be given in full, including the author's name, and is to be an exact transcript of the title page."[14]

With the publication of *Rules for Descriptive Cataloging in the Library of Congress* in 1949,[15] however, the author statement disappeared from LC cards (see Figure 2.1). The rationale behind this change was that the author statement was presumed to be redundant with the romanized author heading unless there was a Hebrew pseudonym on the title page (rule 3:6). AACR1,[16] eighteen years later, explicitly stated that the author statement was to be omitted when the form of the name in the heading is a letter-for-letter transliteration of the name in the author statement (rule 134A2). In spite of the fact that LC's Hebrew romanization scheme is *not* a letter-for-letter transliteration, this rule was applied in the cataloging of Hebraica.[17]

---

[10][NYPL, 1960] New York Public Library. Reference Department, *Dictionary Catalog of the Jewish Collection* (Boston: G.K. Hall, 1960), 14 vols.--*First Supplement* (1975), 8 vols.

[11]Hebrew Union College--Jewish Institute of Religion. Library, *Dictionary Catalog of the Klau Library, Cincinnati* (Boston: G.K.Hall, 1964), 32 vols.

[12]Harvard University Library, *Catalogue of Hebrew Books* (Cambridge, MA: Harvard University Press, 1968), 6 vols.-- Supplement I (1972), 3 vols. , *Appendix: Judaica in the Houghton Library* (in Supplement I, Vol. 1: Classified Listing).

[13]Bella Hass Weinberg, "Judaica and Hebraica Cataloging: Anglo-American Traditions," *Judaica Librarianship* 6 (Spring 1991-Winter 1992): 14.

[14][ALA, 1908] American Library Association, *Cataloging Rules: Author and Title Entries*, American Edition (Chicago: American Library Association, 1908): 43.

[15]Library of Congress. Descriptive Cataloging Division, *Rules for Descriptive Cataloging in the Library of Congress* (Washington, D.C.: Library of Congress, 1949).

[16][AACR1] *Anglo-American Cataloging Rules*, North American Text (Chicago: American Library Association, 1967.

[17]Bella Hass Weinberg, "Judaica and Hebraica Cataloging: Anglo-American Traditions": 14.

In 1978 the International Standard Bibliographic Description (ISBD)[18] was incorporated by AACR2. [19] ISBD distinguished between the form of an author's name on a title page, which is permanent, and the author heading, which is constructed by the cataloger and the cataloging rules and, therefore, subject to change. The author statement, in the original script, was reinstated, demonstrating LC's acceptance of the fact that a name spelled in Hebrew is substantially different from its romanized form. Thus, post-1978 LC Hebraica cards and online records feature full title-page transcription (of all normally-retained words appearing on the title page) in Hebrew characters, excluding the Hebrew dates, which are not converted. The sample LC record in Figure 2.2 shows this change in LC transcription policy from AACR1, mentioning also in the notes that the title page is partially vocalized, i.e., it shows vowel points or *nikud*, but not reproducing it. Another post-AACR2 LC practice seen in Figure 2.2 is the romanization of Hebrew bibliographic data in notes, which are not access points. The classic post-AACR2 printed Hebraica card, then, romanized access points (including short title just below the author, or as the title main entry), and in recent years, bibliographic data in notes as well.

TRADITIONAL BIBLIOGRAPHIES AND PUBLISHED HEBRAICA CATALOGS

Older British catalogs, like LC printed cards, also practiced partial romanization. Both Steinschneider's mid-nineteenth century Latin-language catalog of Hebraica in the Bodleian Library[20] and Cowley's 1929 English-language catalog of Bodleian Hebraica[21] recorded the title proper in Hebrew characters and romanized the author main entry. Zedner's catalog of Hebrew books in the British Museum,[22] published a few years after Steinschneider's catalog, gives fuller title information, place and date all in Hebrew characters, as well as in the roman or Cyrillic alphabet and in Arabic numerals, respectively.

In America, as mentioned above, almost all published Hebraica catalogs with author main entry in roman script provide title access in the original Hebrew script. Hebraica title indexes have been used for many years by Judaica catalogers to find romanized author headings in these catalogs. In fact, the Library of Congress's

---

[18]ISBD (M:): *International Standard Bibliographic Description for Monographic Publications* (London: International Federation of Library Associations and Institutions, Committee on Cataloguing, 1974).

[19][AACR2] *Anglo-American Cataloguing Rules,* 2nd ed. (Chicago: American Library Association, 1978).

[20]Oxford University. Bodleian Library, *Catalogus Librorum Hebraeorum in Bibliotheca Bodleiana,* [ed.] M. Steinschneider, 1st ed., 1852-1860, Zweite (Faksimile) Auflage (Berlin: Welt-Verlag, 1931), 3 vols.

[21]Oxford University. Bodleian Library, *A Concise Catalogue of the Hebrew Printed Books in the Bodleian Library*, by A. E. Cowley (Oxford: The Clarendon Press, 1929).

[22] British Museum, *Catalogue of the Hebrew Books in the Library of the British Museum*, [comp. Joseph Zedner] (London: British Museum, Dept. of Oriental Printed Books and Manuscripts, 1867).

Hebraic Section, in violation of its parent body's principles, for decades maintained a Hebrew-script title catalog. One of the most recent general Hebraica catalogs in America, the *Hebrew-Character Title Catalog of the Jewish Collection*,[23] which the NYPL published in 1981, maintains the Anglo-Saxon tradition of the primacy of Hebraic title access: although most of the records feature romanized author main entry, the author cards have not been reproduced in the published catalog.

---

[23] [NYPL, 1981] New York Public Library. Research Libraries, *Hebrew-Character Title Catalog of the Jewish Collection* (Boston: G.K. Hall, 1981), 4 vols.

Sabine, George Holland. 1880-1961
תולדות תורת המדינה. תרגם לעברית אורי רפ. [תל-אביב]
יחדיו   .1963-

   v. 22 cm.

Includes bibliographies.

   1. Political science--Hist.
           Title transliterated: Toldot torat ha-medinah.

   JA81.S316   He 64-47

Library of Congress   [1]

**Fig. 2.1. Library of Congress card, pre-ISBD:
Hebrew author statement omitted.**[24]

Ṭuḵṭali, Ehud.
  (Galut ben galim)
גלות בין גלים / אהוד טוקטלי, שמואל וגידי קליצנר ; עטיפה
וציורים, מיכאל נצר. -- ירושלים : הוצאת "פרי הארץ",
     c1987-   [1986 or 1987-   747- .

   v. <1   > : ill. ; 23 cm.

  Title page partially vocalized.
  Contents: sefer 1. 'Alilot yalde Tarshish.

  I. Ḵlitsner, Shemu'el.   II. Ḵlitsner, G'udi.   III. Netser, Mikhae'l.
IV. Title.

PZ90.H3T77 1987   87-166787
                                MARC
             90   AACR 2
Library of Congress   HE

**Fig. 2.2. Library of Congress card, post-AACR2:
Hebrew author statement transcribed; vocalization
on title page noted; notes romanized.** [25]

---

[24]Bella Hass Weinberg, "Judaica and Hebraica Cataloging: Anglo-American Traditions": 14.

[25]Bella Hass Weinberg, "Judaica and Hebraica Cataloging: Anglo-American Traditions": 16.

In summary, the predominant pattern in Anglo-American Hebraica catalogs has always been romanized author main entry, but in virtually all of these the importance of Hebrew title access is apparent also. Many of the published catalogs, unlike the 1981 NYPL catalog, do *not* arrange their published work by Hebrew-character title-entry, but virtually all of them offer Hebrew-character *indexes* of titles. The published Hebraica catalogs of Harvard, New York Public Library and Hebrew Union College all feature this essential type of index. The British Museum *Catalogue of the Hebrew Books* goes one step further, offering both an *author* and a *title* index in the Hebrew alphabet to supplement its roman alphabet main entry arrangement.

In spite of the persistence of the Anglo-American pattern of romanized author main entry and with title page transcription and title index in Hebrew characters in its published Judaica Hebraica catalogs and bibliographies, there are some notable exceptions. The bibliography *Koheleth America: Catalogue of Hebrew Books Printed in America from 1735-1925*[26] features Hebrew title main entry, complete title-page transcription in Hebrew, and Hebrew as the language of cataloging, with no author access or indexes whatsoever. Another exception, exhibiting a different pattern, is the catalog of the Yiddish collection of the YIVO Library,[27] published quite recently, in 1990. Like the YIVO card catalog itself, which has always provided Yiddish author main entry, the published catalog is arranged by Yiddish (Hebrew-character) main entry. However, the title, by which Anglo-American Judaica librarians are most accustomed to searching in Hebraica catalogs, is not always available, because older works that have not been recataloged have only author entries.

CROSS-REFERENCE CARD INDEXES

Romanization, in spite of valiant attempts to standardize it by such august institutions as the Library of Congress, was, is, and will always be a very inexact technique whenever non-vocalized scripts such as Hebrew are involved. Nevertheless, English is the spoken language of America and England, and Anglo-Saxon Judaica librarians persist in preferring a catalog that features main entry headings in their native script. Not all of them feel this way, as Weinberg's ironic comment on this situation notes, but for most, "despite all of the errors and inconsistencies in LC romanization practice, the view persists....that romanized headings are official and Hebrew ones are not.[28] One librarian reviewing a bibliography wrote '...the main entries...are always in Hebrew characters, hardly the best possible index to an American university library catalog.' "[29]

---

[26]Ephraim Deinard, *Koheleth America: Catalogue of Hebrew Books Printed in America from 1735-1925* (St. Louis, MO: Moinester Printing Co., 1926).

[27] YIVO Institute for Jewish Research, *The Yiddish Catalog and Authority File of the YIVO Library*, edited by Zachary M. Baker and Bella Hass Weinberg (Boston: G. K. Hall, 1990), 5 vols.

[28]Bella Hass Weinberg, "Hebraica Cataloging and Classification, " In *Cataloging and Classification of Non-Western Material: Concerns, Issues and Practices,* edited by Mohammed M. Aman (Phoenix, AZ: Oryx Press, 1980), p. 327.

Thus, both because they tend to be more comfortable with roman-character headings and to avoid such criticism, Anglo-American libraries and librarians have largely used LC romanized headings. At the same time almost all of them, including the Library of Congress, have maintained Hebrew title indexes in the original script. Furthermore, in recognition of the difficulty involved in finding an item under a romanized personal or corporate heading (particularly when the title is nondistinctive), large Judaica libraries such as the Jewish Theological Seminary and Yeshiva University have maintained Hebrew author cross-reference files to lead the user or librarian directly to the corresponding form, for example,

וינברג, מרדכי גרשון

see

Vainberg, Mordecai Gershon[30]

This cross reference card index, which refers a reader from a Hebrew form of a name that may be found in a book to a non-Hebrew form of the name established in the roman-alphabet author catalog, was intended to replace a catalog of Hebrew author headings and aid the reader who knows the Hebrew form of the author of a book but not its title. Nevertheless, except for very large Judaica libraries such as those mentioned above, most American libraries have not seen the need to establish a card index of Hebrew and romanized names, but have preferred a romanized author catalog and a Hebrew title catalog.

FULL ROMANIZATION

The Anglo-American tradition (the *real* tradition) has always been partial romanization, as on Hebrew LC cards, and the traditional bibliographies and printed catalogs. After MARC cataloging of the JACKPHY languages (Japanese, Arabic, Chinese, Korean, Persian, Hebrew and Yiddish) began in 1983, the desire to create a machine-readable file of its Hebrew collection led the Harvard College Library not only to change over to full romanization, but to retrospectively convert its entire partially romanized card file as well. Dr. Charles Berlin, head of the Judaica Division of the Harvard College Library, explains that decision in a personal interview with Elizabeth Vernon in 1990, pointing out that for Harvard's Hebraica collection "the decision was not romanization per se," but rather that "the goal was automation and romanization was the means then available to achieve that goal."[31] In the online

---

[29]Sheldon R. Brunswick, "Book Review" of Michael Yizhar, *Bibliography of Hebrew Publications on the Dead Sea Scrolls, Jewish Social Studies* 31 (July 1969): 220-221. Brunswick's annoyance at Yizhar's use of Hebrew main entries for "an American university catalog" is particularly confusing since the publication being reviewed is a *bibliography,* apparently based on material from Harvard's catalog of Hebrew books, and not a *catalog,* as his next sentence indicates: "The *Catalogue of Hebrew Books* itself which was published in 1968 by the Harvard University Library has Hebrew character entries, but only for titles and not for main entries!"

[30] Bella Hass Weinberg, "Hebraica Cataloging and Classification," p. 327.

[31]Elizabeth Vernon, "Hebrew and Arabic Script Materials in the Automated Library: The United States Scene," *Cataloging and Classification Quarterly* 14 (1) (1991): 57.

environment, romanization of the complete title page transcription is required. Even today, when the Research Libraries Information Network (RLIN) has Hebrew vernacular cataloging capability, the vernacular fields in records for Hebrew materials are *additional* fields, which do not replace romanized access points, but rather supplement them. Dr. Berlin, in fact, points out in this same interview that he would *still* choose romanization as the most pragmatic option, since he feels that "the vernacular capability does not bring with it a significant enough increase in access to justify the amount of additional work that option demands at present."[32]

Rosalie Katchen proposed in 1990 that RLIN approve the romanization of author and title proper only, rather than requiring complete Hebraica title-page transcription in the roman alphabet.[33] Interestingly, and perhaps ironically, although her proposal was aimed at adapting Hebrew cataloging to the era of automation, the effect of the proposal's implementation would be to emulate the model of the LC printed card in the online environment.

THE ISRAELI TRADITION:
The "Standalone" Approach

In his master's thesis on Israeli cataloging traditions, Bernard Hugo Rabenstein, in 1970, listed a number of reasons for the Israeli practice of maintaining separate catalogs of headings in various alphabets rather than a unified catalog of headings in one alphabet, as in the Anglo-Saxon tradition:

a. In the past immigrants speaking and reading various languages and alphabets immigrated into Israel from many parts of the world and are still arriving.

b. The Israelis frequently read literature in non-Hebrew alphabets. Libraries are obliged to build large collections of non-Hebrew books and to establish catalogs with non-Hebrew headings as well as catalogs with Hebrew headings.

c. The Israelis can read many alphabets. They need no aid from the conversion of alphabetical characters that they can read in the original.

d. Average library workers in Israel (filers, typists, technical assistants, etc.) do not have trouble working with different alphabets that they usually can read.

---

[32]Elizabeth Vernon, "Hebrew and Arabic Script Materials...": 58.

[33]Rosalie Katchen, "Hebrew Online: Current Issues and Future Concerns: A View from the Field," *Judaica Librarianship* 5 (Spring 1989-Winter 1990): 22-25.

e. There is no ideal alphabetical form into which headings of other alphabetical forms can be converted because: 1) Hebrew is an alphabetical form into which conversion of other alphabetical forms is virtually impossible; and 2) the roman alphabet, though an important alphabet, is not native to Israelis.

f. Israeli librarians are concerned with entering author headings into catalogs under forms with which the readers are familiar. According to them, a Cyrillic book ought to be given a heading in Cyrillic rather than in roman.[34]

Either because he felt that the other reasons were self-evident, or because he felt that the first reason of E—"Hebrew is an alphabetical form into which conversion of other alphabetical forms is virtually impossible"—is the most important reason, Rabenstein devotes considerable space to elucidating this reason, above all others, for the Israeli "standalone" approach. He begins by pointing out that there are countries where libraries establish separate catalogs because conversion of headings from other alphabets to the country's primary alphabet is difficult if not impossible. Israel is one of those countries, but its problem with its Hebrew alphabet is not unique. The countries that use the Arabic alphabet, which is similar to the Hebrew alphabet in that it expresses only the consonants and leaves the vowels unexpressed, have the same problems converting headings from other alphabets into their native alphabet. However, Israel's problem transcribing foreign names into its alphabet are unlike China's problem with its ideographic alphabet. Converting the roman-alphabet (which is literal) into Hebrew (which is consonantal) is difficult, but not as difficult as converting roman into Chinese (which is ideographic). Furthermore, the question is whether the conversion of roman into Hebrew is of any value when conversion from other alphabets is difficult, if not impossible.[35] In short, Hebrew is simply not a good "receiving" alphabet, and this accounts for one of the major reasons for its tradition of maintaining separate catalogs for separate alphabets instead of a unified catalog of headings in its native alphabet.

In spite of the inhospitability of Hebrew as a receiving alphabet, and in spite of the fact that no Israeli library has ever "Hebraized" all its catalog entries, these libraries *do* have to contend with the problem of the correct transcription of foreign author names when cataloging translations into Hebrew. One of the specific problems Israeli libraries face in transcribing these author names into Hebrew is that no set of rules can be systematically applied in such situations because so many popular transcriptions of personal and geographic names, not to mention spellings of borrowed words, have become "standard" in Hebrew. This last phenomenon makes a strong case against systematic transcription schemes.[36]

---

[34]Bernard Hugo Rabenstein, "A Survey on the Use of Alphabetical Forms in Author and/or Title Headings in the Catalogs of Israeli Libraries," p. 67.

[35] Bernard Hugo Rabenstein, "A Survey on the Use of Alphabetical Forms in Author and/or Title Headings in the Catalogs of Israeli Libraries," p. 33.

[36] Bella Hass Weinberg, "Hebraica Cataloging and Classification," p. 328.

A, B, C, and D on Rabenstein's list of reasons for the Israeli practice of maintaining separate catalogs for publications in separate alphabets are all variations on another theme he develops fairly extensively—the cosmopolitan nature of Israel's population:

> Israel has a cosmopolitan population. People from all over the world have migrated there. They know Roman languages, and Cyrillic languages, they know or can read Hebrew. A large minority of the native population knows Arabic. All in all, Israel is a four-alphabet country. It is true that in all countries of the world there are elements in the population that can read different alphabets. But in Israel these elements are marked; they are more evident. The librarians in Israel feel the necessity to accommodate these elements; consequently they establish separate catalogs.[37]

Rabenstein's explanation is confirmed by a statement in a 1939 catalog of courses published by the Hebrew University of Jerusalem. In the section that deals with the Jewish National and University Library, the following sentence appears: "Since many languages are spoken in Palestine, and the reading public is very diversified the alphabetical catalog is set up in five sections: Latin script, Hebrew, Yiddish, Russian and Arabic."[38] In contradistinction to the "cosmopolitan population" explanation for the rise of the "standalone tradition," it is also true that in this early period of Israel's development the population of Israel consisted of newly arrived immigrants who often could not understand languages other than their native language, which as often as not was not written in Latin script. Furthermore, in that early period a curious situation existed with regard to Hebrew as the national language. Although the Hebrew language revolution had already taken hold of the native population, Israel really had no predominant language yet. Continuing immigration of people from other countries created a language problem as well as a cultural absorption problem. Therefore libraries were obliged to cater to the needs of the immigrants who spoke different languages and who had lived under various cultural conditions. One of these needs was for books in many languages that were written in a variety of alphabets. As a result, separate catalogs were used to satisfy the linguistically diverse library-using public.

The source of the Israeli standalone tradition (as opposed to the reasons for the tradition, discussed above) can be traced back to the Jewish National and University Library, which is indeed the source of most of Israel's cataloging traditions and policies. However, the JNUL in the 1920s and 1930s was the largest and most important library in Mandate Palestine and, for many years, was the site of the only school of librarianship in Israel, its practices usually became *de facto* standards for all the libraries in the country.[39] For the most part the JNUL approach, which was subsequently adopted by all Israel's libraries, has been to try to adapt traditional approaches

---

[37]Bernard Hugo Rabenstein, "A Survey on the Use of Alphabetical Forms in Author and/or Title Headings in the Catalogs of Israeli Libraries," p. 35.

[38]Ha-Universiṭah ha-Ivrit bi-Yerushalayim, *The Hebrew University, Jerusalem, its History and Development* [Jerusalem: Haaretz Press, 1939], p. 108.

[39]Elhanan Adler, "Judaica Cataloging: The Hebrew Bibliographic and Israeli Traditions": 8.

to international (primarily Anglo-American) standards. One of the conspicuous exceptions to this approach is the practice of maintaining separate catalogs. Americans visiting the JNUL have always found the practice a curious one, or at least one worth noting, as Avram Rosenthal's description of the JNUL catalogs in a 1957 *ALA Bulletin* attests:

> There are five catalogs in the general library. Four of them are author-title catalogs. The most extensive is the one containing materials written in those languages using Latin characters which include primarily the Romance and Germanic languages. Although Arabic and Hebrew are both Semitic languages, the alphabets are sufficiently different so as to require separate catalogs. The last author-title catalog is for Cyrillic/alphabets and includes the Russian, Bulgarian and other Slavic languages....Since the library owns a substantial number of books in each of these alphabets, it would be quite impractical to transliterate all the entries into English or Hebrew. At any rate, it was felt that people tend to use the catalog containing the alphabet with which they are familiar.[40]

In the process of collecting research for his master's thesis on the treatment of various alphabets in Israeli library catalogs, Rabenstein carried on a correspondence in the late 1960s with Kaethe Lewy, one of the JNUL's distinguished librarians. He details at some length Mrs. Lewy's explanations of and critical comments corncerning JNUL practices regarding separate catalogs, noting that her review of data and ideas are not found anywhere in the library literature.[41]

Mrs. Lewy wrote that books in alphabets in which the Jewish National and University Library had only small collections, such as Greek and Chinese, are romanized. Thus, even the library that had the most highly developed system of separate catalogs in Israel united headings of certain alphabets in one catalog. All in all, she wrote, Israeli librarians prefer separate catalogs over a unified catalog, but they do not deny the practicality of unified catalogs. Israeli libraries varied only in the *degree* to which they maintained the practice of separate catalogs for separate alphabets. For example, the University of Haifa Library maintained Arabic separately but romanized Cyrillic.

---

[40]Avram Rosenthal, "Experiences at the Hebrew University Library in Jerusalem," *ALA Bulletin* 51 (February 15,1957): 113.

[41]Bernard Hugo Rabenstein, "A Survey on the Use of Alphabetical Forms in Author and/or Title Headings in the Catalogs of Israeli Libraries," p. 58-61.

In addition to supplying Rabenstein with extensive descriptive information on the separate catalog practices of Israeli libraries, and particularly the JNUL, Kaethe Lewy went on to express some critical comments on the situation to Rabenstein. First, she affirmed that a weakness of a system of separate catalogs is that the reader has to search several catalogs to find works of an author in various languages or translations thereof. In other words, the *collocating* function of the catalog, something which the unified Anglo-American catalog preserved by romanizing author headings, was lost to a large degree in the JNUL's system. Lewy thought that the ideal situation would be separate catalogs complemented by a unified catalog, that would probably contain only romanized author headings (and possibly title headings for books that have no author headings). Even if it proved impossible to construct a unified catalog of those entries that were already in the JNUL catalogs, she commented to Rabenstein, it might be possible to begin a unified catalog for new entries to be made in the future when catalogers, as soon as they have established a Hebrew author could at the same time establish a romanized heading. She saw the unified catalog as a potential union catalog, funded by combining money and other resources of Israeli libraries and library associations. She even took her dream (which apparently remained only wishful thinking) one step further, envisioning the publication, in a few years, of the unified catalog in book form, as a supplement to the separate catalogs of all Israeli libraries.

Mrs. Lewy, however, was not the only Israeli librarian who addressed herself to the problems of separate catalogs. Hana Oppenheimer, who codified cataloging rules in Hebrew for Israeli librarians in her classic 1961 work, *Targilim be-ḳitlug*,[42] felt that the doubling of catalogs caused grave problems in all Israeli libraries. Unlike foreign libraries, which could arrange all their entries in a unified catalog according to the foreign alphabet, using the ALA rules for transcription (see Chapter 3: Romanization and Transliteration Systems), Israeli libraries could not reasonably require their readers to search for a Hebrew book in a foreign alphabet, although they could romanize materials in Greek and sometimes Russian (as previously mentioned, some Israeli libraries romanize Cyrillic and some do not). However, they could not establish Hebrew as the all-inclusive alphabet because they could not overcome the difficulties of transcription of the foreign alphabets into Hebrew. "We saw how hard we had to struggle just to transcribe Hebrew books by people with foreign names in which by them there is no choice but to enter them into the Hebrew catalog. The difficulty would become unbearable if we had to transcribe headings for the thousands of foreign names in foreign books," she wrote.[43] Therefore, in her opinion, there was no choice in Israel but to establish two separate catalogs, although she thought that establishing a separate catalog for every different alphabet was excessive. Romanizing Russian, using the ALA rules, was not only plausible but desirable in Israel, she continued, since the unification of catalogs, wherever possible, makes for less labor and "a Hebrew library is not obligated to consider the needs of the Russian reader to the same degree as those of the Hebrew reader."[44] Oppenheimer makes it

---

[42]Hana Oppenheimer, *Targilim be-ḳitlug* (Jerusalem: [s.n.], 1961).

[43] Hana Oppenheimer, *Targilim be-ḳitlug,* 67. Interestingly, in view of the massive integration from the former Soviet Union to Israel in recent years, Israeli libraries have had to deal with a large Cyrillic-reading-only public, which has led many public libraries to create separate Cyrillic catalogs.

[44]Hana Oppenheimer, *Targilim be-ḳitlug*, p. 67.

clear, however, that even when cataloging publications in languages she feels should be romanized in Israeli libraries, the romanization applies only to headings. The body of the entry was to be written as on the title page, in the predominant Library of Congress tradition.

A few years before Oppenheimer published *Targilim be-ḳitlug*, Zwi Maimon advocated romanization of all headings in Israeli libraries, criticizing the practice of establishing separate catalogs as old and unjustified.[45] He pointed out the weakness of separate alphabetical catalogs—the need to search more than one catalog for all the works by and about one person. He also dealt with the questions of whether romanization should be used only for the headings of the cards or also for the body (a question to which Oppenheimer gave a clear answer four years later), and whether it should be done according to the sound of the reading of the words or names or according to their written symbol, a debate that was still raging thirty years later between Anglo-American proponents of the graphic approach (reversible romanization) and the phonetic approach (ALA/LC romanization).

In addition to the universal objection that separate catalogs slow down bibliographers in their search for works by and about particular persons in all languages (as Rabenstein noted, a bibliographer searching for all works in the JNUL by and about Shakespeare had to search in five catalogs for five different alphabetical forms, and then only if he could read them),[46] a second objection was that an excessive number of separate catalogs makes cataloging and processing of materials more difficult and inefficient.

Weinberg discusses a third problem that arises in institutions such as the JNUL in which materials in different languages written in *Hebrew* characters are held in separate catalogs. Actually, at the JNUL, only two of the three major Hebrew-character languages are separated—Hebrew and Yiddish. The third, Judezmo (also known as Ladino), is integrated into the Hebrew catalog. The reasons for having a separate Yiddish catalog were largely a result of the difficulty of integrating Hebrew *ketiv ḥaser* with Yiddish, with its expressed vowels. Because Yiddish orthography is more phonetic than Hebrew orthography, older Hebrew title pages often feature the name of the author in Yiddish spelling. As a result, separating the Yiddish and Hebrew catalogs resulted in both problems and advantages. In the unified Hebraica catalog a title would be entered only once, even if it was bilingual (Hebrew-Yiddish). However, establishing a single spelling for authors with works in both Hebrew and Yiddish can be very confusing, and reciprocal *see also* references between separate Hebrew and Yiddish author catalogs were a must. Another problem of separation of Hebraica by language was the definition and identification of Jewish languages. Here Weinberg cites Moses Mendelssohn's translation of the Bible into German, which was

---

[45]Maimon, Zwi, ["General Catalog or Catalog by Language"], *Yad Lakore* 4 (September 1956-March 1957):128-129; in Hebrew.

[46]Bernard Hugo Rabenstein, "A Survey on the Use of Alphabetical Forms in Author and/or Title Headings in the Catalogs of Israeli Libraries," p. 69.

printed in most editions in Hebrew characters. Asking rhetorically whether the rightful place of such editions is the Hebrew or Yiddish catalog, she answers in the next sentence that "there is no question that German in Hebrew characters does not belong in the Hebrew language catalog."[47]   By the same token, the entries for Latinized Hebrew or Yiddish books belonged in the roman catalog, with any access point in their original language catalogs made only through added entries. In addition, romanization from Yiddish can often look like German, and from Judezmo, like Spanish. In short, defining and identifying the Jewish languages for inclusion in the proper catalog could sometimes be a problem for the Israeli cataloger. In Israeli *automated* catalogs, by the way, the Hebrew and Yiddish have been merged without any major ill effects.

As for subject access to material in Israeli libraries, an additional and separate subject catalog was the only means by which the subject structure of the catalog system could be united. Historically, subject access was via a classified catalog, which eliminated the need to select a primary language (and not just a script) in a multilingual reader situation. Many Israeli libraries of all types and sizes (from the JNUL to small public libraries) still maintain classed catalogs. Since 1970, several university libraries have instituted English language subject headings (using LCSH) and one university has opted for split subject access (LCSH for non-Hebrew works, local Hebrew headings for Hebrew works).[48]   Recently, the Center for Public Libraries in Israel announced its intention to supply public libraries with cataloging data containing Hebrew subject headings.[49]

Although non-Hebrew cataloging in Israel generally followed international practice, many of the significant differences that have developed in Hebrew cataloging in order to meet the special needs of Israeli readers searching for Hebrew materials, remain a part of Israeli cataloging practice even today.   Israeli libraries have retained the "standalone" approach of Hebrew bibliography—meaning separate Hebrew- and roman-character catalogs and, in the automated environment, separate Hebrew- and roman-character access. With the advent of automated cataloging in Israel's university libraries, the number of nonroman "catalogs" was at first reduced, since early versions of ALEPH, the Israeli academic library network, were able to handle only Hebrew and roman-character scripts. In the mid-1980s ALEPH-Yissum, the research and development company for ALEPH software, began work on a solution for accommodating other nonroman scripts into the ALEPH system. The solution they developed was soft fonts, software in the form of character sets that are resident in the computer, rather than the hardware-based solution of its earlier versions.[50] Soft fonts are available for multinational Latin (L), Hebrew (H), Arabic (A), Cyrillic (S) and

[47]Bella Hass Weinberg, "Hebraica Cataloging and Classification": 330.

[48]Gita Hoffman *et al.*, "Hebrew Subject Headings: Development and Implementation at Bar-Ilan University," *Judaica Librarianship* 6 (Spring 1991-Winter 1992): 24.

[49] Shoshanah Langerman and Rahel Kedar, "[The Bibliography Project for Public Libraries Takes Its First Steps,]" *Basifriyot* 4 (June 1994), 16-17.

[50] Susan S. Lazinger, "ALEPH: Israel's Research Library Network: Background, Evolution, and Implications for Networking in a Small Country," *Information Technology and Libraries* 10 (December 1991), 289.

Greek (R) and can be supported on a wide variety of terminals.[51]   Thus, with the implementation of soft fonts, both Cyrillic and Arabic characters can be input and displayed.

All in all, the system of separate catalogs in Israeli libraries simplified daily use of the catalogs by Israeli readers. True, it entailed the disadvantage of requiring multiple searches in order to locate all items under a specific heading in more than one script, e.g., all works of an author in all languages, but in the final analysis, searching for all items by a known author in all alphabets is not common. The overwhelming majority of nonsubject searches are in advance limited to a single alphabet (most to a single language). Furthermore, as mentioned above, this was a problem only in descriptive cataloging, because subject access in most libraries was and is provided by a subject catalog (or subject file, in the automated environment), classified or alphabetical, which lists works in all scripts. It is true, also, that separate catalogs create complications in cataloging works with multiple title pages in multiple scripts, but here again, the need to catalog multiple title pages in multiple scripts is a relatively infrequent phenomenon. Occasionally it was necessary to catalog an item twice, to be sure, but not so often as to create a serious burden on Israeli catalogers. Thus, in spite of the disadvantages, separate catalogs allow the reader ready access to publications, under access points as they appear in the publications themselves.   Although most Israelis were and are capable of reading nonroman characters, they were not and are not willing to make the effort required to search for Hebrew books in roman characters (an understandable reluctance). Furthermore, romanization systems are not easy to use anywhere, and even more of a problem in Israel than in America, because there is no agreement as to *which* romanization system to use among all the major research libraries. Israeli librarians always understood that readers were likely to search a Hebrew book in a roman catalog under a wrong or misspelled heading from the wrong system or from their own, made-up transcription.

Whatever disadvantages the standalone tradition might encompass, one advantage is difficult to deny: when Hebrew headings are in Hebrew and roman headings are in roman, they are easy to find. Searching on a daily basis meets with less frustration. Thus, as Rabenstein pointed out, the ultimate conclusion one reached in talking with Israeli librarians, was that "separate catalogs help Israeli readers and do not spoil them."[52]

---

[51] For a more detailed discussion of the structure of the soft font package and the equipment which supports it, see Chapter 10: The Israeli Scene: Hebrew in ALEPH.

[52] Bernard Hugo Rabenstein, "A Survey on the Use of Alphabetical Forms in Author and/or Title Headings in the Catalogs of Israeli Libraries," 66.

In conclusion, in spite of the many advantages of the segregated Israeli approach to cataloging, at least for the Israeli user, there is one major, undeniable disadvantage, a disadvantage that surfaced with the advent of the online catalog. The segregated—or full, vernacular record—approach of Israeli cataloging makes sharing Hebrew bibliographic data with the rest of the world in the online environment very difficult. The problems involved in exchanging machine-readable Hebrew cataloging, along with some possible solutions, will be discussed in depth in chapter 11: "Automation and Cooperation: Exchanging Machine-Readable Hebrew Cataloging, Or Synthesizing the Traditions."

3   Romanization and Transliteration Systems

Definitions of the terms *transliteration*, *transcription*, and *romanization* are nearly as numerous and varied as romanization and transliteration systems themselves. In the previous chapter, Bella Weinberg's 1974 definitions of these terms were suggested, because they are clear and workable. Another succinct and accessible definition was proposed a year later by the American National Standards Institute (ANSI): "*Transliteration* denotes the representation of Hebrew writing symbols, while *transcription* denotes the representation of Hebrew speech sounds." *Romanization* is a cover term for both *transliteration* and *transcription*.[1] What ANSI does not make explicit in its definition of romanization, however, is that the object language, or the language into which the nonroman language is converted, is by definition written in the roman or latin alphabet, e.g., English, French, or German. Thus, the definition for romanization proposed in the International Organization for Standardization's ISO/TC46 standard for conversion of one written language into another is more precise: "*Romanization*...is a form of conversion in which letters of the Latin alphabet are made to represent languages using other characters or signs."[2] Sumner C. Spalding, former head of cataloging at the Library of Congress, after defining the general term "romanization" and its two principal varieties, transliteration and transcription, notes the significance of choosing one or the other of these different methods of romanization:

> "Romanization" is the general term for any method which converts names or text written in a nonroman writing system into the letters of the roman alphabet. There are two principal methods by which this may be accomplished. One is transliteration, whereby romanization is accomplished

---

[1] *American National Standard Romanization of Hebrew* (New York: American National Standards Institute, c1975), p. 7.

[2] "General Principles for the Conversion of One Written Language into Another (ISO/TC46 (Sec. 426) 697 (Rev.))," *Journal of Documentation* 21 (1) (March 1965): 15-16.

letter-by-letter according to a table which equates each of the letters of the original (nonroman) alphabet with one or more letters, or letters plus diacritics, of the roman alphabet. The other system is phonetic or phonemic transcription, whereby romanization is accomplished by spelling the proper spoken sound of the name or word as closely as possible according to the orthography of a given roman alphabet, e.g. English. Needless to say, these methods yield quite different results, and in the case of phonetic transcription, quite different results within the same method, depending on the object language that is used, e.g. English or French.[3]

Belgian linguist Jean Poulain, writing on Hebrew transliteration in 1961, further refines the definition and principles of the first method described by Spalding—letter-by-letter romanization:

> Transliteration....is the transcription, letter by letter, of the signs of one alphabet into those of another alphabet, ...it is based on the following three principles which are cited as the introduction to all rules of transliteration: (a) in order to transliterate and re-transliterate, it suffices to identify the language handled; (b) so far as possible, a single Latin character should correspond to a single character in the foreign language, phonetic or etymological value not being the primary consideration; (c) signs which are not found on Latin-alphabet typewriter keyboards should be used as little as possible.[4]

Poulain's last principle—signs not found on Latin-alphabet typewriter keyboards should be avoided insofar as possible—points up a problem that is still with us today, in spite of the fact that cataloging records are produced more frequently using a computer keyboard than a typewriter. Diacritics and other special symbols still create a problem in automated systems. Even in systems such as RLIN, which permit the input and display of diacritics, they usually are displayed as separate characters (rather than attached to, and in the same space, as the letters they modify). Windows-based word processors have begun dealing with the problem of displaying diacritics and special characters in the same space as the letter to which they are attached (for example, in the Hebrew version of Microsoft Word *nikud*, or vowel points, can be added to Hebrew letters), so perhaps in the near future, these nonroman special characters will be able to be input and displayed in bibliographic systems, too, without causing any technical problems.

Bella Weinberg, discussing the complexity of romanizing Hebrew, pointed out that the problem is deeper than simply deciding whether to *transliterate* the letters or writing symbols (graphemes) or *transcribe* the Hebrew speech sounds (phonemes). The decision on whether to represent Hebrew in roman characters according to its

---

[3]C. Sumner Spalding, "Romanization Reexamined," *Library Resources & Technical Services* 21 (1) (Winter 1977): 5.

[4]Jean Poulain, "The Transliteration of Hebrew Characters," *Unesco Bulletin for Libraries* XV (6) (November-December 1961): 329.

graphemes (minimum distinctive units of writing),[5] or its phonemes (minimum units of distinctive sound-feature)[6] involves taking into account that there are *five* possible ratios between the representation of phonemes and graphemes. Type 1 is a single phoneme to a single grapheme, (e.g., *b* as in *boy*). Type 2 is a phoneme with no manifesting mark, or matching grapheme, such as the vowel in *Mc*Cormack. Type 3 is a single phoneme that can be expressed by more than one grapheme, such as the sound *o*, which is written in English in a variety of ways, as witnessed in such words as *oh, so, sew, hoe, beau,* and *though.* Type 4, the opposite situation, is more than one phoneme represented by a single grapheme, such as the letter *c* in *cat* and *cent*. Type 5, a type not found in modern English, is the representation of a vestigial feature, or non-function, of an alphabet by a single mark. An example of this would be the hard sign in Old Style Russian (in New Style Russian it is omitted). The problem in romanization as found in Anglo-American catalogs, Weinberg contends, is that in attempting to represent a foreign alphabet in the roman one, we have been trying to give the letters the spoken values of the English language. Thus, while dealing with *graphic* information, we have been striving for *phonetic* representation.[7]

Hans Wellisch, discussing the prospects for exchanging bibliographic data in nonroman scripts some 15 years ago, went even further in pointing out the multiplicity of conflicting requirements that romanization systems are expected to fulfill. According to him, there are at least six such requirements, which he characterizes as follows: (1) *general applicability*, i.e., the system must be capable of rendering any word or name in the souce script into roman letters; (2) *uniqueness of graphemic representation*, i.e., each letter or character in the source script must be represented unambiguously; (3) *simplicity of graphemic representation*, i.e., a restatement of Poulain's principle that the system should use basic letters only with no, or few diacritical marks; (4) *reversibility*, i.e., the characters of the nonroman script must be unambiguously restorable by simply reversing the transformation process; (5) *traditionality*, i.e., romanization of names, such as biblical names, that have been traditionally spelled in a certain way in a language community, must be preserved; and (6) *pronounceability*, i.e., the combination of roman letters produced by romanization must be pronounceable, particularly for names of persons and places.[8] Wellisch goes on to note that all of these requirements, except the first, clash with each other, and that for any nonroman script, only one or at best two of these requirements can be fulfilled simultaneously, while some, or all of the others, must be sacrificed.[9]

---

[5] Bella Hass Weinberg, "Transliteration in Documentation," *Journal of Documentation* 21 (March 1974): 19.

[6] Bella Hass Weinberg, "Transliteration in Documentation": 19.

[7] Bella Hass Weinberg, "Transliteration in Documentation": 19.

[8] Hans H. Wellisch, "The Exchange of Bibliographic Data in Nonroman Scripts" *UNESCO Journal of Information Science, Librarianship & Archives Administration* 2 (1) (Jan.-Mar. 1980): 14.

[9] Hans H. Wellisch, "The Exchange of Bibliographic Data in Nonroman Scripts," 14.

In an earlier article on the problems of script conversion and bibliographic control, Wellisch distinguishes between the difficulties of romanization for *operators*—i.e., those doing the romanizing—and *users*, who are the people who must decode the romanized texts.[10] He cites six major difficulties for the first group, the operators: (1) *multiplicity of schemes*, i.e., that for every nonroman script there exist today at least three and sometimes up to several dozen different conversion systems; (2) *inconsistent application and local adaptations*, i.e., that even in cases in which only one roman-ization scheme is in use for a particular script, it is often not applied consistently and, in many cases, diluted by locally devised adaptations, often without any indication to outside users what those changes are and when to use them; this situation results in: (3) *variant forms of romanized names*, i.e., names that have been romanized according to different schemes or national usages and which, as a result, appear in quite different forms in various bibliographic control tools; (4) *reversibility*, or more accurately, the lack of reversibility for vowel sounds in languages written in scripts that do not usually indicate vowels, such as Arabic and Hebrew. Wellisch also mentions, in discussing the problem of reversibility, the problem of multiple phonemes for single graphemes within the *same* language, which Weinberg discussed, as well as the related problem of multiple phonemes for the same grapheme in different languages, e.g., *j*, which is pronounced differently in English, French, German and Spanish. Romanization problem, (5) *susceptibility to errors*, is related to the complexity of nonroman writing systems, some of which (including Hebrew) do not express vowels graphically, while others contain letters and letter combinations that are not pronounced, and so on. When combined with the intricacies of certain romanization schemes, these complexities produce inevitable errors and mistakes in conversion that will happen no matter how well the romanizer knows the source language and its script. The final problem for the romanizing operator, (6) *alphabetization,* or the interfiling of entries for documents originally written in Roman script with those that are artificially romanized, results in many inconsistencies and leads to additional errors.[11]

The difficulties of romanization for the user, Wellisch contends, can be summed up more briefly[12] but are no less acute:

> Users are faced with an almost complete lack of keys to a Roman-ization system which is almost never made explicit to users of catalogs or bibliographies. The burden of deciphering a Romanization in order to arrive at the original form of a name is entirely on the user and it

---

[10] Hans H. Wellisch, "Script Conversion and Bibliographic Control of Documents in Dissimilar Scripts: Problems and Alternatives," *International Library Review* 10 (3) (1978): 3-22.

[11] Hans H. Wellisch, "Script Conversion and Bibliographic Control of Documents in Dissimilar Scripts...": 7-12.

[12] Hans H. Wellisch, "Script Conversion and Bibliographic Control of Documents in Dissimilar Scripts...": 12.

amounts in many instances to exercises in cryptography, or the decoding of a message to which the code key is available only to the senders (the librarians) but not to the receivers (the library users).[13]

In his 1976 article on script conversion practices in the world's libraries,[14] Wellisch showed that while most U.S. libraries used the ALA/LC romanization system for converting nonroman scripts (all the romanization schemes mentioned here will be described in more detail in the next section of this chapter), there is little consistency in use of romanization schemes in the rest of the world's libraries: "Some organizations use ISO transliteration standards, some cling to systems with a long bibliographic tradition such as the schemes of the U.S. Library of Congress or those of the Preussische Instruktionen, some use the national standards of their respective countries, and some others use various locally devised adaptations and mixtures of these systems.... None of these systems is unambiguously reversible."[15]

All of the problems discussed thus far are problems involved in romanization of nonroman languages in general, although some (such as the reversibility problem) apply to specific classes of languages, to which Hebrew belongs. In addition to these general romanization issues and problems, there are several problems specific to romanization of *Hebrew-character* materials. First, there is the problem of Sephardic and Ashkenazic pronunciation. Phonemic renderings of texts, and particularly of Hebrew names, by Jewish individuals and communities (especially those of synagogues and other religious, educational, and philanthrophic institutions), approximated the pronunciation of Hebrew in the respective orthography of various countries. Because some of these are based on the Sephardic pronunciation while others are linked to various versions of Ashkenazic pronunciation, the confusion that besets "popular" romanization of Hebrew has been increased even further.[16] Working in the other direction, trying to romanize proper names phonetically, even using dictionaries, is often virtually impossible, as Poulain points out in his paper rejecting the principles of phonetic transliteration and recommending instead a reversible system that romanizes consonants only (to be discussed in detail later in this chapter): "The name written in Hebrew QRSL can be pronounced *Karsal, Kirsal, Karsil, Krisil, Krisel,* etc. In fact, the name is *Kressel,* but this is something one has to know, and it is not always possible, even for a Hebraist, to have such knowledge. In this case, the name can be given in Latin only by the transcription of the Hebrew consonants QRSL."[17] Even aside from such cases as unguessable proper names, unpointed modern written Hebrew requires the romanizer who is trying to produce a voweled, phonetic romanization from an unvocalized Hebrew text to know Hebrew very well indeed.

---

[13] Hans H. Wellisch, "Script Conversion ... Dissimilar Scripts," 12.

[14] Hans H. Wellisch, "Script Conversion Practices in the World's Libraries," *International Library Review* 8 (1976): 55-84.

[15] Wellisch, "The Exchange of Bibliographic Data in Nonroman Scripts": 15.

[16] Hans H. Wellisch, *The Conversion of Scripts--Its Nature, History, and Utilization* (NewYork: John Wiley & Sons, 1978), p. 299.

[17] Poulain, "The Transliteration of Hebrew Characters": 330.

A BRIEF HISTORY OF HEBREW ROMANIZATION SYSTEMS

Probably the most complete review of Hebrew transliteration and transcription systems in the literature was published by Werner Weinberg in the 1969-1970 edition of the *Hebrew Union College Annual*.[18] Weinberg explains and justifies the bewildering multiplicity of such schemes by the geographic scatter of the Jews and the different purposes that romanization schemes serve in terms of phonetic and orthographic representation. Wellisch, in his survey of script conversion practices in libraries, demonstrates statistically that Hebrew has one of the highest percentages of homemade schemes of all nonroman languages found in the world's libraries.[19] In his book on the conversion of scripts, published two years later in 1978,[20] Wellisch covers the whole spectrum of nonroman scripts, not just Hebrew, but his historical survey of Hebrew romanization schemes is quite detailed and complements Werner Weinberg's. Between them, Weinberg and Wellisch present a comprehensive picture of the history of Hebrew romanization schemes from the earliest, dating back to the early Middle Ages, to the one used most widely today (ALA/LC). The following brief history is a composite assembled from both these sources.

The earliest recorded romanization scheme, a rather strict transliteration used by St. Jerome in the Middle Ages, gave way in the Renaissance to romanization systems that aimed at approximating the sounds of Hebrew as spoken in the Sephardic pronunciation. These schemes, and virtually all of the romanization systems used until this century were devised by mostly non-Jewish Hebrew philologists. They are all characterized by attempts to indicate a sometimes conjectural pronunciation, while at the same time striving to express also all written characters, including those not pronounced (Bella Weinberg's Type 5 phoneme/grapheme ratio) and those pronounced identically although written with different letters and diacritical marks (Bella Weinberg's Type 3 ratio).

In the latter part of the 19th century compilers of dictionaries and encyclopedias often devised their own schemes for the benefit of educated laymen. In 1890 the Royal Asiatic Society formed a committee for the transliteration of Oriental characters. Its report was adopted by many Societies at the Geneva Congress of Orientalists in 1894. In 1902, the *Jewish Encyclopedia* (*JE*) published a romanization system[21] that it claimed to be "in the main" the one proposed at the Geneva Congress of Orientalists, although in actuality it constituted a considerable broadening and simplification. This scheme was widely accepted for the romanization of Hebrew in

---

[18] Werner Weinberg,"Transliteration and Transcription of Hebrew," *Hebrew Union College Annual* 40-41 (1969-1970), 1-32.

[19]Hans H. Wellisch, "Script Conversion Practices in the World's Libraries": 55-84.

[20]Hans H. Wellisch, *The Conversion of Scripts--Its Nature, History, and Utilization.*

[21]*Jewish Encyclopedia* (New York: Funk & Wagnall, 1901-1905), Table, vol. II (1902), p. ix.

English-speaking countries and formed the basis for the ALA/LC scheme used by virtually all American libraries today. The *JE* generally uses a scheme almost identical to that of the Library of Congress, except for צ, which is rendered by z (not *ts* as in the LC scheme). The ALA *Catalog Rules* of 1908, speaking both for the American and the British Library Associations, recommended the *JE* romanization without qualification.[22] In 1941, a system based on the *JE* rules was adopted.[23] The Jewish National and University Library of Jerusalem, interestingly, followed the different ALA systems until 1967, when it adopted System I of the *Akademiyah la-lashon ha-'ivrit* (Academy of the Hebrew Language), which will be described in detail later in this chapter.[24]

The *Universal Jewish Encyclopedia* of 1939 introduced several differences from the *JE*, the most significant being *v* for ו and *ts* for צ.[25] The *Encyclopaedia Judaica* of 1928 adopted the usual German realizations for consonants: ו=*w*, ז=*s*, ח and כ = *ch*, י = *j*, צ = *z*, ש = *sch* (none of which are used in the Library of Congress of System, which is naturally based on English-language prononunciations of consonants).[26]

In 1921, the British Royal Geographic Society (RGS) published *Alphabets of Foreign Languages Transcribed into English According to the RGS II System* by E. Gleichen and J. H. Reynolds of the "Permanent Committee on Geographical Names for British Official Use" (PCGN).[27] In 1925, the PCGN published the "First List of Names in Palestine" in consultation with a Palestine subcommittee on Hebrew. Based on this, an insert was prepared to replace the Hebrew section in *Alphabets of Foreign Languages*. The new *RGS II* contained the following changes: ç = *h* (instead of *kh*), ק = *q* (instead of *k*), the first change bringing it closer to the ALA/LC system, the second change moving it further away. The new RGS II was adopted by the Palestine

---

[22]American Library Association, *Catalog Rules: Author and Title Entries,* American edition (Chicago: American Library Association, 1908), p. 69, fn.

[23] American Library Association, *Catalog Rules: Author and Title Entries* (Chicago: American Library Association, 1941), 337; also, [ALA, 1949] American Library Association, *A.L.A. Cataloging Rules for Author and Title Entries* (Chicago: American Library Association, 1949), 248.

[24]Ha-Aḳademiyah la-lashon ha-'ivrit, *Kelalei ha-ta'atiḳ me-ketav' ivri le-ketav latini* (offprint from *Zikhronot ha-Akademiyah* III-IV) (Jerusalem: ha-Aḳademiyah, 1957).

[25] *Universal Jewish Encyclopedia* (New York: Universal Jewish Encyclopedia, 1939-1943), Table, I.202.

[26]*Encyclopedia Judaica*, vols. 1-X (Berlin, 1928-34), Table, vol. I, p. xx.

[27] Royal Geographical Society, *Alphabets of Foreign Languages Transcribed into English, According to the RGS II System,* by E. Gleichen and J. H. Reynolds (London, 1921), 67 f., "Hebrew," revised and printed as insert, 1925, p. 67-69.

Government in 1931 in their pamphlet, *Transliteration from Arabic and Hebrew into English...*[28]

In 1957, the Academy of the Hebrew Language published a double set of romanizations, the "Simple" and the "More Exact" system (Systems I and II) for Israeli use.[29] In 1961, the U.S. Board of Geographical Names (BGN) published a "Hebrew-Latin Transliteration Table."[30] One year later, the PCGN and BGN together adopted System I of the Hebrew Academy. The International Organization for Standardization (ISO) Transliteration of Hebrew was published in 1962[31]. System II of the Hebrew Language Academy served as a basis of the ISO deliberations (ISO Document TZ 46 Secretariat—345 535 F).

Werner Weinberg, in his article on Hebrew romanization, stressed the need for more than one system, and in fact went far beyond the two schemes devised by the Academy of the Hebrew Language. He asserted that no less than five types of romanization are needed: (1) narrow transliteration, (2) narrow phonetic transcription, (3) broad transliteration-transcription, (4) phonemic transcription, and (5) popular transcription-transliteration.[32] Of these five systems, (1) and (5) are roughly equivalent to Academy II and I respectively, (2) is intended for use by phoneticians only, since it depends on dialects, diction, and so forth, and (3) and (4) are intended for philological purposes, using a phonetic alphabet. Primarily as a result of Weinberg's suggestions for multiple romanization systems, the ANSI Standard Z39.25-1975, which was prepared by the Subcommittee for the Romanization of Hebrew and Yiddish of the American National Standards Committee Z39 on Standardization in the Field of Library Work, Documentation and Related Publishing Practices, contains four schemes (which are only partially compatible with each other).

The Subcommittee for the Romanization of Hebrew and Yiddish was organized in the spring of 1970 as a subgroup of Subcommittee 5 on Transliteration, and was charged with the development of romanizations for both Hebrew and Yiddish. Starting with the system for Hebrew, the subcommittee agreed early on that no single all-purpose system was either practical or desirable. Therefore it set as its goal the preparation of a system that would include several systems of romanization, each for a different purpose. The resulting standard included four different systems, presented along with suggestions and guidelines for the intended use of each system.[33]

---

[28]Palestine Government. *Transliteration for Arabic and Hebrew into English...* Jerusalem: Goldberg's Press, 1931.

[29] Ha-Aḳademiyah la-lashon ha-'ivrit, *Kelalei ha-ta'atiḳ me-ketav' ivri le-ketav latini.*

[30]U.S. Board of [on] Geographic Names, *Transliteration Guide (*Washington: 1961).

[31]International Organization for Standardization, *Recommendation R 259: Transliteration of Hebrew* ([Switzerland]: ISO, 1962).

[32]Werner Weinberg,"Transliteration and Transcription of Hebrew."

[33]*American National Standard Romanization of Hebrew.*

Three are intended for conventional writing or printing, while the fourth is designed for use with computer printout facilities. The "general purpose" and "more exact" schemes—the first and second ANSI tables—are designed for English-speaking users and based on Israeli pronunciation. The first one, General-Purpose Romanization, was used by some bibliographers, such as Shimeon Brisman,[34] but has been criticized because its use makes it difficult to match a bibliographic reference to a library catalog entry.[35] ANSI claims that its primary virtue lies in its appropriateness for those whose knowledge of Hebrew is minimal and who need to cite a form that only suggest the original Hebrew. The second ANSI table, the More Exact style, is a combination of transliteration and transcription, because it differentiates between homophonous consonants, but not between homophonous vowels, permitting reversibility of consonants (but not vowels) to the Hebrew original. It is essentially equivalent to the one used by LC, which was to become the *de facto* standard in American libraries.

The third scheme, Narrow Transliteration, which involves subtleties of Hebrew grammar such as doubling of consonants in the case of *dagesh forte*, was never used to a significant extent in the bibliographic community. It is a transliteration scheme intended for scholarly purposes, providing unambiguous one-to-one equivalents made possible by diacritical remarks. It is characterized by nearly complete reversibility.

The fourth and final scheme, Keypunch-Compatible Transliteration was according to ANSI, "ideal for storage of text for any kind of textual study" and "also entirely suitable for bibliographical records, especially where alphabetical interfiling with Hebrew-character material is desired, where romanizers who know Hebrew well are not available, or where both conditions pertain."[36] Unlike systems one and two, the Keypunch-Compatible Transliteration system was *not* English-language oriented and therefore had the advantage of being applicable internationally. Most of the time it used simple and completely reversible consonantal tables composed of characters that were available on the IBM 029 Keypunch, which was state-of-the-art in 1975, as well as on an ordinary typewriter. This system's place in the history of Hebrew romanization was assured by the fact that it was significant in the production of the Hebrew character title sequence of the New York Public Library's Automated Book Catalog.[37]

---

[34]Shimeon Brisman, *A History and Guide to Judaic Bibliography* (New York: Ktav; Cincinnati: Hebrew Union College, 1977) (His Jewish Research Literature, 1), p. x.

[35] For example, by Zachary M. Baker, [Review of]: Brisman, Shimeon, *A History and Guide to Judaic Encyclopedias and Lexicons, Judaica Librarianship* 4 (2) (Spring 1988-Winter 1989), 142.

[36]*American National Standard Romanization of Hebrew,* p. 12.

[37]New York Public Library. Research Libraries, *Dictionary Catalog of the Research Libraries* (New York: NYPL, 1972-1981).

THE GRAPHIC APPROACH:
Reversible Romanization

While the conversion of alphabets is not in itself a computer-related topic, in Judaica librarianship the connection between romanization and automation has been historically important, as Bella Weinberg noted in her 1991 article on automation and Judaica libraries.[38]

As they watched the development of the MARC (machine-readable cataloging) format by the Library of Congress in the 1960s, Judaica librarians realized that this would be "good for the Jews" only if a MARC format was developed to accomodate Hebrew data. Since computers at that time were not yet able to handle nonroman character sets, in 1969 Herbert Zafren of Hebrew Union College proposed using reversible romanization to represent Hebrew characters in machine-readable form.[39]

Dr. Zafren served as the representative of the Association of Judaica Libraries (AJL) to ANSI Committee Z39 and chaired the committee that developed the American National Standard for the Romanization of Hebrew. The keypunch machine referred to in ANSI table 4, Keypunch-Compatible Transliteration, became obsolete within five years after the standard's publication, but reversible romanization was to remain an issue in Judaica librarianship until well into the late 1980s.

Why? What were the arguments for this system, which today looks so quaint and bizarre and absolutely unreadable? What caused librarians as prominent and diverse as Zafren, Ben Ami Lipetz , chairman of the American Society for Information Science (ASIS) Standards Committee, and Jerrold Orne, chairman of Z39 and also chairman of the general subcommittee on transliteration (SC/5) all, at various times, to support so staunchly the concentration of efforts on "developing new conversion systems for international use, designed for machine input and output, completely reversible, and having no major concern for conventions of alphabet, spelling or phonetics"?[40]

Wellisch, in his book on conversion of scripts, traces the concept for reversible romanization of Hebrew to E. A. Goldman, who in 1971 published an article detailing a computer-compatible "semitic alphabet" in the Hebrew Union College Annual.[41]

---

[38]Bella Hass Weinberg, "Automation and the American Judaica Library during the First Quarter Century of the Association of Jewish Libraries, 1965-1990," *Judaica Librarianship* 5 (2) (Spring 1990-Winter 1991): 167.

[39]Herbert C. Zafren, [Letter], *AJL Bulletin* 4 (1) (Dec. 1969): 4.

[40] Ted Brandhorst, "ANSI Z39 Romanization Standards and 'Reversibility': A Dialog to Arrive at a Policy," *Journal of the American Society for Information Science* 30 (1) (January 1979), 59.

[41]E. A. Goldman, et al, "A 'Computer-Compatible' Semitic Alphabet," *Hebrew Union College Annual* 42 (1971): 251-278.

The idea here, Wellisch continues, is not to code an already existing transliteration system, but rather to develop a transliteration scheme with a strict one-to-one relationship between a Hebrew character and its conversion into a character found on any standard computer printout device.[42] Goldman and his colleagues claimed that conversion from Hebrew to computer-compatible transliteration was almost automatic, and that it could be done by any typist who knows the 22 letters of the Hebrew alphabet and the conversion code.

The June 1977 issue of the *Bulletin of the American Society for Information Science* (p. 35) carried a short position statement prepared by Ben Ami Lipetz on the subject of "Standards for Romanization of Languages That Use Nonroman Alphabets."[43] The statement recommended that ANSI Z39 reexamine the basic premises behind its romanization work, and that it establish "reversibility" as the guiding principle for all future work. "Reversibility" was defined as the ability to transliterate both forward (from original to rendered version) and backward (from rendered version to original) without ambiguity or loss of information in either direction. The statement regarded reversibility in transliteration as essential in an age of machine-readable bibliographic records.

The implications of Lipetz's premise are twofold. First, it means that romanization standards must be designed to convert the original unavailable character set into a limited and widely accepted set of Roman characters, such as the 26 letters of the English language plus a few very widely used punctuation marks. The second implication is that the romanized rendering of a record from a nonroman language should be indicative of original spelling, but not necessarily indicative of proper pronunciation. In Lipetz's opinion, the "fatal flaw" in the Z39 romanization standards program was, in all but the fourth table, an obsession with pronunciation: "What we are trying to cope with in romanization is the written record; so our focus should be on writing, not sounds. English and other Western languages are not written entirely phonetically, so why should we need fully phonetic romanization?[44]

The primary advantage to using reversible romanization as the international standard, Lipetz felt, was that it would open up tremendous opportunities both for inexpensive processing and for interchange of records in languages that were currently impossible to deal with. Romanization would rely on the limited set of roman characters, plus those punctuation marks and other special characters that are commonly available in English printing. It would *not* employ unusual symbols (such as phonetic symbols), which were unavailable in computer processing environments and were likely to remain so for the foreseeable future.

---

[42]Hans H. Wellisch, *The Conversion of Scripts--Its Nature, History, and Utilization,* p. 308.

[43]Ben Ami Lipetz, "Standards for Romanization of Languages of Languages that Use Nonroman Alphabets," *Bulletin of the American Society for Information Science*: 35.

[44]Ben Ami Lipetz, "Standards for Romanization of Languages of Languages that Use Nonroman Alphabets": 35.

In the same year, 1977, S. Michael Malinconico and Walter R. Grutchfield published an article describing what was to go down in history as the only large-scale application of the principle Lipetz so passionately felt was the only way to handle nonroman material.[45]

The New York Public Library (NYPL), in order to handle the input and display of data in nonroman vernacular scripts in its Automated Bibliographic Control system, developed and implemented facilities using input conventions derived from the ANSI standard for Computer Compatible Transliteration of Hebrew. Malinconico and Grutchfield describe both *how* NYPL implemented ANSI's "Keypunch-Compatible Transliteration Style" and, perhaps more significantly, *why* they adopted it for the important NYPL Jewish collection.

Because of the absence of vowels from LC cataloging of Hebrew vernacular records and, in fact, from most texts, they explain, romanization of Hebrew is a thorny problem. In addition, due to its right-to-left writing mode, it creates many complex problems for an automated system since such a system must be able to handle a mixture of Hebrew and roman alphabet text within the same entry. Because of these difficulties, and because of the importance of NYPL's Jewish collection and the large number of Hebrew and Yiddish language readers in New York City, the NYPL decided in 1974 to implement Hebrew as the first nonroman script in its automated system.

At the same time, they continue, ANSI was in the process of drafting a computer-compatible transliteration standard. In January 1975 the transcription was adopted by ANSI for promulgation as a standard. One of its major advantages was unique representation of each Hebrew character by a normal alphabetic or special character. Data transcription was thus greatly simplified since romanizing the unwritten vowel sounds was not required; instead, only a character-for-character transliteration was required. This attribute had a further, obvious advantage— *a-priori*—assurance that all data input under such a scheme would be able to be displayed in vernacular script whenever the mechanical capability came to exist. This would not be the case with traditional transliteration schemes since they are rarely, if ever, completely reversible by a computer program.

An additional advantage to the scheme, they claimed, was that any reader familiar with the language, after learning twenty-seven correspondences, could read the "transliterated" text. It is toward this aspect of the system that Maliconico and Grutchfield demonstrate an optimism that few other proponents of Keypunch-Compatible Transliteration ever showed. Even those who enthusiastically proclaimed the system's ease of use and efficacy for bibliographic exchange, rarely denied that the results are not readily readable, and are not readable at all for anyone unfamiliar with the scheme.

---

45 S. Michael Malinconico and Walter R. Grutchfield, "Vernacular Scripts in the NYPL Automated Bibliographic Control System," *Journal of Library Automation* 10 (September 1977): 205-255.

Unreadability notwithstanding, the NYPL decided to begin data input at the earliest possible time using the proposed ANSI computer-compatible transliteration and to display Hebrew script in the book catalog in that manner until the additional work could be done to produce true vernacular text. All input and display were done in roman characters, using the table shown in Fig. 3.1.[46] The October 1974 edition featured reversible romanization, but in December 1975, Hebrew characters appeared.

NYPL was one of the founding members of the Research Libraries Group, and after joining, discontinued its Automated Book Catalog in the summer of 1981. Because many other libraries were inputting ALA/LC Romanization, the continued use of reversible romanization would have led to a split in the Hebrew subset of the RLIN database. NYPL therefore discontinued use of that system.

Although nothing is left of reversible romanization in contemporary processing of Hebrew materials in the online environment, it was an important concept in the early days of Judaica library automation, when nonroman scripts could neither be displayed nor printed by computers. NYPL employed this transliteration system successfully in the production of its own book catalog. In a network environment, however, there was pressure to conform to the practice of the majority of libraries, and the alternative romanization scheme was abandoned.[47] NYPL's bibliographic records featuring reversible romanization on RLIN have yet to be converted back to Hebrew characters, and the only lasting influence that the ANSI Standard had on LC was to prompt LC to add diacritics to certain letters in its romanization table to make consonants reversible[48] (LC, 1976). This "peppery" romanization, as Bella Weinberg likes to call it—because it consists mainly of dots under letters—is an inconvenience to the Hebraica cataloger working online, because the diacritic is input in RLIN as a separate character before the letter, and this impedes legibilility.

A final postscript on reversible romanization resurfaced in the late 1980s when it became known that RLIN required parallel romanization of the core fields of Hebrew bibliographic records.[49] Proponents of the ANSI reversible scheme argued that it required a lower level of linguistic knowledge and therefore was less time-consuming to use than LC's phonetic romanization system. Bella Weinberg, who helped draft an earlier AJL resolution of romanization supporting reversible romanization of Hebrew in machine-readable records,[50] now withdrew her support for using this scheme in parallel romanization of Hebrew records in RLIN for three

---

[46]S. Michael Malinconico and Walter R. Grutchfield, "Vernacular Scripts in the NYPL Automated Bibliographic Control System," *Journal of Library Automation* 10 (3) (September 1977): 209.

[47]Bella Hass Weinberg, "Automation and the American Judaica Library during the First Quarter Century of the Association of Jewish Libraries, 1965-1990": 68.

[48]"Hebrew and Yiddish" [Romanization table], *Cataloging Service,* Bulletin 118 (Summer 1976): 63.

[49]Joan M. Aliprand, "Hebrew on RLIN," *Judaica Librarianship* 3(1-2) (1986-1987): 12.

[50]Bella Hass Weinberg, "Automation and the American Judaica Library during the First Quarter Century of the Association of Jewish Libraries, 1965-1990": 68.

reasons: (1) reversible romanization should be only a temporary solution to the unavailability of Hebrew characters; (2) reversible romanization would be redundant to the Hebrew bibliographic data in RLIN, and if useful to those with roman-only terminals, should be generated automatically; and (3) the use of reversible romanization by some libraries and ALA/LC romanization by others would create a split in the Hebraic subset of the RLIN database in which the romanized data is the basis for *clustering* or matching records.[51]

As it turned out, many if not most Judaica librarians agreed with her, and RLG's committee on bibliographic standards did not approve an alternative to ALA/LC romanization standard for Hebrew. Thus, peppery romanization aside, the NYPL automated system went the way of the dinosaur, and its Hebrew data was declared non-standard by RLIN.

[51] Bella Hass Weinberg, "From Copy Cataloging to Derived Bibliographic Records: Cataloging and Its Automation in American Judaica Research Libraries from the Sixties Through the Eighties, " *Judaica Librarianship* 4 (2) (Spring 1988-Winter 1989), 118.

Fig. 3.1. NYPL Hebrew Transcription Table.

Hebrew Character		NYPL Input Representation
א		*@*
ב		**B**
ג		**G**
ד		**D**
ה		**H**
ו		**W**
ז		**Z**
ח		**II**
ט		**T**
י		**Y**
כ,ך		**K**
כ	in final position	**K̸**
ל		**L**
מ,ם		**M**
מ	in final position	**M̸**
נ,ן		**N**
ן	in final position	**N̸**
ס		**S**
ע		**&**
פ,ף		**P**
פ	in final position	**P̸**
צ,ץ		**C**
צ	in final position	**C̸**
ק		**Q**
ר		**R**
ש		**S**
ת		**T**
'	**Single**	**abbreviation mark**
"	**Double**	**abbreviation mark**

The Hebrew character set also includes: space, arabic numerals (0-9), and normal punctuation (**. , : ; ( ) ? ! ' "" - /**).

ALA/LC ROMANIZATION:
The American Standard

The de facto standard for romanization in America and in much of the rest of the world is the system developed by the Library of Congress and the committees of the American and British library associations beginning in the late 19th century. The Anglo-American code of 1908, compiled by two important committees in the Anglo-American library community, contains an "Appendix 2" which devotes eight pages to romanization. The first item in the appendix is a report given in 1885 by an ALA Transliteration Committee, that recommends adoption of the general principles recently set forth by the Royal Geographical Society with respect to roman orthography in transliteration systems. These principles which, generally stated, were to use consonants with their English values and vowels with their German or Italian values, have dominated Anglo-American romanization for libraries ever since. This appendix included, in addition, specific tables for Semitic languages, compiled by Professor C. H. Toy of Harvard University.[52]

The Hebrew romanization scheme contained in ALA 1908 was essentially the one used by the *Jewish Encyclopedia*, and in ALA 1949 that scheme was reprinted, but in a revised edition (including variant romanizations for Yiddish), which had been adopted by the Library of Congress in 1948 (see Fig. 3.2. The ALA/LC 1948-1976 Romanization Table[53]). Prior to 1948 Yiddish words of German origin retained their German spelling in romanization. For example, the Yiddish word for "history" was romanized as "geschichte." After 1948, this became "geshikhte."[54]

Until March 1948 the ALA/LC Hebraica romanization table was based on German spelling, a practice that appears to go back to Cutter's recommendation to use *The Jewish Encyclopedia* of 1901-1905 as the basis for Hebrew romanization.[55] *The Jewish Encyclopedia* was also used as the standard reference authority for Hebraica cataloging, e.g. in establishing forms of headings. The main differences from the later romanization system involved the vav, tsadi, and tav. The vav was romanized as "w"(currently, "v"), the tsadi as "z" (currently, "ts"), and the tav without dagesh as "th"(currently "t"). The Hebrew word for "country," for example, was romanized as "arez" or "erez"; after 1948 this became "arets" or "erets."[56]

---

[52]American Library Association, *Catalog Rules: Author and Title Entries,* American edition.

[53]Paul Maher, *Hebraica Cataloging: A Guide to ALA/LC Romanization and Descriptive Cataloging* (Washington, DC: Cataloging Distribution Service, Library of Congress, 1987), p. 71.

[54]Paul Maher, *Hebraica Cataloging: A Guide to ALA/LC Romanization and Descriptive Cataloging,* p. 10.

[55]Charles A. Cutter, *Rules for a Dictionary Catalog,* 4th ed. (Washington: G.P.O., 1904). Cf. Appendix I, p. 150, footnote.

[56]Paul Maher, *Hebraica Cataloging: A Guide to ALA/LC Romanization and Descriptive Cataloging,* p. 10.

Fig. 3.2. The ALA/LC 1948-1976 Romanization Table

א	initial and final disregarded; otherwise ´ (prime)	ל	l
ב	b	מ (final, ם)	m
בּ	v (in Yiddish, b)	נ (final, ן)	n
ג	g	ס	s
ד	d	ע	' (inverted comma)
ה	h	פ	p
ו	v	פ (final, ף)	f
וו	v	צ (final, ץ)	ts
ז	z	ק	k
ח	h	ר	r
ט	t	שׁ	sh
י	y (at beginning of word or syllable; otherwise, i)	שׂ	s
כ	k	ת	t
(final,ך)	kh	ת	t (in Hebrew words; in Yiddish, s)
ך			

Vowels used in Hebrew

ָ	a
ַ	a
ֶ	e
ֵ	e
וֹ	o
וּ	u̲
ֻ	u
ִ	i
ִי	i
ְ	e

Vowels used in Yiddish

א	a or o
או, ו	u
אוי, וי	oi
אי, י	i
ע	e
איי, יי	ay (as ai in aisle) or ey (as ei in weigh)

In 1974 Hans Wellisch conducted a survey of script conversion practices among 321 libraries throughout the world with substantial holdings of works in nonroman scripts. His reason for the survey was, in his words, that "no attempt has ever been made, so far as is known, to ascertain the degree of diversity in script conversion practices of libraries on a world-wide scale, nor has it been found out which of the many existing conversion schemes has the largest following among libraries."[57] The results, published in 1976, indicated that the ALA/LC romanization system was used by more libraries than the two next romanization schemes and that it was the most widely used romanization system for the eight most important nonroman scripts throughout the world. Furthermore, on the American continent, the ALA/LC romanization scheme was found to be used almost exclusively.[58] Wellisch attributed the predominance of the ALA/LC scheme to "the excellent organization that stands behind the system, and even more to the provision of catalogue cards in some three dozen scripts covered by the Library of Congress." Thus, in the mid-1970s, it was the convenience of being able to use LC's catalog cards that was the driving force behind the willingness of America's libraries to standardize (or at least attempt to standardize) their romanization, just as ten years later the potential for being able to use RLIN cataloging records convinced the Judaica librarianship community in America to give up the advantages of reversible romanization and standardize the cataloging of their Hebrew materials using ALA/LC romanization.

In 1976 inferior dots were added to "v" and "t" in order to distinguish vet (v) from ṿaṿ (v) and ṭav (t) from ṭet (ṭ); the miagkii znak, or prime (´) for alef was changed to alif ('); the acute was added to the "s" to distinguish samekh (s) from śin (s), and the grave was added to the "s" in romanized Yiddish to distinguish the sav (ṡ) from samekh (s) and sin (ś).[59] The resulting romanization table is shown in Fig. 3.3, which presents both the ALA/LC Consonantal Table for Hebraic Languages (1976-Present), and Vowels Used in Hebrew and Vowels Used in Yiddish (neither of which changed in 1976).

Hebraica Cataloging: A Guide to ALA/LC Romanization and Descriptive Cataloging, which Paul Maher, LC's Senior Descriptive Cataloger, prepared in 1987, is the definitive guide to romanization of Hebrew-alphabet materials using this, the world's most widely-recognized romanization system. It is full of examples that, in attempting to simplify and clarify the rules Maher defines, inevitably demonstrate how endlessly complex the process of romanization of Hebrew really is. Maher devotes a large portion of his manual to elucidating fine points of romanization with examples to cover nearly every ambiguous situation (and there is a discouraging number of them). What follows is a selection of what we consider some of the more important applications of the ALA/LC romanization tables for Hebrew which Maher illustrates.

---

[57]Hans H. Wellisch, "Script Conversion Practices in the World's Libraries": 55.

[58]Hans H. Wellisch, "Script Conversion Practices in the World's Libraries": 64-65.

[59]Paul Maher, *Hebraica Cataloging: A Guide to ALA/LC Romanization and Descriptive Cataloging*, p. 10.

Fig. 3.3. The ALA/LC Consonantal Table
for Hebraic Languages (1976-Present)

א	initial and final disregarded; otherwise '	ל	l
ב	b	מ (final, ם)	m
ב	v (in Yiddish, b)	נ (final, ן)	n
ג	g	ס	s
ד	d	ע	'
ה	h	פ	p
ו	y	פ (final, ף)	f
וו	v	צ (final, ץ)	ts
ז	z	ק	ḳ
ח	ḥ	ר	r
ט	ṭ	ש	sh
י	y (at beginning of word or syllable; otherwise, i)	ש	ś
כ	k	ת	t
(final,)	kh	ת	t (in Yiddish, ⟨ṡ⟩)
ך			

Vowels used in Hebrew

ָ	a
ַ	a
ֶ	e
ֵ	e
וֹ	o
וּ	u
ֻ	u
ִ	i
ִי	i
ְ	e

Vowels used in Yiddish

א	a or o
או, ו	u
וי, אוי	oi
אי, י	i
ע	e
יי, איי	ay, if pronounced ai as in aisle, or ey, if pronounced ei in as in weigh

Alef

...When it is used in a word merely to indicate the presence of a vowel...., the special character (') is not used.

ALA/LC romanization

rosh [<u>not</u>: r'osh]	ראש
ḳamerit [<u>not</u> ḳ'amerit]	קאמרית

....The alif (') is used for alef however, in other cases where the vowel appears under, **not before,** the alef.

ALA/LC romanization

ḳeri'ah [reading]	קריאה
Yisra'el [Israel]	ישראל

Alef/ʻAyin initials

Aleph and ʻayin initials present a special situation since they may carry virtually any vowel. When romanizing names in Hebrew and a given name is represented by an abbreviated alef or ʻayin, the letter is romanized according to the vocalization, i.e., by supplying the vowel—sl, of the name for which it stands.

ALA/LC romanization

(all the following have initial alef):

A. [Aharon]	א. [אהרן]
E. [Eliyahu]	א. [אליהו]
I. [Iris]	א. [איריס]
O. [Ofir]	א. [אפיר]
U. [Uri]	א. [אורי]

(all the following have initial ʻayin):

ʻA. [ʻAmos]	ע. [עמוס]
ʻE. [ʻEzra]	ע. [עזרה]
ʻI. [ʻImanu'el]	ע. [עמנואל]
ʻO. [ʻOded]	ע. [עודד]
ʻU. [ʻUzi]	ע. [עזי]

If the given name that the initial represents is unknown and no clues are available as to what its correct vocalization might be, the Hebrew letter is romanized as "A" for alef and as "'A" for 'ayin. LC MARC authority records for such names are coded as provisional until it is known precisely what roman letter is appropriate.

Special Characters....

Apostrophe (Hebrew)

[to indicate consonantal sounds not found in the Hebrew alphabet--sl]

G'imi [Jimmy]	ג׳ימי
Z'aḵ [Jacques]	ז׳ק
Ts'urts'il [Churchill]	צ׳ורצ׳יל

In the vernacular a *geresh* (apostrophe) or *gershayim* (double quote mark) may also be used to indicate an abbreviation. In such cases the *geresh* or *gershayim* is retained in the vernacular record, but a **period** is used in the roman record.

ALA/LC romanization

Y. Shmidṭ [not: Y' Shmidt]   י׳ שמידט

....A miagkii znak (prime) is placed between two letters representing two distinct consonants when the combination might otherwise be read as a digraph.

ALA/LC romanization

Hildes ′haimer [personal name]	הילדסהיימר
hats ′harah [translation: declaration]	הצהרה

Vowels

General

Vowels for Hebrew words and forenames, etc. are supplied on the basis of the vocalization in Even-Shoshan's <u>ha-Milon he-hadash</u> in conjunction with the traditional grammars....

All initial schwas (and therefore cases of schwa n'a) in Hebrew words are transcribed as "e" regardless of pronunciation.

ALA/LC romanization

teḵufah [not: tḵufah (era)]	תקופה
teshuvah [not: tshuvah (response)]	תשובה

<u>Yod</u>

....the <u>yod</u> in Hebrew is romanized as "y" only when it is followed by a vowel. Thus:

ALA/LC romanization

matsui [<u>not</u>: matsuy (found)]   מצוי

ḥaverai [<u>not</u>: haveray (my friends)]   חבריי

Foreign Loan Words

Foreign loan words with initial consonantal clusters are not *generally* considered to have initial schwa n'a ....The initial clusters retain the effect of vowel "heightening," i.e., the schwa of the indefinite prefix for be-, ke-, and le- becomes hirik: bi-ki, li.

ALA/LC romanization

Israel. Lishkah ha-merkazit **li**-sṭaṭisṭiḳah.
Universiṭah ha-'Ivrit **bi**-Yerushalayim. Makhon **li**-kriminologyah....

A few loan words are also treated as though exempt from the rules governing the aspiration/non-aspiration of b/v, k/kh, and p/f when preceeded by an open syllable.

be-Polin [<u>not</u>: be-Folin (translation: in Poland)]
u-bibliyografyah [<u>not</u>: u-vibliyografyah (translation: and bibliography)....

Hebrew Hyphenation

The definite article (ha-, he-), the conjunction (u-, va-, ve-), and certain prepositions (e.g., b, k, l, m) are prefixed in the vernacular. In romanization these articles, conjunctions, and prefixes are separated by hyphenation from the word to which they are prefixed. No distinction is made between a <u>makef</u> (a hyphen appearing in the vernacular source), and a hyphen supplied by romanization....

ALA/LC romanization

Shelomoh ha-Melekh veha-devorah שלמה המלך והדברה ...

A special case arises with הלוי and הכהן. When either of these names appears as a surname it is romanized as Halevi or Hakohen, respectively. When appearing as an attributive title associated with a name, the ALA/LC systematic romanization becomes ha-Leyi or ha-Kohen.

ALA/LC romanization

Haleyi, Le'ah	הלוי, לאה
Hakohen, Devorah	הכהן, דבורה
Natanzohn, Yosef Sha'ul, ha-Leyi	נתנזוהן, יוסף שאול, הלוי
Yisra'el Me'ir, ha-Kohen	ישראל מאיר, הכהן

Multiple prefixes

Multiple prefixed articles, conjunctions, and prepositions are separated by only one hyphen from the "base word" unless one of the prefixes is the first word of a title.

ALA/LC romanization

u-Ve-reshit [if "and Genesis"]
uve-reshit [if "and in the beginning"].[60]

Yiddish Romanization

Maher also gives examples of applications of the LC romanization tables for Yiddish materials. In general, he states, the vocalization of Yiddish is much less complicated than that of Hebrew, and the romanization of any non-Hebrew word in a Yiddish text is virtually letter by letter, especially for consonants:

ALA/LC romanization

Rozshanski[not: Rozhanski]	ראזשאנסקי
Tshernoyits [not: Chernoyits]	טשערנאוויץ

Hebrew words in Yiddish

Questions do arise however, regarding the vocalization of Hebrew words in a Yiddish context. For this, Weinreich's *Modern English-Yiddish, Yiddish-English Dictionary* is followed. This applies for the most part to *vowels,* not to consonants.

Weinreich:

bikhides	ביחידות
biksa´v	בכתב
moyre	מורא

---

[60]Paul Maher, *Hebraica Cataloging: A Guide to ALA/LC Romanization and Descriptive Cataloging,* p. 12-22.

Hebrew personal names in Yiddish

If a Hebrew personal name appears in a Yiddish source, it is romanized according to its Hebrew form rather than attempting to approximate a Yiddish pronunciation....

ALA/LC romanization

Mosheh [not: Moysheh]   משה

...Names that are common in both languages are romanized according to context:

ALA/LC romanization

Rozenshṭain (if Hebrew)   רוזנשטיין
Rozenshṭeyn (if Yiddish).[61]

Wellisch treats the romanization of Yiddish as a more problematic area than Maher implies, both because of the differences in orthography from Hebrew, especially regarding the use of consonants to indicate vowels in Yiddish, and because of the additional complexity caused by the "phonetic" orthography of Yiddish as written in the (former) Soviet Union. He contends that the romanization of personal names is particularly difficult because it is common for a writer with a name of German or Slavic origin to spell his name according to Hebrew orthography when writing in Hebrew. Conversely, he adds, a name of Hebrew origin (or one containing Hebrew elements) is not subjected to the rules of Yiddish orthography, but is written as other Hebrew words in Yiddish, namely in "defective" Hebrew spelling, i.e., without indication of vowels, see Chapter 4: Special Problems of Hebrew: Variant Orthography, while Yiddish spelling rules are applied to non-Hebrew parts of a name.[62]

The YIVO Institute for Jewish Research had been instrumental in standardizing Yiddish orthography in the mid 1930s,[63] when the Institute's headquarters were still in Vilna, then one of the chief centers of Yiddish culture. In 1949 YIVO published a phonetic romanization scheme intended for English-speaking users,[64] since by then America had become the center of Yiddish language and literature after the Holocaust. This scheme was adopted by LC and published in ALA 1949, together with the one for Hebrew, and it is to this scheme that Maher refers his applications in his 1987 manual. A more detailed explanation of the system published

---

[61]Paul Maher, *Hebraica Cataloging: A Guide to ALA/LC Romanization and Descriptive Cataloging,* p. 22-23.

[62]Hans H. Wellisch, *The Conversion of Scripts--Its Nature, History, and Utilization,* p. 304.

[63]YIVO, *Takones fun yidishn oysleyg* (Vilna: YIVO, 1937).

[64]Uriel Weinreich, *College Yiddish* (New York: YIVO, 1949), p. 26.

by YIVO in 1949 in Weinreich's *College Yiddish* can be found in Weinreich's Yiddish-English dictionary, published in 1968.[65] Although the YIVO scheme is a phonetic one, applied to the standard orthography it is largely reversible except for the Hebrew-Aramaic component. A completely reversible transliteration scheme for Yiddish was also published by Weinrich in 1954,[66] but it is used mainly by linguists to render the orthography of Old Yiddish.[67]

Writing in 1978, Wellisch notes that the third major Hebrew-character language, Ladino, "has not been the subject of a transliteration scheme, so far as is known, although the rules for transliteration of Hebrew cannot be applied without modification to this language either."[68] He speculates that the reason for the lack of a specific transliteration scheme for Ladino is that few libraries outside of Spain or Israel have sizeable holdings of books and manuscripts in Ladino and the few specialists who study this "now almost extinct language" use their own ad hoc transcriptions for philological purposes. Interestingly, the usually thorough Wellisch seems to have overlooked the detailed romanization scheme for Ladino published by David Bunis four years earlier in his book *The Historical Development of Judezmo Orthography.*[69]

THE ISRAELI DEBATE:
LC Versus Academy of the Hebrew Language

When the State of Israel was established in 1948 it became clear that there was a need to codify and standardize the romanization of Hebrew for uniform rendering of personal and geographic names for governmental and cartographic use. The Academy of the Hebrew Language had actually begun to deal with the problem long before 1948, but with the establishment of the State, it intensified its efforts, devising a double-layered romanization system which it published in 1957.[70] The system is composed of a "simple" scheme and a "more exact" scheme that are mutually compatible but designed for different purposes.

---

[65] Uriel Weinreich, *Modern English-Yiddish Yiddish-English Dictionary* (New York: YIVO and McGraw-Hill, 1968), xx-xxv.

[66] Uriel Weinreich, ed., *The Field of Yiddish* (New York: Linguistic Circle of New York, 1954), vi-vii.

[67] Bella Hass Weinberg, "Hebraica Cataloging and Classification," in *Cataloging and Classification of Non-Western Material: Concerns, Issues and Practices,* edited by Mohammed M. Aman (Phoenix, AZ: Oryx Press, 1980), 329.

[68] Hans H. Wellisch, *The Conversion of Scripts--Its Nature, History, and Utilization,* 305.

[69] David Bunis, *The Historical Development of Judezmo Orthography,* Working Papers in Yiddish and East European Jewish Studies, 2 (New York: Max Weinreich Center for Advanced Jewish Studies, 1974).

[70] Ha-Aḳademiyah la-lashon ha-ʻivrit, *Kelalei ha-taʻatiḳ mi-ketavʻ ivri li-ketav latini.*

composed of a "simple" scheme and a "more exact" scheme that are mutually compatible but designed for different purposes.

The simple scheme, which came to be known as "Academy I," has several homographs for different Hebrew letters having the same or very similar pronunciation (such as ת and ט), but it differentiates ב and ו (*v, w*), ח and כ (*ḥ, kh*), כ and ק (*k, q*). The vowels are reduced to *a, e, i, o, u.* Special forms are: ', *ḥ, k̲* (for easier use on the typewriter or, more recently, the computer keyboard). It is shown in Figure. 3.4. Academy of Hebrew Language I: "Simple" Romanization Table.[71] Academy I is used for the romanization of names and words in official publications (such as passports and birth certificates) in Israel, as well as in Highway Department (but not municipal) road markers and traffic signs. More importantly, while ALA/LC transliteration is used by virtually all of Israel's university libraries, the Jewish National and University Library uses the Academy I system when romanization is required (as in cross references from the romanized form to the Hebrew form or in entries for Israeli corporate bodies in Roman alphabet publications). This causes a problem of cataloging consistency for romanized headings in the ALEPH network, because such headings, when cataloged by the JNUL use a different romanization system than the same headings when cataloged by other Israeli academic libraries. For example, the town קרית שמונה is romanized as ***Kiryat Shemonah*** by libraries using ALA/LC romanization, but ***Qiryat Shemonah*** by the JNUL, a spelling which, of course would file in an entirely different place and require a separate search to retrieve.

The more exact scheme ("Academy II") was intended for use when it is important to distinguish the original Hebrew letters in romanization. Among other things, System II differentiates ט from ת (*ṭ, t*), and ש from ס (*s', s*). The ISO Transliteration of Hebrew (ISO/R259)[72] published in 1962 was based on and is, in fact, almost exactly the same as the more exact scheme of the Academy, the only difference being the rendering of ח by *h* rather than *ḥ̲*. Like ISO/R259, Academy II is noteworthy for not ever being used in anything anywhere, so far as is known.

---

[71]Ha-Aḳademiyah la-lashon ha-ʻivrit, *Kelalei ha-taʻatiḳ mi-ketav ʻivri li-ketav latini.*

[72]International Organization for Standardization, *Recommendation R 259: Transliteration of Hebrew.*

Fig. 3.4. Academy of Hebrew Language I:
"Simple" Romanization Table [part 1]

The Letters

'	א
B, b	בּ
V, v	ב
G, g	ג, ג
D, d	ד, ד
H, h	ה
W, w	ו
Z, z	ז
<u>**H**</u>, <u>**h**</u>	ח
T, t	ט
Y, y	י
K, k	כּ
Kh, kh	כ
L, l	ל
M, m	מ
N, n	נ
S, s	ס
'	ע
P, p	פּ
F, f	פ
<u>**Z**</u>, <u>**z**</u>	צ
Q, q	ק
R, r	ר
Sh, sh	שׁ
Ś, ś	שׂ
T, t	ת, ת

Fig. 3.4. Academy of Hebrew Language I: “Simple″ Romanization Table [part 2]

The Vowel Points

	{	(ַ)	pataḥ
a	{	(ָ)	kamats gadol
	{	(ֲ)	ḥataf-pataḥ
	{	(ֶ)	segol
	{	(ֵ)	tsirei
e	{	(ֱ)	ḥataf-segol
	{	(ְ)	sheva n‘a
i	-	(ִ)	ḥiriḳ
	{	(ֹ)	ḥolam
o	{	(ָ)	ḳamats ḳatan
	{	(ֳ)	ḥataf-ḳamats
	{	(וּ)	shuruḳ
u	{	(ֻ)	ḳubuts

CONCLUSION: You Can't Live With It, You Can't Live Without It

Figure. 3.5. Comparative Table of Keypunch-Compatible (Reversible), ALA/LC, and Academy I (Israeli) Romanization Schemes for Hebrew Consonants, compresses the three romanization systems discussed in detail above into one table, for easy comparison and contrast of the differences and similarities. These three systems, of course, in no way represent an exhaustive picture of the variety of romanization and transliteration systems which have been devised, or even of those which have actually been used (since some, like Academy II, remained essentially academic exercises).What they do represent is a picture of the major systems that have been, and in the case of all but reversible romanization continue to be, used in America and Israel, the two main centers of Hebrew cataloging.

Romanization, by any system, is far from an accepted given among those who are involved in the cataloging of Hebrew materials. The debate between those who feel that romanization is the only feasible way to catalog and present Hebrew bibliographical data to the English-speaking public (such as Charles Berlin of the Harvard University Library) and those who think that "the more we think of users, the less rationale we find for transliteration,"[73] like Bella Hass Weinberg, continues to rage. The arguments against romanization are many. First, there is no single romanization scheme for alphabetic nonroman scripts which is used by all, or even nearly all, of the world's libraries with large collections of documents in nonroman scripts, making exchange of romanized bibliographic data on the international level problematic. Second, since there is almost never a one-to-one relationship between the spelling and pronunciation in a source script and that of a target script, the result of script conversions that are neither uniform nor mutually consistent and sometimes generate great confusion.[74] Third, the unsuitability of romanization for bibliographic control becomes obvious when it is recognized that it does not allow for universal applicability: English, French or German names and titles cannot be Cyrillicized, Arabicized, Hebraized or Japanized by one-to-one transliterations schemes of the type used in the romanization of Cyrillic or Greek script (where reversibility and thus reconstruction of the original is mostly possible), but only by phonetic transcription, which approximates the *sound* (phonemes) but not the *written symbols* (graphemes) of foreign words.[75] Fourth, romanization demonstrates a basic and non-productive anglocentricity: "We invest millions of dollars a year in acquiring material in foreign alphabets, and then proceed to document them in the roman alphabet, as if it were somehow more 'official' or 'scientific.' The attitude of many English-speaking people is 'why can't all scripts be latinized?' "[76]

---

[73]Bella Hass Weinberg, "Transliteration in Documentation": 28.

[74]Hans H. Wellisch, "Script Conversion and Bibliographic Control of Documents in Dissimilar Scripts...": 6.

[75]Hans H. Wellisch, "Multiscript and Multilingual Bibliographic Control: Alternatives to Romanization," *Library Resources & Technical Services* 22 (2) (Spring 1978): 180.

[76]Bella Hass Weinberg, "Transliteration in Documentation": 20.

Fig. 3.5. Comparative Table of Keypunch-Compatible (Reversible), ALA/LC, and Academy I (Israeli) Romanization Schemes for Hebrew Consonants

Hebrew Character	Keypunch-Compatible (Reversible)	ALA/LC	Academy I
א	@	.....	.....
ב	B	b	b
ב	B	v	v
ג	G	g	g
ד	D	d	d
ה	H	h	h
ו	W	v	w
ז	Z	z	z
ח	Ḥ	ḥ	ẖ
ט	Ṭ	ṭ	t
י	Y	y (at beginning of word or syllable ; otherwise i)	y
כ,ך	K	k	k
כ,ך	K̸	kh	kh
ל	L	l	l
מ,ם	M	m	m
נ,ן	N	n	n
ס	S	s	s
ע	&	ʻ	ʼ
פ	P	p	p
פ,ף	P̸	f	f
צ,ץ	C̸	ts	ẕ
ק	Q	ḳ	q
ר	R	r	r
ש	Š	sh	sh
ש	Ṣ	ś	ś
ת	T	t	t

Adapted from Table 4.15, Romanization Schemes for Hebrew (a) Consonants, in: Hans Hanan Wellisch, *The Conversion of Scripts—Its Nature, History, and Utilization* (NewYork: John Wiley & Sons, 1978), p. 302.

Judaica research libraries have predominantly opposed romanization of Hebrew bibliographic data, even though the only Hebrew access point provided in the catalogs of most of these libraries, at least until their automated records began appearing with added Hebrew fields when RLIN acquired Hebrew capabilities, was Hebrew title.[77] In the late 1970s when the plans of LC and OCLC to provide nonroman scripts in computerized cataloging did not materialize, there appeared to be a threat that LC would provide Hebrew bibliographic data only in romanization. In 1977, a resolution opposing this was formulated and later approved by both the Association of Jewish Libraries (AJL) and the Council of Archives and Research Libraries in Jewish Studies (CARLJS).[78] In practice, when RLIN finally acquired Hebrew vernacular capabilities, instead of solving the problems brought about by romanization, it merely increased the workload of the Hebrew cataloger, since network standards require all access points to be romanized as before, with Hebrew fields added *in addition to*, and not instead of, romanized entries. Bella Weinberg summed up the ironic situation with regard to the romanization issue in American Hebraica cataloging in 1989, stating that in assessing this issue, her conclusion was that "Judaica librarians have won the battle and lost the war. We have a Hebraic capability in a major bibliographic utility, but are now required to do more romanization than ever before, using a system with complex rules that assume sophisticated knowledge of Hebrew grammar."[79]

In summary, it appears that romanization, with all its difficulties and drawbacks is not about to disappear from the cataloging of Hebrew materials, not even with vernacular cataloging capabilities available online. In spite of the distaste of many Judaica librarians (at least in major research libraries) for romanizing the records of their Hebrew collections, romanize they must for the foreseeable future. While on one hand, the very difficulties of phonetic (ALA/LC) romanization, no matter how carefully it is codified, documented, and "simplified," make exchange of romanized bibliographic data difficult; on the other hand, the desire for standardization in order to do exactly this—exchange records—requires catalogers in the RLIN network to romanize access points, whether or not they add Hebrew. The great romanization paradox—if you want to standardize your records for bibliographic exchange, you must/must not romanize—seems farther than ever from solution. Still, an occasional optimistic voice, such as that of Elizabeth Vernon in her recent article on Hebrew and Arabic script materials in the automated library, is heard in the romanization wilderness: "With advances in computer technology, it is quite possible that the future may bring new possibilities that will permit 'vernacular only' cataloging for Hebrew and Arabic script materials, and even for all nonroman script materials."[80] Who is to say she is wrong?

---

[77]Bella Hass Weinberg, "Hebraica Cataloging and Classification," p. 327.

[78]Amnon Zipin, "Romanized Hebrew Script in the Online Catalog at the Ohio State University Libraries," *Judaica Librarianship* 1 (2) (Spring 1984): 53.

[79]Bella Hass Weinberg, "From Copy Cataloging to Derived Bibliographic Records...": p. 118.

[80] Elizabeth Vernon, "Hebrew and Arabic Script Materials in the Automated Library: The United States Scene," *Cataloging & Classification Quarterly*, 14 (1) (1991), 65-66.

4 Special Problems of Hebrew: Variant Orthography

One of the most distinctive features of the Hebrew language is its use of certain characters both as consonants and as so-called "mothers of reading" or *matres lectionis*, i.e., as characters which represent vowel signs. For example, ו in the word אכשיו (*akhshav*) is pronounced like and romanized as the English consonant "v," while ו in the word חוק (*ḥok*) is romanized as the English vowel "o" and in the word צוק (*tsuk*) as the English vowel "u." Similarly, י is pronounced like and romanized as the English consonant "y" in the word יד (*yad*), but is romanized as "i" in the word דין (*din*) and represents a vowel sound which can be expressed in English as "i" or "ee" or "e" (pizza, peek, Pete). While the *matres lectionis* are actually four in number, including א and ה, as well as י and ו, the latter two *matres lectionis* pose an additional problem to catalogers of Hebrew materials because of their inconsistent use not only diachronically, within different historical periods, but also synchronically, or within the same chronical period. Which brings us to the second problem of Hebrew orthography.

Another distinctive, although not exclusive, feature of Hebrew is that it has two officially recognized orthographies. One is called *defective* (in Hebrew, *ketiv ḥaser*) because vowels are only partially represented by *matres lectionis* and must either be indicated by diacritical marks, the so-called *points* (or *niḳud*) or not indicated at all and left to the reader to fill in mentally. In this orthography the second two *matres lectionis* mentioned above, the letters ו (*vav*) and י (*yod*) are omitted. The Bible and most liturgical works, poetry (both classical and modern) and children's books are written in this orthography *with* points, while access points in records for Hebrew materials in Israeli university libraries, for example, are written in this orthography *without* points. The other orthography is known as *plene* or full (in Hebrew, *ketiv male*), because it retains both these *matres lectionis*. It is traditionally written without points and is used for most modern Hebrew literature, all newspapers, governmental publications, textbooks and in the daily writing of letters, notes and other texts by most Israelis. There is one officially approved version, the rules for writing in the plene form which were published by the Academy of the Hebrew Language in 1969,[1] and any number of unauthorized modifications.

---

[1] Aḳademiyah la-lashon ha-ʿivrit, ["Rules For the Unpointed Script"], *Leshonenu la-ʿam*, maḥzor 21, ḳuntres 6 (1969); in Hebrew.

A BRIEF HISTORY OF HEBREW ORTHOGRAPHY

One of the more interesting facts of Hebrew orthographical scholarship is that possibly the most thorough study of Hebrew orthography ever written was published in English, not Hebrew. It was written by Werner Weinberg and appeared in 6 parts in the *Hebrew Union College Annual* between the years 1975-1980.[2] The scope and detail of this study can only be hinted at in this chapter, of course, but a few highlights from Weinberg's monumental 6-part work may help put the complexity and historical significance of Hebrew variant orthography in perspective.

The oldest Canaanite and Hebrew inscriptions were entirely consonantal, e.g. בת (בית), ז (זה), לפנ (לפני), שערם שערים (שעורים). Sometime between the tenth and the ninth century B.C.E. the first vowel letters were introduced. In the *Shiloah* inscription, around 700 B.C.E. and the *Lakhish* Letters, contemporary with the destruction of the First Temple, they were well established, at least at the end of the word, e.g., אמא, הכו, היה, וזה. Once writers had grown accustomed to seeing in י and ו the graphic presentation of vowels, they introduced them also into places where there had never been a consonantal י and ו before. They were purposely inserted, י to express /e/ or /i/, and ו to express /o/ or /u/. From that time on we have *matres lectionis*, both *with* and *without* an etymological history. The letter ה is found at the end of words; it can express any of the vowels /a, e, o/. א was originally consonantal also at the end of a word or syllable. As a vowel letter it is found both at the end and within the word, and it can express any of the vowels /a, e, i, o, u/.[3]

The progression from a purely consonantal orthography to the use of *matres lectionis* to express vowel sounds has been neither linear nor consistent, however. In fact, the entire developmental direction of Hebrew orthography can perhaps best be summed up in these two sentences taken from the first part of Weinberg's study ("From Antiquity to Haskalah"):

> While the trend away from totally defective writing is apparent, no regular or even logical expansion in the use of *matres lectionis* took place, which might eventually have led to the establishment of a standard spelling with vowel letters. Rather has the process been characterized, diachronically by both increases and decreases in the use of *matres lectionis*, and synchronically by diverse customs governing their use or non-use, resting large degree it simply seems arbitrary.[4]

Another problem of Hebrew orthography is posed by the terminology itself:, i.e., What is meant by "*plene*" and what by "defective"? The answer is that both

---

[2] Werner Weinberg, "A History of Hebrew *Plene* Spelling," Parts 1-6, *Hebrew Union College Annual* 46-50 (1975-1980).

[3] Werner Weinberg, "A History of Hebrew *Plene* Spelling," Part 1: 457-458.

[4] Werner Weinberg, "A History of Hebrew *Plene* Spelling," Part 1, 459.

terms are / relative. *"Plene"* never means that every vowel /o/ and /u/ is rendered by ו, every /i/ and /e/ by י . On the other hand "defective" never means that not a single *mater lectionis* is used. In spite of this, most people would call a printed Mishnah *plene*, as opposed to a printed Bible, because Mishnah editions contain more words and, especially, more word-patterns in *plene* script than does the Bible. Inversely, most people would refer to the Bible spelling as defective, even though it contains a great many *matres lectionis* as compared to early Hebrew inscriptions. It has become the custom to refer loosely to a text as defective, if it does not contain more *plene* patterns than the MT (Massoretic Text), and as *plene* if it does.[5]

The National Renaissance in the second half of the nineteenth century left a legacy of large numbers of Hebrew-reading Jews. This potential readership caused a sudden proliferation of printed Hebrew that logically might have led to a standardization of *plene* spelling. In fact, however, it did not. Writers as well as editors kept changing from *plene* to defective writing of the same word on the same page. As Weinberg points out: "It seems that every writer and publisher wrote, at the same time, *plene* and defective, used more or less auxiliary pointing according to what he deemed more expedient for his readers to understand him. It seems further that the readers, in turn, were not disturbed by the lack of uniformity...in Hebrew spelling."[6]

Weinberg in this passage is referring to Hebrew-reading Jews of the last century, but the situation he describes still exists today, in spite of numerous attempts by the Language Council, and after the establishment of the State of Israel of the Academy of the Hebrew Language, to standardize Hebrew spelling. Both of the elements have persisted to the present day, in fact: (1) every writer and publisher still writes according to what he deems expedient, and (2) Israeli readers somehow seem undisturbed by the lack of uniformity.

By the beginning of the twentieth century, however, one trend was clear: A number of *plene* writings had been accepted by everyone, even the most highly literate groups in Hebrew-speaking society. In the long run, some sort of natural development toward a more *plene* spelling had taken place. This situation changed dramatically when at the end of the nineteenth century schools began to function in Palestine in which Hebrew was the language of instruction. The teachers became aware that each of them was teaching his pupils a different orthography and that this was poor pedagogy. In 1903 they founded their professional organization, The Jewish Teachers Federation in Palestine, and immediately began urging their new president David Yellin to find a solution to the problem of what spelling to teach. Yellin in response came forward with a system that falls into the category of what is considered defective (biblical) spelling.[7] It abolished *plene* patterns that had become established by the turn of the century, thereby creating many homographs and consequently ambiguities and sources for mistakes in reading unpointed Hebrew.

---

[5]Werner Weinberg, "A History of Hebrew *Plene* Spelling," Part 1: 460.

[6]Werner Weinberg, "A History of Hebrew *Plene* Spelling," Part 2: 245.

[7]Werner Weinberg, "A History of Hebrew *Plene* Spelling," Part 2: 253.

In 1948 the Language Council, which had been established in 1904, published a set of rules for *ketiv male*, the *plene* or full Hebrew spelling used without vowel points, under the title "Rules of the Unpointed Script" in vol. 16 of the journal *Leshonenu*.[8] The 1948 rules constituted a deliberate compromise between opposing schools of thought concerning the historical (etymological) versus the phonetic (or phonemic) approach, in an attempt to satisfy the democratic process. The result was a system with which no writer could easily familarize himself, since he could not find guiding principles to foster the consistency written Hebrew lacked. The rules left all /a/s, most /e/s, and many /i/s and /o/s unexpressed, creating a multitude of partially or completely unvocalized homographs which led to uncertain and faulty reading.[9] In 1949 the introduction to *ha-Entsiḵlopediyah ha-ʻivrit*, which began publication in the same year, stated that it would follow the Language Council's recommendations *for the most part*.[10] This policy engendered a host of minor modifications of the rules, which finally rendered them obsolete, and some 20 years later a new set of rules was necessary featuring substantial differences from its predecessor.[11]

The 1969 rules were not the end of official attempts to standardize Hebrew orthography, but they remain the officially authorized version in use today. Further efforts by the members of the Academy of the Hebrew Language to improve on these rules failed to bring the inconsistencies of Hebrew orthography to an end any more successfully than previous attempts had done and even the rules that *do* exist are by no means universally enforced, as a look at Israeli street signs or newspapers will show. In effect, four ways of spelling Hebrew have established themselves in different areas of writing in Israel: (1) unpointed *plene*, which comprises ninety percent or more of all printing—books, newspapers, journals and magazines, private and business correspondence, many street signs, etc.; (2) pointed *plene*, which is used primarily in newspapers for new immigrants and in language courses; (3) pointed-defective, which is used in printing children's books, Bibles, prayerbooks, poetry, grammars and dictionaries; and (4) unpointed-defective which, by now, is used primarily by academic libraries in Israel in order to inculcate some measure of orthographic consistency in their Hebrew cataloging records.

---

[8]Vaʻad ha-lashon ha-ʻivrit be-erets yisraʼel, ["Rules For the Unpointed Script"], *Leshonenu* 16 (1948); in Hebrew.

[9]Werner Weinberg, "A History of Hebrew *Plene* Spelling," Part 2: 268.

[10]["On the Order of Entries in the Encyclopedia and on Editorial Policy on Spelling and Transcription"], *ha-Entsiḵlopediyah ha-ʻivrit*, vol. 1, Added t.p.: Encyclopaedia Hebraica (Tel Aviv: Encylopedia Publishing Co., 1949), col. 39-46; in Hebrew.

[11]Aḵademiyah la-lashon ha-ʻivrit, ["Rules For the Unpointed Script"].

VARIANT ORTHOGRAPHY AND THE LIBRARIAN

The lack of a standard Hebrew orthography causes innumerable problems for Israeli catalogers of Hebrew materials. The Jewish National and University Library, at its inception, decided that the best solution to variant spelling of access points would be to normalize all access points to defective spelling in cataloging. While this solution to the dilemma may sound simple and straightforward, it is in fact fraught with difficulties and inconsistencies.

First, normalizing variant spelling is a major variation from accepted international cataloging practice with which, for the most part, Israeli libraries prefer to stay in tune. In non-Hebrew cataloging, bibliographic data is normally transcribed as it appears in the item cataloged and variant spelling of access points is retained: *labor* and *labour* coexist, and no one would dream of uniting *Shapiro* and *Schapiro*.[12] The result of forcing all Hebrew access points into a standardized form, regardless of how they appear in the item is equivalent to deciding that all authors named Shwarz, Shwartz, Schwarz, Schwartz, etc. should all be entered under one standard form.[13] The alternative, however (i.e., not normalizing spelling in Hebrew access points) would require alternate-form *see also* references for the majority of the headings in the catalog because the reader cannot be expected to know which orthographic form was used in a specific publication or edition (e.g., *shulḥan* with or without a *vav*). Thus recording authors, titles, etc. as they are found in the specific work would have led to bibliographic chaos.

The Israeli solution to this problem, then, has been to normalize all access points to a single orthographic form, while retaining exact transcription of the title page in the descriptive data fields. As mentioned above, for both historical and practical reasons—it is easier to decide simply to remove *matres lectionis* consistently than to try and figure out when to insert them—the brief classical form (defective or *ketiv haser*) has prevailed, despite the fact that the trend of modern Hebrew is more and more towards the fuller *plene* or *ketiv male*.[14]

Furthermore, the *ketiv ḥaser* or *defective* form is not used consistently in all types of Israeli libraries. While the JNUL and, at least officially, the academic libraries use the official defective form, public libraries have opted for a compromise, "*half-defective*" spelling (omitting the *yod* but including the *vav*), in accordance with the cataloging of the former Center for Public Libraries (recently renamed simply the Center for Libraries). This form has dubious linguistic justification but is somewhat closer to popular (*plene*) spelling.

---

12 Elhanan Adler, "Judaica Cataloging: The Hebrew Bibliographic and Israeli Traditions," *Judaica Librarianship* 6 (1-2) (Spring 1991-Winter 1992): 9.

13 Elhanan Adler, "Hebrew Cataloging and the Computer--The View from Israel," *Information Technology and Libraries* (September 1982): 241.

14 Elhanan Adler, "Judaica Cataloging: The Hebrew Bibliographic and Israeli Traditions": 9.

The decision of the seven Israeli university library systems to use uniform software (the ALEPH system) and the advent of networking technology that facilitated copying cataloging records between institutions led to a need for more stringent standardization of spelling of access points *between* Israeli libraries as well as *within* them. As a result, the Subcommittee on Cataloging and Conversion, founded for this purpose in 1983 by the Standing Committee of the National Library and the University Libraries, felt it necessary in 1991 to issue a reaffirmation of the decision to use defective spelling throughout Israel's academic libraries.[15]

The Subcommittee opens the section on "Hebrew Spelling" in the 1991 document on cataloging decisions with a categorical statement that Hebrew spelling in access points will be *defective* in all cases. This unambigous statement is followed by a rather lengthy explanation/justification of this decision, beginning with a reiteration of the need for uniform spelling in Hebrew access points:

> The question of Hebrew speeling is perhaps the most problematic subject in Hebrew cataloging. Since there is no uniformity in the spelling which appears in publications, and we do not wish to confuse the reader with a mixture of spellings (מלון_and also מילון ; וייס, ווים, וייס_and also ויס), it is and always has been accepted practice to write all access points in a <u>uniform</u> spelling.[16]

The Subcommittee concedes that *ketiv male,* or *plene* spelling, is used more on a daily basis. Nonetheless, it continues, there are a number of linguistic and technical problems that mitigated in favor of *defective* spelling: a) The *plene* spelling in use today (in newspapers, for example) is not precise *plene* spelling and is inconsistent: on one hand it is still mixed with *defective* spelling, and on the other hand it includes extra occurences of the letters *yod* and *v̯av* beyond even those required by the rules of *plene* spelling (שימעון instead of שמעון , etc.); b) the <u>correct</u> use of *plene* spelling (according to the rules of the Academy of the Hebrew Language) is a difficult task which requires considerable knowledge of Hebrew grammar and for which there are no convenient reference tools; in contrast, the rules for *defective* spelling are simpler and can be clarified by the use of dictionaries and by other pointed books; c) the libraries with the biggest collections in Hebrew, and above all the Jewish National and University Library, have consistently used *defective* spelling. A decision to change the spelling, except for linguistic problems, would be, from a technical standpoint, "an unbearable decree" (i.e., perhaps proper but not feasible).[17]

---

[15] Elhanan Adler, editor, ["Cataloging Decisions and Rule Changes in Israeli University Libraries"], *Yad Lakore* (January 1991): 69.

[16] Elhanan Adler, editor, ["Cataloging Decisions and Rule Changes in Israeli University Libraries"]: 69.

[17] Elhanan Adler, editor, ["Cataloging Decisions and Rule Changes in Israeli University Libraries"]: 69.

In light of the above, and since without uniform Hebrew spelling in all the libraries there is no point in a national network with regard to Hebrew material, the Subcommittee concludes that only *defective* spelling is to be used.

In spite of the Subcommittee's supposedly binding decision, a comparison of Hebrew access points in various ALEPH files of Israel's university libraries, shows that in practice, there is still no uniformity: many of the large libraries and the old libraries (including the JNUL) continue to use *defective* spelling more or less consistently, while other university libraries (particularly the science and technology libraries with limited Hebrew collections) have opted for leaving the existing plene forms or even filling out occasional defective forms to plene. Even among the libraries which have consistent defective-form access points, there are differences in display formats (e.g., whether to display the normalized [defective] title or the actual title transcription) and in decisions about whether to include the transcription title and statement of responsibility in the word indexes (thereby allowing some plene form retrieval).

The main problem all this spelling inconsistency causes for the non-Israeli librarian, of course, is romanization difficulty. As Bella Weinberg so aptly put it in her 1980 survey of Hebraica cataloging and classification practices the "burden of transcription" is on the librarian: "For example, whether the title-page form is קהלת or קהילת the Library of Congress will romanize it as as *ḳehilat* (unless of course the former is to be read as *ḳohelet*!). Thus a librarian/user trying to find a romanized citation in a Hebrew title catalog would have to look under all possible original spellings of the word or name. Names are of course subject to even more orthographic variation than words."[18] Bella Weinberg's comment, however, is only relevant to a non-normalized catalog (one that uses exact title-transcription). In a consistent catalog, whether *haser* or *male*, this would not be a problem.

Conversely, romanizing titles of Hebrew books in *ketiv haser* requires a knowledge of Hebrew pronunciation beyond the capability of many experienced catalogers with even a solid knowledge of Hebrew. The variant orthography of the Bible, as Weinberg notes, demands that the cataloger "practically be a walking concordance to read and to romanize correctly such unvocalized titles as משפט אהב (*ohev*) (Psalms 37:28) or תולדת נח (*toldot*) (Genesis 6:9), since they are more naturally read *ehov* and *toldat*."[19] In short, the Hebrew cataloger, in addition to knowing cataloging and Hebrew, also needs a thorough grounding in the Bible.

Further complexities of Hebrew variant orthography can be seen in the treatment of Yiddish in Israeli library catalogs. As long as separate Yiddish catalogs were maintained, Yiddish was recorded in its fairly standard full form. However, with

---

[18]Bella Hass Weinberg, "Hebraica Cataloging and Classification," in *Cataloging and Classification of Non-Western Material: Concerns, Issues and Practices,* Edited by Mohammed M. Aman (Phoenix, AZ: Oryx Press, 1980), p. 325.

[19]Bella Hass Weinberg, "Hebraica Cataloging and Classification," p. 324.

the merging of Hebrew and Yiddish in the computerized files of ALEPH, an interesting compromise was reached: titles and other uniquely Yiddish headings remain in their full Yiddish form, while personal name entries have been reduced to Hebrew *ketiv ḥaser* form.[20] In the Subcommittee on Cataloging and Conversion's 1991 "Decisions and Changes..." the decision on the spelling of Yiddish names is succinctly recorded in a single sentence, as follows: "Names will be written in Hebrew *defective* spelling, with cross references from the full form, for example: (מאנגער *see* מנגר)."[21]

CONCLUSION: Blissfully Ignoring It

Werner Weinberg, in the final part of his history of Hebrew *plene* spelling, puzzles over the failure of mid-twentieth century defenders of *ketiv haser* to come to terms with the the overwhelming percentage of unpointed *ketiv male* or *plene* spelling that was going on in the "real world" of Israeli society: "Did they blissfully ignore it? Did they really think they could abrogate it? Or did they relate it...to some kind of free-for-all scribbling that did not deserve the name of orthography and was not worth being regulated?"[22] Although he ponders various theories, he never settles on a single, undisputed explanation of the willingness of the Hebrew-speaking community, both scholarly and popular, to live with dualism as the dominant feature of its orthography. In the end he simply points out that dualism, the coexistence of pointed-defective and unpointed *plene* Hebrew orthographies, has existed *de facto* for over a thousand years. Furthermore, in spite of the fact that the concept of dualism also implied that the two spellings could not be mixed (for instance, there could be no pointed-*plene* script), in practice even this rule has not held. The fact is that there exists not two, but *four* Hebrew spellings—unpointed defective, pointed defective, unpointed *plene* and pointed *plene*—each of which is used in certain circumstances and/or for certain groups within Israeli society. Speaking of the utter failure of Israel's linguistic scholars to standardize Hebrew spelling by the 1970s, the period in which Weinberg wrote his study, he notes: "There existed four Hebrew spellings at the beginning of the 20th Century, when the process of spelling reform gained momentum. With all the genius and energy invested in solving the problem, there still existed four spellings when the decision about the experimental introduction of *plene* spelling into the school system was made."[23]

It is perhaps indicative of the Israeli people's ability to deal with uncertainty that, in spite of the lack of uniformity in their orthography, for the most part they

---

[20] Elhanan Adler, "Judaica Cataloging: The Hebrew and Bibliographic and Israeli Traditions": 10.

[21] Elhanan Adler, editor, ["Cataloging Decisions and Rule Changes in Israeli University Libraries"]: 74.

[22] Werner Weinberg, "A History of Hebrew *Plene* Spelling," Part 5: 325.

[23] Werner Weinberg, "A History of Hebrew *Plene* Spelling," Part 5: 330.

manage to read and write Hebrew all their lives barely noticing its inconsistencies--
"blissfully ignoring it," as Weinberg so accurately observed. The average Israeli who
received his training in the school system would probably be hard pressed to define
exactly any of the spellings or to focus his observation beyond the fact that there are
pointed and unpointed scripts. Many Israelis are inclined to play down the problems
of Hebrew orthography, comparing them to "neglecting to dot one's i's or cross one's
t's."[24] Yet while the recognition of four essentially different spelling systems in
modern Hebrew may require some sophistication, they most definitely exist and
apparently, in spite of all the efforts of the scholars to unify them throughout countless
years of arguing over, codifying, defending and decrying various sets of
orthographical rules, they are here to stay.

As for the problems of reading the unpointed *plene* script which dominates in
everyday life, in spite of the fact that learners, whether children or adults, can read
only those words which they already know or recognize for sure in a given
environment, for the vast bulk of the adult, native population of Israel, unpointed
plene presents no real problem. Unpointed *plene* is a way of writing Hebrew that
implies the ability of a phonetic interpretation by the reader. Still, Werner Weinberg
concludes, "people who know Hebrew read unpointed-*plene* fast and quite correctly,
and when they misread they usually notice their error soon enough. Much that has
been said to the contrary is exaggerated."[25] Nonetheless, the fact that most Israeli
libraries are using either defective or partially defective spelling means that while a
reader seeing such a heading (e.g., אגדה [agudah]) can decipher it, he would have a
hard time locating it in the first place.

---

[24] Werner Weinberg, "A History of Hebrew *Plene* Spelling," Part 5: 330.

[25] Werner Weinberg, "A History of Hebrew *Plene* Spelling," Part 5: 330.

5 Headings and Uniform Titles: American and Israeli Practices

Some of the most significant diferences between American and Israeli Hebraica (and even Judaica) cataloging relate to the forms used for author and uniform title headings. While some of these differences derive from the Hebrew-primacy orientation of Israeli cataloging, many derive from much older, basic differences of approach between traditional Jewish bibliography and general bibliography. In many cases, American Jewish libraries of Judaica (i.e., libraries in Jewish institutions) have followed or created practices that are closer to their Israeli rather than American counterparts. While some of these may be questions of convenience of access, some are much more philosophical and even theological (for example: exactly which texts are included under the term, *Bible*).

An understanding of these differences is crucial to any use of an Israeli (or even traditional Jewish) reference work or library catalog.

THE ANGLO-AMERICAN AUTHOR ENTRY TRADITION VERSUS THE JEWISH TITLE ENTRY TRADITION

Bella Weinberg has noted that: "What most distinguishes the Anglo-American tradition of Judaica cataloging from the Hebrew bibliographic tradition is that the latter opts for *title* main entry while the former features *author* main entry."[1] Traditional Jewish Hebraica bibliography has always prefered arrangement or entry under title.[2] The three major printed milestones of Hebrew bibliography: Shabbatai Bass's *Sifte yeshenim* (1680), Isaac Ben-Yaakov's *Otsar ha-sefarim* (1880), and C. D. Friedberg's *Bet 'eked sefarim* (2d ed., 1950-1956) are all arranged primarily by title, with secondary indexes by author (Ben-Yaakov's author index was never published).

---

[1] Bella Hass Weinberg, "Judaica and Hebraica Cataloging: Anglo-American Traditions," *Judaica Librarianship* 6 (1-2) (Spring 1991-Winter 1992): 13.

[2] Johannes Buxtorf's *Bibliotheca rabbinica* (Basel, 1613) was actually the first scientific work of Hebrew bibliography to be arranged by title.

The major exception to this tradition is the current, ongoing Institute for Hebrew Bibliography project—planned to be the ultimate bibliography of Hebrew script publications—whose specimen brochure, published in 1964, indicates author main-entry. [3]

Arranging a bibliography under title has particular advantages in traditional Hebraica:

> Title main entry ... has several advantages in arranging Rabbinic literature. It avoids the problem of entering many works of Midrash and Kabalah under their attributed authors. Uniform title entries also interfile more readily with titles than with authors ... Problems of form of ancient and medieval names also seem less significant when they appear in a secondary index rather than as main entries. Probably the most obvious benefit of title entry in Rabbinic literature is the fact that, in practice, author's names were not known, or were ignored. [4]

Each of these points is still very much valid today.

The vast majority of ancient Hebrew and Jewish literature (from the Bible through the Apocrypha, the Dead Sea Scrolls, Talmudic, Midrashic and early Kabalistic literature) falls under the heading of what were once called "Anonymous classics" (a term no longer used in cataloging and absorbed into the broader but less expressive "Uniform titles"). Even the smallest library of Judaica or Hebraica will have a significant representation of this literature, which still is widely studied today. Many of these works are traditionally attributed to Biblical or Tannaitic authors—attributions which are not accepted by the scholarly world, but which are virtually matters of faith to many traditional Jews. For example, the question whether the Kabalistic classic *Zohar* was composed by the second century Rabbi Shimon bar Yohai (as tradition and most title pages hold) or by the thirteenth century mystic Moses de Leon (as modern scholarship claims) is much more than a cataloging question and has widespread theological implications. Indeed, the decision of the religious publishing house Mossad Harav Kook to withdraw from partnership in the Institute for Hebrew Bibliography project was motivated, at least partially, by disagreement over such sensitive cataloging questions. [5] Uniform title entries (***Zohar, Pesiḳta de-Rav Kahana***, etc.) avoid these problems, however, interfiling them with author entries can be very confusing to the reader. Entering all works under title creates a much more homogenous listing.

Another problematic aspect of Rabbinic literature is the fact that even works of known, undisputed authorship are often best known by title—to the extent that many Rabbinic scholars would be hard put to name the authors of many works they use

[3]Mif ʻal ha-bibliyografyah ha-ʻivrit, *Ḥoveret le-dugmah* [*Specimen Brochure*] (Jerusalem, 1964).

[4]Elhanan Adler, "Judaica Cataloging: The Hebrew Bibliographic and Israeli Traditions," *Judaica Librarianship* 6 (1-2) (Spring 1991-Winter 1992): 8.

[5]Protocol of a Meeting of the Editorial Committee of the Institute for Hebrew Bibliography, Dec. 25, 1960.

currently and extensively. The standard form of citation in Rabbinic literature throughout the ages has been title only (unless the title was a generic one such as *Responsa*). Indeed in Jewish tradition it is has become virtually an honor for a person to be known, or even exclusively identified by the name of his primary work—referring to the person simply as "the author of ..." (e.g., **ba'al ha-ma'or** for Zerahiah ha-Levi, the author of the work *ha-ma'or ha-gadol*) or even by the name of the work alone (e.g., Israel Meir Kahan, known as the **Ḥafets Ḥayyim** after one of his works with this title). This point can be further illustrated by the fact that Simon Moses Chones' popular bio-bibliographical lexicon of Rabbinic literature *Toldot ha-poskim* (first published 1910) was arranged alphabetically not by the name of the biographee but by the title of each one's best known work.

Furthermore, even title-page authorship is not always a convenient access point. In many countries surnames that were imposed on the Jewish community were ignored by authors who preferred to retain the traditional patronymic form (A... *son of* B...). Even current Hassidic literature often ignores surnames and indicates only forename and Hassidic dynasty (occasionally only the dynasty is mentioned, requiring the cataloger to determine who was the head of the dynasty at the time the work was written).

In catalogs or bibliographies with a single entry, there is, therefore, a high likelihood that title entry would serve as a more useful and accurate point of access for much Hebraica. This is particularly true for single-entry records for items in process (acquisitions records or temporary cataloging records) where authority work has not been done on the personal or corporate access points. In the published card catalog of the Klau Library of Hebrew Union College, while cataloged items (both Hebrew and non-Hebrew) follow standard American practice of preferring author main entry, uncataloged items are represented by one temporary card arranged for best access: "Books in Hebrew characters have a title card only; other books have an author (main entry) card only."[6]

M. Nabil Hamdy considers title main entry to be an Oriental tradition followed, even today, by a few countries in Asia and the Middle East, as opposed to the Western school, which is based on the determination of authorship responsibility for the selection of a main entry.[7] He notes:

> Historically, the title unit entry is attributed to the Orient or the East. For many years and "even today in the Orient the traditional entry for a book is its title."[8] China, Japan until recently and some of the Arab countries, especially Egypt, are examples of the nations adopting this concept... In the

---

[6]Hebrew Union College--Jewish Institute of Religion, *Dictionary Catalog of the Klau Library, Cincinnati* (Boston: G.K. Hall, 1964), Introduction by Herbert C. Zafren: v. 1, p. iv.

[7]M. Nabil Hamdy, *The Concept of Main Entry as Represented in the Anglo-American Cataloging Rules* (Littleton, Co.: Libraries Unlimited, 1973), p. 17.

[8]Ruth French Strout, "The Development of the Catalog and Cataloging Codes," *Library Quarterly* 26 (October 1956): 257.

Arab world it is suggested that the lack of family names in modern Arabic or Islamic names is a reason for the use of a title unit entry rather than a main author entry. While this might be true, it is apparent from the literature that titles of books have always been favored over the names of their authors, even when there existed names similar to family names.[9]

Hamdy concludes his discussion of the Oriental tradition with the comment:

> It has been advanced in the literature that the use of the title entry rather than the author entry in the East can be attributed in some way to the East's lack of emphasis on the importance of the individual. This assumption lacks evidence and it is questionable whether it can really explain a cataloging tradition.[10]

While the Jewish bibliographic tradition of title entry for Hebrew works developed in Europe rather than in the Middle East, there are parallels between Hamdy's explanations for preference of title entry and those we have advanced above. Title main entry in Hebrew avoided many problems of name form and, for users of Rabbinic literature, was probably the most important identification. The fact that this tradition has been dropped by 20th century Hebraica catalogers and bibliographers (both in Israel and abroad) in favor of author main entry is due to the adoption of universal (primarily American) cataloging and bibliographic standards by the Judaica/Hebraica bibliographic world. In addition, as the corpus of Hebrew literature became more and more secular (non-Rabbinic), and contemporary Hebrew names less problematic, the rationale behind title main entry has virtually disappeared.

ISRAELI CATALOGING PRACTICE

While the professional cataloging standards of Israel are based primarily on American practice, there remain significant differences in how Israeli libraries (and in some cases non-Israeli Judaica libraries) establish forms of headings. In addition there are some difficulties in defining and documenting Israeli practice.

While American cataloging has largely followed the lead of the Library of Congress in its cataloging standards (primarily because of the desire to use its cataloging), contemporary American cataloging rules have always been compiled and authorized by various committees of the American Library Association and therefore binding as standard national practice. These rules are the 1908 *Catalog Rules: Author and Title Entries* [11](hereafter ALA-1908), the 1948 *A.L.A. Cataloging Rules for*

[9]M. Nabil Hamdy, *The Concept of Main Entry as Represented in the Anglo-American Cataloging Rules,* pp. 19-20.

[10]M. Nabil Hamdy, *The Concept of Main Entry as Represented in the Anglo-American Cataloging Rules,* p. 21.

[11]American Library Association, *Catalog Rules: Author and Title Entries* (Chicago: American Library Association, 1908).

Author and Title Entries[12] (hereafter ALA-1948), and the first,[13] second,[14] and second-revised[15] editions of the *Anglo-American Cataloging Rules* (hereafter AACR1, AACR2, and AACR2-rev).

Establishing Israeli cataloging practice is somewhat more problematic and a distinction must be made between practice and its codification:

> The Israeli cataloging tradition grew out of the practices of the Jewish National and University Library (JNUL) in the 1920s and 1930s—the formative years when attempts were made to adapt modern methods of librarianship to Judaica and Hebraica cataloging. Since the JNUL was the largest and most important library in Mandatory Palestine and, for many years, was the site of the only school of Librarianship in Israel, its practices usually became *de facto* standards for all the libraries of the country. Its bibliographical quarterly *Kiryat sefer*[16] (1924-) was also a means for disseminating bibliographic data as recorded in the JNUL catalogs.
>
> The JNUL approach, subsequently adopted by all Israeli libraries, has been to try to adapt traditional approaches to international (primarily Anglo-American) standards. This process continues even today, although with the development of many other large libraries of Judaica in Israel the JNUL serves more as the "first among equals" than as the unquestioned standard-setter. Cataloging rules for Judaica in the academic libraries are set today by an inter-university Subcommittee on Cataloging ...[17]

The Israeli cataloging "tradition" was therefore established by the JNUL practice; however, it was never formally codified (published as a code of rules) either by the JNUL or by a national professional body. The first formulation of Hebrew cataloging rules was Reuven Levi's brief 1958 *Principles of Cataloging*[18] followed by Hanna Oppenheimer's cataloging textbook *Exercises in Cataloging* which appeared in 1961[19] (Oppenheimer 1963) and again, adapted to AACR1 in 1974[20] (Oppenheimer

---

[12]American Library Association. Division of Cataloging and Classification, *A.L.A. Cataloging Rules for Author and Title Entries* (Chicago: American Library Association, 1949).

[13]*Anglo-American Cataloging Rules. North American Text* (Chicago: American Library Association, 1967).

[14]*Anglo-American Cataloguing Rules*, 2nd ed. (Chicago: American Library Association, 1978).

[15]*Anglo-American Cataloguing Rules,* 2nd ed., 1988 revision (Ottawa, Canadian Library Association, 1988).

[16]*Kiryat Sefer* (Jerusalem, Jewish National and University Library, 1924-).

[17]Elhanan Adler, "Judaica Cataloging: The Hebrew Bibliographic and Israeli Traditions": 8.

[18]Reuven Levi, [*Principles of Cataloging: a Manual for Librarians*] (Tel-Aviv: Mifale Tarbut ve-hinukh, 1958).

[19]Hana Oppenheimer, *Targilim be-ḳitlug* (Jerusalem: [s.n.], 1963).

1974) (A preliminary edition appeared in 1961[21] and a "proofread edition" in 1966[22] as well). The first orderly compilation of cataloging rules and practice was Adler and Shichor's *Cataloging* which first appeared in 1978[23] (Adler-Shichor 1978). In the introduction to this work the authors state:

> There are no comprehensive and accepted cataloging rules in Israel today. There is an established custom that Israeli cataloging is based on the American cataloging rules however these ... do not meet the special needs of cataloging Hebrew material in a Hebrew speaking country. Over the years an "unwritten tradition" developed which included the "agreed" changes which were practiced in Israel... Any unwritten tradition which does not have a higher authority behind it, responsible for its maintenance, will naturally split into different traditions and practices. To this natural trend must be added the need to adapt this "tradition" to changing American and international rules ... without the existence of a higher Israeli cataloging authority. The inevitable result has been serious inconsistency...
>
> The task we have taken upon ourselves has not been easy for we have had to make professional decisions which should have been made in a national decision-making body...[24]

Despite the above, since this work was the only available Hebrew cataloging manual, was widely used by Israeli libraries, served as the textbook in all professional and paraprofessional courses in cataloging and was followed by the Center for Public Libraries centralized cataloging service, its rules became de-facto national practice for all Israeli libraries. A second edition in 1984[25] (Adler-Shichor 1984) updated and adapted these rules to account for the changes of AACR2. The third, 1995 edition[26] (Adler-Shichor-Kedar 1995) not only updated these rules to account for the 1988 revision of AACR2 but also took into account the published decisions of the inter-university Subcommittee on Cataloging[27] (set up in 1983) which currently serves as

---

[20] Hana Oppenheimer, *Targilim be-ḳitlug*, New ed., adapted to the Anglo-American Cataloging Rules (Jerusalem:[s.n.], 1974).

[21] Hana Oppenheimer, *Targilim be-ḳitlug* (Jerusalem: [s.n.], 1961).

[22] Hana Oppenheimer, *Targilim be-ḳitlug*, Proofread ed. (Jerusalem: [s.n.], 1963.

[23] Elhanan Adler and Aviva Shichor, *Ḥa-kitlug: sefer'eḳronot ve-kelalim* (Jerusalem: Center for Public Libraries in Israel, 1978).

[24] Adler-Shichor 1978, Introduction (translated).

[25] Elhanan Adler and Aviva Shichor, *Ha-ḳitlug: sefer'eḳronot ve-kelalim*, 2nd ed. expanded and adapted to AACR2] (Jerusalem: Center for Public Libraries in Israel, 1984).

[26] Elhanan Adler, Aviva Shichor and Rochelle Kedar, *Ha-ḳitlug: sefer'eḳronot ve-kelalim*, 3rd ed., expanded and adapted to AACR II], 2nd rev. (1988) (Jerusalem: the Center for Libraries in Israel, 1995).

[27] Elhanan Adler (editor), ["Cataloging Decisions and Rule Changes in Israeli University Libraries"], *Yad Lakore* 25(2) (Jan. 1991): 69-74; in Hebrew.

the only national arbiter of cataloging policy. This third edition also includes a lengthy (84 page) appendix of Hebrew Judaica uniform title entries approved by the Subcommittee on Cataloging and will be used, unless stated otherwise, as the authoritative source for current Israeli practice and particularly for the differences between Israeli and Anglo-American practice.

In the following sections we will discuss these differences as they apply to the rules for establishing headings and the reasons behind them.

UNIFORM TITLE HEADINGS

As noted above, a large body of ancient Hebrew literature is either anonymous or of traditionally attributed authorship. The cataloging of such literature has always been problematic, including questions of when such attribution is worthy of entry or even being noted (e.g. King David as the author of *Psalms*) and when works are to be considered independent or part of a larger corpus (*Psalms* alone, or as part of *Bible*).Various types of liturgical works are also currently treated as part of this literature.

The American 1949 rules of entry referred to this type of literature as "anonymous classics" defined and specified as:

> **Definition**: An anonymous classic is a work of unknown or doubtful authorship, commonly designated by title, which may have appeared in the course of time in many editions, versions and/or translations.

> **Specification**: The term includes (1) single anonymous texts ... (2) composite anonymous texts collectively known by a specific title ... Some of these composite texts form organized literary units; others are simply unorganized collections.[28]

A footnote at the beginning of these rules noted that:

> These definitions, specifications and rules can only be considered as tentative. A series of studies applying the rules to specific literary groups is essential before basic principles of entry can be considered standardized and necessary exceptions can be formulated. A list of established headings is a desirable adjunct.[29]

The 1967 Anglo-American Cataloging Rules tried to generalize the treatment of religious "anonymous classics" (the term itself no longer appears) within the framework of Uniform titles (chapter 4), however retaining exceptional treatment for

---

[28]ALA 1949, p. 62.

[29]ALA 1949, p.62, footnote 25.

sacred scriptures and liturgical works under the heading **Special Rules** (AACR1 rules 108-119).

The 1978 second edition and its 1988 revision, while avoiding the "Special Rules" heading, retain exceptional treatment for these works (**Sacred Scriptures** in AACR2 rules 25.17-25.18 and **Liturgical Works** in AACR2 rules 25.19-25.23).

As mentioned above, the form of heading used for religious texts is not only a question of cataloging expediency, but can be theologically offensive, particularly if the approach or form used indicates preference of one religious tradition over another. While some of the differences between Israeli and American Hebraica and Judaica headings are questions of convenience or of the practices of preferred reference sources, some are deeply rooted in the religious significance implied by various headings (particularly **Bible**) where the use of the American standard heading would be religiously offensive.[30] In the latter cases, American libraries of Judaica associated with Jewish institutions (and therefore free to express this sensitivity) often use headings closer to their Israeli counterparts than to standard American usage. In the following section we will present some of the major differences between American and Israeli practice in uniform title headings and the reasons behind them.

As mentioned above, an extensive list of Israeli Judaica uniform title headings has been compiled by the inter-university Subcommittee on Cataloging and was recently published as an appendix to the third edition of the current Israeli cataloging manual.[31] This list contains also romanized forms of the headings for use in cataloging translations of these works. Current Israeli practice is to use systematic Academy of the Hebrew Language romanization for most uniform title headings and their subdivisions (with the exception of **Bible**, **Apocrypha** and **Dead Sea Scrolls**) while current Anglo-American practice is to base these headings on the forms found in the *Encyclopaedia Judaica*[32] (see, for example, AACR2, rules 25.18.B1 and 25.18.E1). Both these practices have changed over the years. Previous to AACR2 the standard Anglo-American forms were based on the 1901-1906 *Jewish Encyclopedia*[33] (see, for example, AACR1 rules 115.A.1 and 115.D.1, and ALA 1949 rule 35.A). Israeli practice has changed many times, from systematic ALA romanization in the first (1963) edition of Oppenheimer's cataloging textbook,[34] to systematic Academy of the Hebrew Language romanization in the second (1974) edition,[35] to the

---

[30]While there is great sensitivity to the use of "Christian-oriented" alphabetic headings in Judaica, most Israeli and many American Judaica libraries use the Dewey Decimal Classification (DDC) in which Judaism (296) follows Christianity (210-289) and the "Old" and "New" Testaments (221-224 and 225-228 respectively) are parts of a single whole (Bible: 220-229). Even Israeli adaptations and expansions of DDC retain these orientations. Apparently the theological implications are less offensive when expressed as numbers than as verbalized headings.

[31]Adler-Shichor-Kedar 1995, appendix 6 (84 p.)

[32]*Encyclopaedia Judaica* (Jerusalem: Keter, 1971).

[33]*Jewish Encyclopedia* (New York: Funk & Wagnalls, 1901-1905).

[34] Oppenheimer 1963, p. 78.

[35] Oppenheimer 1974, v. 1, p. 74.

Encyclopaedia Judaica forms in the 1978 and 1984 editions of Adler-Shichor (rules 5.9 and 5.11) and back to Academy romanization in the current 1995 edition (Adler-Shichor-Kedar 1995 appendix 6).

Bible

The heading "Bible" is perhaps the most problematic of all Judaica headings because it means different things to believers of different religions. The Jewish Bible consists solely of the books that the Christian Bible designates as the **Old Testament**. The use of the terms **Old Testament** and **New Testament** in the Christian Bible has theological implications (the "New" replacing or amending the "Old"), which are unacceptable to Jewish libraries.[36] From a Jewish standpoint these are two completely separate works—sacred scripture of two different religions—and uniting them under a common heading would be equivalent to combining the Bible with the Koran under a common heading. Christianity, of course, sees these as two parts of a single unit and international cataloging rules (and classification tables) follow this approach.

While collocation of all Biblical works in catalogs and bibliographies goes back to the beginnings of library cataloging (and derives from classified arrangement), the use of a common heading beginning with the word **Bible** is more recent. Maunsell's 1595 catalog[37] lists all works of the Bible together, a practice found also in Hebrew bibliography. Bass's 1680 *Sifte yeshenim* collects all editions of Biblical books alphabetically under the heading תורה (*Torah*--literally The Pentateuch), however the entry form of each book is its specific title (Joshua, Psalms, etc.). Ben-Yaakov's 1880 *Otsar ha-sefarim* has similar arrangement, but uses the more more accurate heading (תנ״ך) כתובים, נביאים, תורה, (Pentateuch, Prophets, Hagiographa followed by their common acronym: **TNKh** pronounced Tanakh). The caption title for this section is the acronym תנ״ך alone, however here also the entry for each individual entry is its specific title. Friedberg's *Bet eked sefarim* (1st ed. 1928-1931 and 2nd ed. 1950-1956) follows modern rules of entry and enters each book under the uniform heading תנ״ך followed by the name of the specific book.

From the standpoint of rules of entry, a case could be made for entering each book of the Bible **directly** under its own title (e.g., **Psalms**) rather than collecting them all together in **indirect** form under a common heading (**Bible. Psalms**) since the Bible (whether Jewish or Christian definition) is a collection of many works of different authorship written over a period of several centuries. Charles Ammi Cutter makes note of this point in his *Rules for a Dictionary Catalog*,[38] one of the earliest American cataloging codes:

---

[36]For a recent discussion of this problem, including such options as substituting "First" for "Old" and "Second" for "New", see: David E. Suiter, "Establishing Uniform Headings for the Sacred Scriptures: a Persistent Issue in Hebraica-Judaica Cataloging," *Judaica Librarianship* 9 (1-2) (1996): 83-85.

[37]Andrew Maunsell, *The First Part of the Catalogue of English Printed Bookes...* (London, 1595).

[38]Charles A. Cutter, *Rules for a Dictionary Catalog,* 4th ed., rewritten (Washington: Government Printing Office, 1904).

123. Enter the BIBLE or any part of it (including the Apocrypha) under the word **Bible.**

This is the best heading--in an English catalog--for the Bible and for any of its parts in whatever language written and under whatever title published. This is the British Museum rule. It is of a piece with putting all periodicals under the heading **Periodicals** and all publications of learned societies under the heading **Academies.** It would be much more in accordance with dictionary principles, but much less convenient, to put the separate books of the Bible each under its own name as given in the revised English version (**Matthew**, Gospel of, not **Gospel** of Matthew), with all necessary references.[39]

Cutter clearly sees the heading **Bible** (particularly when used for individual parts or books) to be an artificial one—a heading of "convenience" to bring all books of the Bible together under a single uniform heading. He attributes this convention to Panizzi's 1841 rules for the British Museum catalog.[40] Panizzi's rule no. LXXIX states that "The Old and New Testament and their parts, to be catalogued under the general heading "Bible" ..." and goes on to indicate order of arrangement (complete editions, translations, separate Testaments and their parts, etc.). That this is an artificial arrangement is inferred from Panizzi's following rule no. LXXX: "All acts, memoirs, transactions, journals ... of academies, institutes ... to be catalogued under the general name "Academies" ..." (of course, there is a major difference between "Bible," an actual title, and "Academies," a purely artificial heading). Donald Lehnus notes in his comparison of Pannizi's rules and AACR1 that "Sections 1-10 of rule LXXIX have set the pattern for all modern cataloging of the Bible as well as other sacred scriptures ...."[41]

While Panizzi's rule may well be the basis for modern practice in cataloging the Bible and its parts, there is one noteworthy variation which developed in American cataloging. In the British Museum catalog, as well as other contemporary British catalogs, the specific part of the Bible was entered after the uniform heading **Bible** in what we would call today "direct entry" (**Bible. Psalms,** or **Bible. Matthew**) without indication of any hierarchical arrangement (indirect entry). In the 1908 ALA *Catalog Rules*, however, appears a subdivision <u>by Testament</u>, followed by direct entry by specific book[42] (**Bible. Old Testament. Genesis**) but not full indirect entry (**Bible. Old Testament. Pentateuch. Genesis**). This is the arrangement which appears also in

---

[39]Charles A. Cutter, *Rules for a Dictionary Catalog,* 4th ed., rewritten, p. 57.

[40] Antonio Panizzi, "Rules for the Compilation of the Catalogue," in British Museum, *The Catalogue of Printed Books in the British Museum* 1 (London, 1841), v-ix.

[41]Donald J. Lehnus, *A Comparison of Panizzi's 91 Rules and the AACR of 1967* (Urbana: University of Illinois at Urbana-Champaign, Graduate School of Library Science, 1972) (University of Illinois Graduate School of Library Science Occasional Papers, no. 105), p. 32.

[42]ALA 1908, p.35.

the Library of Congress printed catalog to 1942[43] and has been standard American cataloging practice ever since. It should be noted that whether or not the Testament was entered as part of the heading, virtually all pre-computer-age catalogs arranged the entries themselves in hierarchical rather than alphabetical order (Old Testament before New, Genesis before Exodus, etc.).

For Israeli libraries, the division of the Bible into *Old* and *New* Testaments is unacceptable and the two must be treated as separate, independent entities. For Hebrew editions the solution is relatively simple since, with the exception of a few missionary editions, Hebrew editions are limited to the Hebrew Bible only. The Israeli uniform title is therefore תנ״ך--the acronym for the three parts of the Hebrew Bible: *Torah* (Pentateuch), *Nevi'im* (Prophets) and *Ketuvim* (Hagiographa). Subdivision is by the Hebrew name of the specific book. The Apocrypha is not part of the Hebrew Bible and is entered independently (see below). The New Testament is considered a separate work and entered directly under its Hebrew title: ברית חדשה (*Berit hadashah*) with specific title subdivisions as appropriate.

For non-Hebrew editions (or even Hebrew editions with non-Hebrew title pages) the problem is somewhat more complicated. In Israeli cataloging the term **Bible** is used for the Hebrew Bible only, and the uniform titles **Apocrypha** and **New Testament** are used for these works when they appear independently (or at least with separate title pages). For editions of the Christian Bible containing both the Old and New Testaments, with a single title page, Israeli cataloging has invented a compound uniform title: **Bible + New Testament**.[44]

Some Judaica libraries outside Israel follow Israeli practice; others prefer to remain aligned with their national cataloging standards. As Bella Weinberg notes: "Not all Judaica libraries make an issue of theology in cataloging. Some prefer to keep the Christian view if it will cut down their cataloging costs, but sometimes institutional pressure can be considerable."[45] Participation in regional or national information networks and use of automated authority control services are also factors which discourage non-conformity in cataloging.

Another exception made by Israeli libraries is the omission of the language for Hebrew texts of the Bible (or any other uniform title entry), thereby causing them to file first (e.g., **Bible. 1960** for a Hebrew edition with a non-Hebrew title page, followed by **Bible. English. 1955**, etc.).[46] The English forms of the names of the books of the Bible, however, retain standard Anglo-American usage (i.e., the

---

[43]Library of Congress, *A Catalog of Books Represented by Library of Congress Printed Cards Issued to July 31, 1942* (Paterson: Rowman and Littlefield, 1963), v.14, introduction to heading **Bible** and catalog cards.

[44]Adler-Shichor-Kedar 1995, rules 5.6-5.7.

[45]Bella Hass Weinberg, "Hebraica Cataloging and Classification," in *Cataloging and Classification of Non-Western Material: Concerns, Issues and Practices*, edited by Mohammed M. Aman (Phoenix, AZ: Oryx Press, 1980), p. 334.

[46]Adler-Shichor-Kedar 1995, rule 5.6.

Authorized Version), even though some of the headings may seem strange to the Israeli reader familiar with the Hebrew names (*Leviticus* rather than *Vayikra*, *Ecclesiastes* for *Ḳohelet*, etc.)

Apocrypha

In addition to the Old and New Testaments themselves, The term **Bible** is commonly understood (in non-Jewish context) to include various works not officially part of the Biblical canon and known collectively as **Apocryphal literature.** Jewish canon excludes these works from the Bible (even those of Jewish origin such as **Wisdom of Solomon** or **Judith**). They are never published as part of the Hebrew Bible, and are known in Jewish tradition as "outside books" (*sefarim ḥitsoniyim*). Even within the Christian canon there are differences regarding which apocryphal books are considered part of the Bible. Pre-AACR cataloging rules distinguished between three groupings: (1) **Bible. O.T. Apocrypha**, (2) **Bible. O.T. Apocryphal books** [those not in the Authorized Version], and (3) **Bible. N.T. Aprocryphal books**. AACR1 simplified this arrangement by limiting entry under **Bible** to **Bible. O.T. Apocrypha** only and listing the twelve specific titles to be included under this heading (AACR1 rule 109C, AACR2 rule 25.18.A5), all other apocryphal books to be entered directly under their own titles (AACR1 rule 114, AACR2 rule 25.18.A14).

The Israeli cataloging tradition has always been to treat the Jewish apocryphal works as completely separate from the Bible. For non-Hebrew headings the uniform title heading **Apocrypha** is used (without **Bible**). For Hebrew headings the uniform title used today is ספרים חיצוניים (*Sefarim ḥitsoniyim*).[47] Previously, many Israeli libraries used an older form of heading: כתובים אחרונים (*Ketuvim aḥaronim* = later writings) based on the title of the first Hebrew collection of Apocryphal books (published in Leipzig, 1830). This heading was changed to the more common *Sefarim ḥitsoniyim* in the 1978 cataloging rules.[48]

Since Jewish tradition considers these works to be non-canonical, there is no clear definition as to exactly which books constitute the Jewish Apocrypha. The current Israeli cataloging rules use A.S. Artom's Hebrew edition of the Apocrypha[49] as their "canon"—any books appearing in this edition are to be entered under the **Apocrypha** heading; any others are to be entered as independent works.[50]

---

[47]Adler-Shichor-Kedar 1995, rule 5.8.

[48]Adler-Shichor 1978, rule 5.8 (footnote).

[49] Bible. O.T. Apocrypha. 1958, [Apocrypha with commentary by E.S. Artom] (Tel-Aviv: Yavneh, 1958-1967), v. 9; in Hebrew.

[50] Adler-Shichor-Kedar 1995, rule 5.8 (footnote).

Talmudic Literature (Mishnah, Tosefta, Talmud Bavli, and Talmud Yerushalmi)

The major corpus of Talmudic literature consists of four works: The Mishnah, the Tosefta, the Jerusalem Talmud (Talmud Yerushalmi), and the Babylonian Talmud (Talmud Bavli).[51] These four works are collections of both legal (halachic) and non-legal material composed and redacted (edited) in ancient Israel and Babylonia. All four have the same structure: they are divided into six major classes or orders (sedarim) and subdivided into 63 individual tractates (masekhtot). While there is no disagreement on the basic approach to cataloging this body of literature, there are differences in the details.

Anglo-American practice has always been to use the term **Talmud** alone to refer to the Babylonian Talmud (Talmud Bavli), and the term **Talmud Yerushalmi** for the Jerusalem Talmud[52]—despite the fact that the Babylonian Talmud is always designated as such in its various editions. The Hebrew bibliographic tradition and Israeli cataloging practice has been to designate the Babylonian Talmud by its full and correct name: **Talmud Bavli**.

Individual orders and tractates are recorded as subheadings of the larger work. Israeli Hebrew headings, of course, use the actual Hebrew or Aramaic forms. Anglo-American catalogs and Israeli entries for translations of the orders and tractates use romanized forms. Israeli libraries today use systematic Academy of the Hebrew Language romanization, American libraries currently follow the forms of the *Encyclopedia Judaica* (AACR2, rule 25.18.B1). Previous to AACR2 the source for uniform heading forms was the 1901-1906 *Jewish encyclopedia* (AACR1 rule 115.A.1).

While most of the Talmudic literature is of legal nature, there is one exceptional tractate devoted entirely to ethical statements—the tractate *Avot* (literally "fathers," often known as *Pirke Avot*, and in English editions as *Chapters of the Fathers* or *Sayings of the Fathers*). This tractate, which appears only in the Mishnah, has often been given exceptional treatment—both because of its different subject matter and because it has been published independently (both in Hebrew and translation) more often than any other tractate. Current Anglo-American practice is to treat this tractate no differently than any other, entering it under the heading **Mishnah. Avot** (AACR2, rule 25.18C), however up to and including AACR1 (rule 115.2.B) it was entered directly under the independent heading **Aboth** (note older *Jewish Encyclopedia* style romanization). Israeli practice was and continues to be entry under the direct heading אבות (**Avot**).[53]

---

[51]Other works dating from this period are part of the Midrashic literature, Apocrypha or Dead Sea Scrolls literature.

[52]ALA 1949, rule 35.A(1), AACR1, rule 115.A.1, AACR2, rule 25.18B1.

[53]Adler-Shichor-Kedar 1995, rule 5.9. The 1984 Adler-Shichor rules, adapted to AACR2, changed the heading to the AACR2-style משנה. אבות or **Mishnah. Avot**, however the previous, direct-entry form was reinstituted by the inter-university Subcommittee on Cataloging.

Another difference between Anglo-American and Israeli practice is in entry of the body of literature known as the "minor tractates" (Hebrew: *masekhtot ḳeṭanot*—literally: "small" tractates)—a group of brief works from post-Talmudic period Babylon that are often included in editions of the Babylonian Talmud. Anglo-American practice has been to enter this literature as a subheading of the Babylonian Talmud using the heading **Talmud. Minor tractates** for editions of all or multiple tractates and subdividing further for individual tractates, e.g., **Talmud. Minor tractates. Semahot** (AACR2, rule 25.18.B2). Israeli practice is to treat the minor tractates as an independent body of literature entered under the Hebrew heading מסכתות קטנות (*masekhtot ḳeṭanot*) and subdividing for individual works (מסכתות קטנות. שמחות).[54] Translations are currently entered directly under the Academy of the Hebrew Language-style romanized heading **Massekhtot qetanot** (subdivided as above) but were previously entered under the translated heading **Minor tractates**.[55]

Midrashic Literature

The midrashic literature differs from Biblical or Talmudic literature in that it is a group of mostly anonymous independent works written or compiled over a period of over 1000 years (from the Mishnaic age to the Middle Ages) that was never "canonized," treated or published as a single work. The titles of many (but not all) of these works begin with the word *Midrash*, which in some cases is an intrinsic part of the title (i.e the work *Sifre* is often titled *Midrash Sifre*—the word midrash being superfluous—however the headings for *Midrash rabba* ("great" midrash) or *Midrash Mishle* (midrash on Proverbs) cannot stand alone without the word *Midrash*). In addition, several midrashim are arranged as commentaries on several books of the Bible and have been published in partial editions that require distinguishing subheadings.

Early American practice as seen in the LC printed card catalogs and codified in the 1949 ALA rules was to treat most of the midrashic texts as a unified body of literature:

> Enter early anonymous midrashic material under the uniform heading MIDRASH with the name of the particular midrash as a subheading ...
>
> **Midrash**. Mekilta
>
> ...
>
> **Midrash**. Tanhuma
>
> ...

For the sake of uniformity prefer the use of the period in the heading even in cases where the word Midrash is an integral part of the particular midrash.

> **Midrash**. Ḳohelet
>
> *not* Midrash Ḳohelet

---

[54]Adler-Shichor-Kedar 1995, rule 5.10.

[55]Adler-Shichor 1978 and 1984, rule 5.10.

nor Midrash. Midrash Kohelet[56]

Although the ALA rules do not specifically indicate how to treat collections from several midrashim, LC practice as indicated in the printed card catalogs was to enter them under the artificial uniform title **Midrash** without any subdivision.

AACR1 recognized the fact that the midrashim should be treated as independent works and simply stated:

> 1. Enter an anonymous midrash under its vernacular title, generally in the form found in the *Jewish Encyclopedia*.
> **Mekilta**
> **Midrash Tanhuma**
> **Tanna debe Eliyahu**
> 2. Enter a separately published component of the *Midrash ha-gadol, Midrash rabbah* or *Sifre*, however, under the uniform title for the collection, with a subheading consisting of the English name of the book of the Bible with which it deals.
> **Midrash ha-gadol.** Numbers[57]

AACR2 (rule 25.18.E1) continues this practice (aside from changing the source for forms to the *Encyclopaedia Judaica*). It also indicates further sophistication in understanding the midrashic literature in mandating the use of the headings *Midrash ha-gadol, Midrash rabbah* and *Sifrei* while recognizing the fact that these are actually collections rather than individual works, any other collections of midrashim to be treated under the general rule for collections (rule 25.18.E2).

Israeli libraries, more aware of the diverse nature of the midrashic literature, never accepted the ALA uniform title approach. Oppenheimer's 1966 cataloging textbook states:

> According to ALA 35A6 we are to bring together all midrashim, halachic and agadic, under the common heading "Midrash." This rule is not accepted in any [Israeli] libraries and we will not follow it here. In our opinion midrashim cannot be united as a single bibliographic unit: there are no complete editions of all the midrashim as there are complete editions of the books of the Bible or the Apocrypha. Therefore we prefer to catalog each midrash under its specific name.[58]

The Israeli approach is the one subsequently adopted in AACR1 and AACR2, although there are minor differences in some specific uniform titles as well as

---

[56]ALA 1949, rule 35A(6)

[57]AACR1, rule 115D.

[58]Oppenheimer 1966, p. 81 (translated).

differences in romanization (AACR2 following the *Encyclopaedia Judaica* while Israeli libraries use systematic Academy of the Hebrew Language romanization).

Dead Sea Scrolls

The so-called Dead Sea scrolls are a collection of writings, largely fragmental, found in and around the caves near the ancient town of Qumran in the Judean Desert. Not all the scrolls have been published yet and scholarly opinion is still divided regarding whether they originated in Qumran and belong to a single sect (and if so which one) or perhaps were brought to Qumran from other parts of the country. The scrolls cover a wide range of topics and their prime uniting factor is their common provenance.

While understandibly there is no mention of the scrolls in the 1949 ALA rules (the first scrolls were discovered in 1947), LC practice has been consistent in entering collections and anthologies under the heading **Dead Sea scrolls** and individual works, as published, under their unique titles. While AACR1 does not address the scrolls directly, they appear as examples of rule 103 (Anonymous works without title): the heading **Dead Sea scrolls** as an example of entry under a manuscript group (AACR1 rule 103B) while the heading for a single scroll: **Habakkuk commentary** appears as the example for entry of an anonymous work under a title assigned subsequent to its writing (AACR1 rule 103A). AACR2 retains **Dead Sea scrolls** as an example of entry under a manuscript group (rule 25.13); single works do not appear as examples but are presumably treated as independent works under rule 26.6A1: "If a separately cataloged part of a work has a title of its own, use the title of the part by itself as the uniform title."

As for Israeli practice, Oppenheimer's 1966 textbook notes that:

A rule has not yet been established for cataloging the Judean Desert scrolls, nor is there uniform practice amongst the various libraries. We recommend treating the scrolls similar to the books of the Bible and the Apocrypha. We will therefore list all the scrolls under a common heading and in cataloging a specific scroll we will add its name to that joint heading.[59]

Based on the above, and JNUL practice, Oppenheimer indicates entry for the scrolls under the most common hebrew form: מגלות גנוזות (literally: the hidden scrolls) with references from the alternate forms מגלות ים המלח (Dead Sea scrolls) and מגלות מדבר יהודה (Judean Desert scrolls). The specific title War of the Sons of Light and the Sons of Darkness is entered as a subordinate work: מגלות גנוזות. מלחמת בני אור ובני חשך.

The 1974 edition follows the same approach but prefers the uniform title form מגלות מדבר יהודה (Judean Desert scrolls) with references from the other two forms.

---

[59]Oppenheimer 1966, p. 74 (translated).

The 1978 and 1984 editions of Adler-Shichor (rule 5.13) follow AACR practice and mandate entering individual scrolls directly under their unique titles (in the example above, directly under מלחמת בני אור ובני חשך--War of the Sons of Light and the Sons of Darkness). Collections of the scrolls are to be entered under the "hidden scrolls" heading (מגלות גנוזות) with references from the alternate forms. The 1995 edition, however, reflects a decision of the inter-university Subcommittee on Cataloging to revert to pre-AACR Israeli practice and prefer entry of all scrolls (with the exception of the Isaiah Scroll which is a Biblical text) as subordinate headings.

Liturgical Works

The 1949 ALA rules treated liturgical (prayer) books as pseudo-corporate entries. Rule 116F in chapter III (Corporate Bodies as Authors) states: "Enter liturgies of the Eastern and Latin rites ... under the name chosen for the church, adding the form subheading LITURGY AND RITUAL" and allowing for further subdivision for separate works (e.g. **Catholic Church.** Liturgy and ritual. Missal*)*." Rule 120G indicates similar treatment for Protestant denominations. With regard to Jewish liturgy, rule 121 states: "Enter Jewish creeds, hymnals and service books under the heading JEWS. LITURGY AND RITUAL." (as if JEWS was the name of a corporate body!) Rule 121 does note that: "No single Jewish organization represents all Jews, but the continuity of liturgical rites and forms justifies an entry in this form."

The compound Church + *Liturgy and ritual* heading was retained by AACR1 (rule 29) although now called a uniform title heading rather than a corporate one and with an apologetic footnote indicating its retention because of "long-established usage." With regard to Jewish liturgy, rule 29C states: "Enter a Jewish liturgical work under the heading JEWS. *Liturgy and ritual."* A footnote refers the reader to the Library of Congress published catalogs for subheadings. With regard to this practice Bella Weinberg has noted: "Most American Judaica libraries cross out the word *Jews* but follow LC otherwise."[60]

AACR2 did away with both the pseudo-corporate ... *Liturgy and ritual* (for all religions) and the artificial heading *Jews.* Liturgical works pertaining to an organized church or denominational body are entered under its corporate entry form alone. The title under this heading is entered as a bracketed uniform title (AACR2 rule 21.39A1). Since there is no Jewish corporate body, Jewish liturgical works are to be entered directly under uniform title (AACR2 rule 21.39C). Rule 25.21 supplies two examples: **Haggadah** and **Kinot** and refers to the *Encyclopaedia Judaica* as the source for uniform titles for all Jewish liturgical works. While this approach is logical and eliminates the offensive *Jews*, it also has the unfortunate result of scattering the vast literature of Jewish liturgy (dozens of different liturgical works and thousands of editions) throughout the catalog. Bella Weinberg has noted many cases of inconsistency in Library of Congress application of this rule.[61]

---

[60]Bella Hass Weinberg, "Hebraica Cataloging and Classification," p. 335.

[61]Bella Hass Weinberg, "The Cataloging of Jewish Liturgy by the Library of Congress: a Critique," *Judaica Librarianship* 1 (2) (Spring 1984): 70-74.

Israeli libraries never accepted the *Jews. Liturgy and ritual* headings, preferring the single Hebrew word for prayers תפלות and using its romanized form *Tefillot* for non-Hebrew editions. Specific prayer books (with the exception of the Passover Haggada) were entered as subdivisions of this heading (e.g. תפלות. סדור and *Tefillot. Siddur* but הגדה של פסח and *Haggadah*).[62] The 1984 Adler-Shichor rules (rule 5.14) attempted to institute independent uniform title entry in accordance with AACR2, however this approach was never fully accepted by the major Judaica libraries. The 1995 edition (rule 5.14) reflects the decision of the inter-university Subcommittee on Cataloging to return to centralized entry under *Tefillot* with subdivisions, however, with four direct-entry exceptions: *Haggada shel Pessah, Selihot, Qinot* and *Tiqqunim.*

An additional problem relating to the cataloging of Jewish liturgical works is indication of the specific rite or custom to which the work belongs. The term "rite" in Jewish context is often quite difficult to determine. While there are some clearly defined and localized rites (Yemenite, Iraqi, etc.) Eastern European prayer books are often an amalgam of Western European (Ashkenazi) rite with Hassidic-Sephardic rite. In addition, specific rites are in many cases not indicated on the title page and would in some cases require an expert in Jewish liturgy to make a correct identification. Oppenheimer's 1966 text notes that:

> A special problem is that of customs [*minhagim*]. Two prayer books with the same title might be completely different works if they belong to different customs. A reader requiring a certain custom and receiving a different one would find it useless. Therefore a library which collects prayer books of different customs must indicate the custom, even when it is not mentioned on the title page. It is not always easy to determine the custom and may occasionally require assistance of an expert, but it is necessary.[63]

She goes on to note that entry in some catalogs (such as Zedner's British Museum catalog[64]) has been based on subdivision by custom/rite, further subdivided by the specific type of work (e.g., LITURGIES. GERMAN RITE. *Fastday Prayers*), however she rejects this approach as impractical:

> This order [subdivision by rite] is without question the most scientific, however it assumes that the librarian will be able to always determine the custom—otherwise there will be no place for the work. In addition, when he wishes to identify a book in hand in the catalog he will not be able to do so without knowing its custom. Therefore other catalogs make do with a more mechanical arrangement: arranging everything by type of prayer book, within

---

[62] Oppenheimer 1966, p. 86; Adler-Shichor 1978, rule 5.14.

[63] Oppenheimer 1966, p. 87 (translated).

[64] British Museum, *Catalogue of the Hebrew Books in the Library of the British Museum* [compiled by J. Zedner] (London: British Museum, Dept. of Oriental Printed Books and Manuscripts, 1867).

type by year of publication, and indicating the custom in a note if it does not appear on the title page—to the best of the librarian's ability. In this work we catalog according to this mechanical principle, however each library should consider its needs and resources and decide on its own procedure.[65]

This "mechanical" arrangement (indicating custom or rite in the description rather than in the access forms) has been followed by virtually all Israeli libraries. The list of uniform Judaica headings of the inter-university Subcommittee on Cataloging follow this practice and indicates exceptions for only three very unique sects: the Samaritans, the Karaites and the Beta-Israel (Ethiopian) Jews.

The *Anglo-American Cataloguing Rules* ignore the problematics of determining and defining rite. AACR2 (rule 25.22A) states:

> If the item being catalogued contains an authorized or traditional variant or special text of a liturgical work, add in parentheses (in this order of preference):

> 1) the name of a special rite (e.g. ... a rite other than the unmodified Ashkenazic rite for Jewish works)

> ...

> **Haggadah** (*Sephardic*)

> ...

> 2) the name of the place ... in which the variant is authorized or traditional ...

> ...

> **Kinot** (*Russia*)

> ...

> 3) ... If a single term is insufficient to identify the variant text, add a second term (e.g., the name of the editor).

> **Haggadah** (*Reform, Guggenheim*)

> ...

While AACR1 (rule 119C1) contains virtually the same rule, its examples are solely from Catholic liturgy while AACR2 adds examples of Jewish liturgy as well under each of the three cases. Current Library of Congress practice seems to be to add the rite to the heading only when it is indicated on the piece itself, with no attempt at verification or to establish rites not clearly indicated.

HEBREW PERSONAL NAMES

Israeli Hebrew cataloging uses Hebrew vernacular forms for all descriptive access points—forms usually found on the item itself (although "normalized" to standard orthography). Anglo-American cataloging, however, requires Roman alphabet forms of names. Even in Israel, Roman alphabet forms of Hebrew names are often needed in cataloging translations and as personal name subject entries

---

[65]Oppenheimer 1966, p. 87 (translated).

(depending on treatment of personal subjects—see chapter 7). While many current Hebrew publications provide a Roman alphabet form of the author's name (either on the verso of the title page or on a separate English language title page) this is true primarily in Israeli publications intended for the international market—it is rare in current Rabbinic literature and in older Hebraica.

Establishing a non-Hebrew form of a Hebrew name raises many questions: Should systematic Romanization be used even in cases where there is a non-standard form prefered by the author (and perhaps even appearing on the publication)? Should surnames originally Hebraized from Roman alphabet forms be restored to their original forms (e.g. should the Hebrew name שורץ or שווארץ (pronounced *shvarts*) be restored to the original German *Schwarz*[66])? How should one establish Jewish authors with different Hebrew and non-Hebrew forenames, a common practice amongst 19th and 20th century diaspora Jews (e.g., the 19th century German-Jewish scholar Adolf Jellinek who used the Hebrew forename *Aharon* in his Hebrew publications)? Furthermore, many older Hebrew names have been recorded over the years in non-Hebrew literature and reference works in forms that would hardly be recognized by the persons themselves, but that are well established (*Maimonides* or even *Moses ben Maimon* for the Hebrew name *Moshe ben Maimon*).

Commenting on the problematics of systematic romanization as currently practiced by LC, Barry Walfish notes that

> ...While this problem [supplying vowels] is for the most part manageable as it affects book titles, it is far more serious with regard to personal names. For any given name several equally possible and plausible pronunciations may suggest themselves. ... This situation, it should be pointed out, does not affect the majority of Hebrew and Yiddish names but it does affect enough of them to pose a serious problem and to call into question the whole enterprise of systematic romanization, at least as it is practiced by LC.[67]

Rule 53 of the 1908 ALA rules ("Hebrew writers") distinguishes between persons living before and after the 19th century (when Jewish surnames became more or less universal). Names prior to the 19th century are to be generally entered under the given name:

> Hebrew writers prior to the 19th century, unless decidedly better known under a European form of name, are to be entered under the given name of the author followed by that of his father or by some designation referring to the city of his birth or residence, to his profession, or to his rank.

---

[66]This is particularly problematic with names of German origin where Hebraization and subsequent romanization (according to American practice) cause *Sch* to be "restored" as *sh*, *w* as *v* and *z* as *ts*. Romanization according to the Academy of the Hebrew Language table would produce a result closer to the original.

[67]Barry Walfish, "Hebrew and Yiddish Personal Name Authorities under AACR2," *Cataloging & Classification Quarterly* 3 (4) (Summer 1983): 60.

With regard to variant forms of a name, this rule goes on to state that:

> Refer from the various forms in which the names of many Hebrew writers have become current. The Biblical names are to be given, as far as possible, in the form in which they appear in the authorized version.

The "Hebrew writers" rule does not address the question of romanization. It is, however, discussed in Appendix 2 (Report of the A.L.A. Transliteration Committee, 1885), which both contains a "Semitic Transliteration" table and states:

> *Biblical* names are to be written as we find them in the English Bible, and the names of post-Biblical Jews, if derived from the Scriptures, should retain their Anglicized form. On the other hand, a strict transliteration is demanded of rabbinical and other more or less pure Hebrew names which are not taken from Scriptures, and therefore have no popular English forms, to which, again, there is an exception in the case of a few celebrated Jewish authors, as Maimonides, where an un-Hebrew form has been fully adopted in English literature.[68]

The 1949 ALA rules contain a lengthy three page section devoted to Hebrew names (rule 65). It continues the division of pre- and post-19th century Hebrew names but expands this division not only to the forename/surname entry question, but to romanization as well. Rule 65A(6) establishes that "For Hebrew writers before 1800, given names of Biblical origin are to be spelled in the form in which they are given in the Authorized Version. Other Hebrew names are to be faithfully transliterated from the original, e.g., Yom-Tob, Hayyim."[69]

With regard to post-1800 persons, however, ALA rule 65B allows "Hebrew or Yiddish form" of Biblical names (e.g., *Shlomo* instead of *Solomon)*, but only if the bearer "consistently uses" this form. This rule also addresses the problem of both Jewish and non-Jewish given names (prefer the best known form; in case of doubt prefer the Jewish name) and recognizes the trend of Israelis adopting Hebrew surnames (prefer the Hebrew unless the previous form is predominant).

AACR1 addresses Hebrew names only in the context of rule 44B (Names not in the roman alphabet). This rule indicates preference for existing romanization whenever such a form exists in English language reference sources or in an author's works. If no such form exists then systematic romanization is to be used. Rule 44B1 provides the order of preference for existing forms:

> 1. Use the form preferred by the person whenever it is known
> 2. Use the form appearing in any work ... that an author has written in English ...

---

[68]ALA 1909, p. 66.

[69]Therefore *Moses* rather than *Moshe.* It is interesting to note that the opposite approach is used with Biblical names in Arabic. Rule 64H states: "Give Arabic given names of Biblical origin in their native form, e.g., Yusuf, not Joseph; Musa, not Moses; Ibrahim, not Abraham."

3. Use the form found in the authorized version of the Bible for names of Biblical characters and for given names and patronymics of Biblical origin borne by persons whose language is Hebrew or Yiddish unless the person is a resident of twentieth century Palestine or Israel or unless another romanized form appears in a work he has written and that has been published in his own country.

4. Use the form appearing in any work of an author published ... in Israel (as first choice) or in any other country if his language is Hebrew or Yiddish

5. Use the form that has become established through common usage in English-language reference sources ...

6. If the name is found only in a romanized form, use it as found ...

Rule 44B2 states:

Systematic romanization. If there is no existing romanized form or no form that meets the conditions stated above, romanize the name according to the romanization table for the person's language, adding vowels to names that are not vocalized.

Exception: Use the form found in the Authorized version of the Bible for given names and patronymics of Biblical origin borne by people whose language is Hebrew or Yiddish unless they are residents of twentieth century Palestine or Israel.

According to the above, a Hebrew author whose non-Hebrew form of name is known, or a Hebrew name of sufficient importance to appear in English-language reference works would follow "existing" romanization (with the exception of some Biblical names). All other Hebrew names would be systematically romanized, except for Biblical given names outside of 20th century Palestine or Israel (i.e., an American Hebrew author named *Moshe* would become *Moses*, but a 20th century Israeli would remain *Moshe*). Because most pre-20th century Hebrew authors did not indicate (or perhaps even have) a romanized form of name and relatively few made their way into English-language reference works, a large number of Hebrew names were consigned to systematic romanization.[70] A Hebrew author named שוואַרץ might be entered as *Schwarz, Swartz,* etc. (if such a form could be found in one of the sources in rule 44B1), otherwise he would be entered in the unlikely but systematic form: *Shvarts.* A searcher looking for a Hebrew author would be hard put to know when "existing" romanization was used and when "systematic".

In an apparent attempt to solve this problem, AACR2 mandated systematic romanization **only**. Rule 22.3C2 states:

---

[70]AACR1 has an alternate rule 44B which allows preferring entry under "the form most frequently found in English-language translations and reference sources" rather than the form preferred by the person himself. This alternate rule is intended primarily for libraries which do not collect materials in the language of a name to be romanized. It would, of course, be no help with names which do not appear in such sources.

Persons entered under surname. If the name of a person entered under surname (see 22.5) is written in a nonroman script, romanize the name according to the table for the language adopted by the cataloguing agency...

...

        Mordekhai Ze'ev Fai'erberg

not   Mordecai Zeev Feierberg

AACR2, however, has an *alternate* rule 22.3.C2 (applicable selectively by language) which states:

Persons entered under surname. Choose the romanized form of a name for a person whose name is in a language written in a nonroman script and who is entered under surname (see 22.5) that has become well established in English-language reference sources. However, in the case of a person using Hebrew or Yiddish who lives in twentieth-century Palestine or Israel, prefer the romanized form appearing on items issued in Palestine or Israel.

...

        Mordecai Zeev Feierberg

not   Mordekhai Ze'ev Fai'erberg

This alternate rule in effect returns the AACR1 approach although without the complicated order of preference. Forms are to be established according to English language reference sources with the exception of 20th century Israeli Hebrew authors who are to be entered according to the romanized form appearing in their publications. Non-Israeli contemporary Hebrew authors and all pre-20th century Hebrew authors are not covered by this exception and would be entered either under established English-language form (if existant) or under systematic romanization. The Library of Congress has opted to follow this alternate rule.[71]

The 1988 revision of AACR2 altered the special exception with regard to Hebrew. Alternate rule 22.3C2 states:

For a person who uses Hebrew or Yiddish and whose name is not found to be well-established in English-language reference sources, choose the romanized form appearing in his or her works.

The revised rule removes the geographic and period limitations. All Hebrew and Yiddish authors can be entered under the romanized form appearing in their works, however English-language reference works take precedence over any "personal" romanization.

Summarizing the changes in LC practice, Paul Maher states:

AACR2 22.3C, the footnote, and their LCRIs [Library of Congress Rule Interpretations] have gone through several revisions since 1981. This history is perhaps best viewed as an evolutionary process. There appears to be

---

[71]*Cataloging Service Bulletin* 16 (Spring 1982): 39.

no completely satisfactory solution to the questions raised by the necessity of romanizing personal names.[72]

As noted above, the romanized-form personal author problem in Israel is relatively minor. Translations of works by Hebrew authors are treated independently of their Hebrew originals, i.e., being in a separate catalog, the authors names are established according to the standard rules of entry for roman alphabet headings based on known preference, most frequent form (in the roman alphabet publications only!), etc. Indeed, this approach can lead to radically different headings in the Hebrew and roman-character catalogs (e.g., *Maimonides, Moses* in the roman-character catalog, the patronymic form משה בן מימון (*Moshe ben Maimon*) in the Hebrew catalog). The need for romanized forms of names appearing only in Hebrew is encountered primarily by the few Israeli libraries in which all subject access is via English language subject headings (usually LCSH). Biographical subject entries in these catalogs require a romanized form which might not be known or available. This question is not directly addressed by any of the Israeli cataloging manuals. In practice, the libraries involved seem to follow current LC practice, with systematic romanization as the last resort.

HEBREW CORPORATE BODIES

As with personal names, Israeli libraries use Hebrew vernacular forms as headings for Hebrew (primarily Israeli) corporate bodies. Here again, Anglo-American cataloging requires roman alphabet forms for all publications of such bodies while Israeli libraries need such headings only for roman alphabet publications of these bodies.

Prior to AACR1 there is virtually no mention of the problematics of nonroman corporate headings and no example of such a heading. The 1908 rules indicate preference for an authorized English form for international societies with authorized names in many languages (ALA 1908, rule 73, carried over virtually verbatim to ALA 1949 rule 97). The 1949 ALA rules mention nonroman headings in the context of governmental bodies of nations with more than one official language, stating that "For governments not using officially a roman, Greek or Slavic alphabet, prefer an English form of name."[73]

Examination of Israeli corporate headings in the 1953-1957 *National Union Catalog*[74] indicates a clear preference for English language forms of Hebrew corporate headings, both governmental (e.g., *Israel. Ministry of Foreign Affairs*) and

---

[72]Paul Maher, *Hebraica Cataloging* (Washington, D.C.: Cataloging Distribution Service, Library of Congress, 1987), p. 47.

[73]ALA 1949, rule 72A, footnote 3.

[74]Library of Congress, *National Union Catalog,* 1953-1957 (Paterson, N.J.: Rowman and Littlefield, 1961).

non-governmental (e.g. *General Federation of Jewish Labour in Israel*). The few headings that apparently had no English language forms were romanized (e.g., *Mifleget po'ale Erets Yisra'el*).

AACR1 devotes a lengthy general rule (no. 64) to the question of language form of corporate entries in general and non-roman headings in particular. English forms are to be preferred only if English is one of the official languages of the country, otherwise the official language is to be used, even if this requires romanization. Rule 64B deals specifically with romanization:

> 1. If the language that is used is one that is not normally written in the roman alphabet, romanize the name for the purpose of the heading by the application of the appropriate transliteration or romanization scheme adopted for library purposes.

> 2. If the publications of the body present its name in its own romanized form, however, use that form (unless it is known that the body uses more than one romanized form) with a reference from the standard library form, if necessary.

Following this rule, and not considering English to be an official language of the state of Israel,[75] the Library of Congress changed all Israeli corporate headings to romanized form (from *Israel. Ministry of Foreign Affairs* to *Israel. Misrad ha-huts* and from *General Federation of Jewish Labour in Israel* to *ha-Histadrut ha-kelalit shel ha'ovdim ha-'ivrim be-Erets Yisra'el*).[76]

AACR2 (rule 24.1A) and its 1988 revision (rule 24.1B) mandate systematic romanization of corporate headings exclusively. Use of a non-standard romanized form preferred by the body itself is allowed only as an alternate rule.

An alternate rule to AACR2 rule 24.3A (and to AACR1 rule 64) allows using an alternate form in the language suitable to the users of the catalog [i.e. English] if the body's name is in a language that is not familiar to the library's users (example given: using *Japan Productivity Center* rather than *Nihon Seisansei Hombu*). This alternate rule could have been used to allow English forms of Hebrew corporate names, however it has not been followed by the Library of Congress and seems to have been intended for use with languages which are rarely found in the library's catalog (which would hardly apply to the major American Judaica collections). This limited intent is much clearer in the AACR1 version where this alternate rule is

---

[75]Although English is often thought to be an official language, only Hebrew and Arabic are the official languages of the state of Israel.

[76]Actually the Library of Congress instituted this change for government agencies long before AACR1. According to *Cataloging Service Bulletin,* 42 (July 1957), p. 8 the 1949 ALA rule 72A and its footnote were changed to remove the instruction to use English forms for government agencies whose official languages were not in the "Roman, Greek or Slavic alphabet." As a result, the 1963-1967 edition of the *National Union Catalog* (published 1969) lists all Israeli government ministries in romanized form, however the labor federation still appears in English form.

limited to headings "in a language that is not one in which the library normally collects materials."[77]

As with personal name headings, Israeli libraries require roman alphabet corporate entries only for roman alphabet publications. There is, however, a major difference between the two. While romanized personal name headings usually match, more-or-less, the form of name on the piece itself, romanized corporate entries are almost always completely different from the usually *translated* headings on the publications (e.g., English language publications of the University of Haifa always use the English form of name; they would never use the romanized *Universiṭat Ḥefah*). Here the searcher would have to depend almost always on the cross references in the catalog to lead him to the romanized, unfamiliar (and to an Israeli, unwieldy) form. Israeli practice prior to 1990 was inconsistent, with some libraries holding out for English forms. One of the decisions of the inter-university Subcommittee on Cataloging was to follow AACR practice and romanize all Israeli corporate headings (except for exceptional cases where the Hebrew form cannot be ascertained).[78] This is now accepted Israeli practice.[79]

GEOGRAPHIC NAMES

Geographic names, as parts of headings, are used both as the names of governments and as distinguishing qualifiers in other headings. These names are uniformly established according to the English form found in gazetteers and other English language reference sources, using the vernacular form only if no such English form can be established (AACR2-rev, rule 23.2).

The use of Hebrew geographic names in non-Israeli cataloging headings is limited to places in the state of Israel. The roman alphabet forms of Israeli place names (as seen in Israeli municipal publications, highway signs, maps etc.) are highly inconsistent--sometimes using archaic or "English" forms and sometimes romanization (with various tables and results). Thus, while *Jerusalem* is generally preferred to *Yerushalayim* and *Haifa* to *Ḥefah*, *Zefat* is more predominant than *Safed* and *Akko* more common than *Acre*. While American libraries will follow the forms found in general, English language sources, Israeli libraries follow the official forms set by the Israeli government committee on geographic names (these forms can most easily be found in government publications such as those of the Central Bureau of Statistics).

In Israeli Hebrew cataloging, of course, the Hebrew forms themselves are used. In addition, Israeli Hebrew cataloging may require Hebrew forms for places outside of Israel (for example, a Hebrew translation of a non-Israeli government

---

[77]AACR1, rule 64, footnote 4.

[78]Elhanan Adler (editor), "Cataloging Decisions and Rule Changes ...," pp. 70-71.

[79]Adler-Shichor-Kedar 1995, rule 4.1.

publication). In this case the forms are established according to Hebrew gazetteers and reference works.[80]

---

[80]Adler-Shichor-Kedar 1995, rule 4.6.

6 Description: American and Israeli Practices

Aside from the questions of entry and access forms discussed in the previous chapter, there are also unique considerations and problems relating to Hebrew descriptive cataloging that require special attention and treatment. In addition, there are also differences between American and Israeli practice. Many of these derive from questions of primary language or cultural orientation (what language and script should be used for cataloger-supplied information, or how to transcribe Hebrew-character numbers and Jewish-era dates). In this chapter we will discuss the primary questions of descriptive cataloging that relate to Hebrew materials and the differences between American and Israeli practice.

LANGUAGE AND SCRIPT OF DESCRIPTION/CATALOGING

AACR2-rev rule 1.0E distinguishes between the language and script of the item being cataloged and that of the cataloging agency itself. While key bibliographic information ("Title and statement of responsibility, Edition, Publication, distribution, etc.,[1] Series") are to be transcribed in the original language and script (whenever possible), virtually all other information is to be supplied "in the language and script of the cataloguing agency." Thus, for example, title information relating to a book in Spanish would always be transcribed in Spanish—however the language of cataloger-supplied note would differ according to the country and language of the cataloging agency. For an American library cataloging a Hebrew item, only the above key information is to be transcribed in Hebrew (either vernacular or romanized). All other information (collation, notes, etc.) would be supplied in English. For an Israeli library the "language of the cataloguing agency" would, of course, be Hebrew and therefore

---

[1] Historically, there was a period when Hebrew imprint information was considered insufficient. The 1949 Library of Congress Descriptive Cataloging Rules contain a special rule for Hebrew and Yiddish imprints (only!) which states: "A Hebrew or Yiddish imprint ... is followed by an imprint in one of the other languages ... If there is no such imprint in the work, the place of publication is supplied using the English equivalent of the name." (Library of Congress, *Rules for Descriptive Cataloging in the Library of Congress (Adopted by the American Library Association)*. (Washington, D.C., Library of Congress, Descriptive Cataloging Division, 1949), rule 3:10F.

the entire record would be in Hebrew.[2] Many of the differences between American and Israeli practice derive from this question of basic language and script orientation.

TITLE TRANSCRIPTION STATEMENT OF RESPONSIBILITY

Seemingly the most elementary rule of descriptive cataloging would be to transcribe data (particularly regarding the title) exactly as it appears on the piece being cataloged.[3] Transcribing Hebrew titles raises two basic questions: is the cataloger required to transcribe any vowel points that actually appear in the title of the item, and conversely, is the cataloger obligated to supply missing vowel points.

Regarding the first question, AACR2-rev (rule 1.1B1) seems to be clear:

> Transcribe the title proper exactly as to wording, order, and spelling, but not necessarily as to punctuation and capitalization. Give accentuation and other diacritical marks that are present in the chief source of information.

If the Hebrew *nikud* (vowel pointing) marks are indeed a form of diacritic, then this rule would seem to mandate their transcription when found as part of the title itself (as is common in Hebrew children's literature, poetry, prayer books and other generally pointed texts). Webster's 3rd unabridged dictionary defines *diacritic* in our context as:

> A modifying mark or sign over, under, after or through an orthographic or phonetic character or combination of characters indicating a phonetic or semantic value different from that of the unmarked or otherwise marked character.[4]

While this definition clearly includes such markings as the *dagesh* (distinguishing, for example, between the characters *bet* and *vet*), it is not clear whether it would include the Hebrew vowel points which systematically *supplement* rather than *modify* the consonantal characters which are unreadable without them. The definition of *diacritic* which appears in the recent Unicode Standard glossary is broader:

> (1) a mark applied or attached to a symbol in order to create a new symbol that represents an entirely new value; (2) a mark applied to a symbol irrespective of whether it changes the value of that symbol. In the latter case,

---

[2]Assuming that a cataloging agency has only one language, this rule could be interpreted to mandate Hebrew notes, collation, etc. in Israeli non-Hebrew cataloging. In Israeli practice, English is assumed to be the "agency language" for all roman character cataloging, Arabic for Arabic cataloging, etc.

[3]Even in Israeli libraries where headings are "normalized" to a standard orthographic form, the title itself is transcribed "as is" although the title may be coded not to serve as an access point.

[4]*Webster's Third New International Dictionary of the English Language, Unabridged*, s.v. "diacritic."

the diacritic usually represents an independent value, e.g., an accent, tone, or some other linguistic information.[5]

The second definition would clearly include the Hebrew vowel points as well. Unfortunately, the glossaries in the various editions of the Anglo-American Cataloging Rules do not define the term *diacritic* as used in those rules. In the introduction to her proposed Hebrew character set for RLIN, Bella Weinberg differentiates between vowel points and diacritics, but still considers both mandatory:

> While this proposal features a full set of vowel points and diacritics, it is not intended that cataloging be corrective in any way (even though AACR2 calls for insertion of missing diacritics according to standard usage in the language). These special characters are included in the proposal to enable the cataloger to record them when they occur in the work being cataloged.[6]

Despite the above, it has been almost universal Hebrew cataloging practice to transcribe the consonantal characters only, omitting all vowel points, accents (*dagesh*) and any other markings. This practice is first and foremost one of convenience—most Hebrew typewriters and even computer printers were unable to print the vowel points and other markings. Producing a pointed catalog card would have required manual additions after printing, or sophisticated typesetting capability. Recognition of these technical limitations can be found in rule 133A of AACR1 dealing with recording of the title: "The title proper ... is transcribed exactly as to order, spelling, accentuation, and other diacritical marks (if possible) ..." The Library of Congress printed catalog to 1942[7] does contain some pointed Hebrew typeset cards from the 1930s but this seems to have been a temporary exception to the general practice. Even today, despite the fact that the RLIN system currently enables entering, storing and displaying all the common Hebrew markings, use of this feature is minimal.[8]

In explaining the current (1987) practice at the Library of Congress, Paul Maher wrote:

> ... there may be some merit to transcribing the <u>nikud</u> as found in the source of information ... Doing so, however, would introduce unnecessary complications: is the <u>nikud</u> absent from the bibliographic record because it did not appear in the item described, was it simply omitted during transcription,

---

[5] Unicode Consortium, *The Unicode Standard, Version 2.0.* (Reading, MA, Addison-Wesley, 1996), Glossary, G-3.

[6] Bella Hass Weinberg, Proposed Hebraic Character Set for the Research Libraries Information Network (March 1985), typescript.

[7] Library of Congress, *A Catalog of Books Represented by Library of Congress Printed Cards Issued to July 31, 1942* (Paterson: Rowman and Littlefield, 1963).

[8] A recent survey by the authors shows that 9 out of 10 responding RLIN Hebraica libraries do not enter vowel points which appear on the title page (for further details see chapter 8).

was it lacking in the graphic facilities available at the time the record was created, or is there some other reason?[9]

If we accept the view that existent vowel points and diacritics *should be* transcribed (even though, in practice, most libraries are not doing so), then the our second question needs to be addressed: should missing vowel points and diacritics be supplied? Supplying vowels and diacritics would resolve many problems of ambiguity in the unpointed texts, however it would also require an expert-level knowledge of Hebrew grammar on the part of the cataloger.

Rule 1.0G1 of AACR2-rev ("Accents and other diacritical marks") states:

> Add accents and other diacritical marks that are not present in the data found in the source of information in accordance with the usage of the language used in the context.

Bella Weinberg (quoted previously) notes this rule, but still feels that Hebrew cataloging should not be corrective. In a later paper she states specifically: "I consider descriptive cataloging in the original alphabet the only permanent element of a Hebraica catalog record. I feel everything should be transcribed from the title page non-correctively."[10] Paul Maher, presenting the Library of Congress interpretation of this rule, lists several reasons why it should not be applied to Hebrew:

> This rule, as applied by the Library of Congress, is not interpreted to include Hebraica nikud ... There are several principles involved in this decision. Most nekudot (dots) are properly vowels, not diacritics. Even though certain nekudot such as the dagesh are true diacritics, the rule calls for application based on "the usage of the language" in question. Since the preponderance of Hebrew texts ... do not use nikud, it cannot be considered as part of the standard usage of the language for purposes of this rule. Witness also the multiple systems of nikud for Hebrew ... Nor can this rule be applied to Yiddish since its usage of nikud is even less predictable than Hebrew's ... In many cases due to the differences of ketiv male and ketiv haser, adding the nekudot not found in the source of information would result in a violation of the rules of Hebrew grammar.[11]

In actual practice, whether for theoretical or practical reasons, no major Hebraica library attempts to supply vowel points or diacritics.

In Israeli practice both questions (transcribing or adding vowels and diacritics) are moot points, not even mentioned in the cataloging manuals. It is

---

[9]Paul Maher, *Hebraica Cataloging* (Washington, D.C.: Cataloging Distribution Service, Library of Congress, 1987), p. 36.

[10]Bella Hass Weinberg, "Judaica and Hebraica Cataloging: Anglo-American Traditions," *Judaica Librarianship* 6 (1-2) (Spring 1991-Winter 1992): 19.

[11]Paul Maher, *Hebraica Cataloging* , pp. 35-36.

understood that only Hebrew consonants are transcribed. Since no current Israeli automated cataloging system uses the extended character set necessary to represent more than the basic consonants, this question has not been raised recently. In non-Israeli romanized cataloging, of course, the vowels and some other diacritics (such as the distinction between *bet* and *vet*) have already been supplied and therefore these questions are not relevant.

Many Rabbinic Hebrew titles begin with separable words such as *sefer* (book), *kovets* (collection), or *she'elot u-teshuvot* (responsa).[12] While the title must be transcribed as is, its access is another question. Library of Congress practice is to make both forms of titles with the separable *sefer* retrievable by using a uniform title to express the title without the initial, separable word.[13] For titles beginning with the other separable words, title added entries (without the word) are made. Common Israeli practice is to simply ignore or suppress the initial word(s) in filing.

STATEMENT OF RESPONSIBILITY

There are two particular problems in transcribing Hebrew statements of responsibility: whether to transcribe titles of address that begin with a prefix which itself should be transcribed but cannot stand alone (e.g., *leha-rav* = by Rabbi), and how to transcribe names containing patronymic forms (A *son of* B, e.g.,, *Yosef ben Ya'akov*), which are often accompanied by lengthy, rather complicated abbreviation strings. Both of these problems are quite common in cataloging Rabbinic literature. They exist in both vernacular Hebrew and romanized Hebrew transcription.

Rule 1.1F7 of AACR2-rev states: "Include titles and abbreviations of titles of nobility, address, honour, and distinction ... if: a) such data are necessary grammatically...." In applying this rule to Hebrew, Maher adds:

> Titles of address such as Rabbi, etc. are not generally transcribed in the statement of responsibility even though they are transcribed if they appear in a bibliographic title. However, if a preposition or conjunction indicating authorship or other responsibility is prefixed to such a title, then it is necessary to transcribe the title of address appearing in the statement of responsibility.[14]

His examples include not only the prepositional *lamed* indicating "by" (*le-Rabenu* = by our Rabbi) but also the conjunctional *vav* (*Devorah ṿeha-Rav Menaḥem Hakohen* = Devorah and Rabbi Menahem Hakohen).

With regard to patronymics, Maher states that:

[12]These words are not always separable ,e.g. *Sefer Moreh nevukhim* (a book: guide to the perplexed) as opposed to *Sefer Bialiḳ* ("Bialik book"). Each case must be carefully considered.

[13]Paul Maher, *Hebraica Cataloging* , p. 45.

[14]Paul Maher, *Hebraica Cataloging* , p. 36.

When a patronymic appears in an author's name and also precedes the surname, if the patronymic is imbedded in a single abbreviation string in the vernacular, then the entire abbreviation string is given in the statement of responsibility. ... Patronymics which follow a surname are not usually transcribed in the statement of responsibility ...[15]

The example given is משה בלאאמו"ר נחמן (romanized: Mosheh b.la-a.a.m.ve-r.[16] Naḥman, translated: Mosheh son of my lord, my father, my teacher, and my Rabbi Nahman).

Israeli practice is somewhat simpler. Adler-Shichor-Kedar rule 7.6 contains a section dealing specifically with Rabbinic literature:

Deletions and additions in Rabbinic literature. In Rabbinic literature it is customary to shower the author or his father with various and multiple titles of honor (Rabbi, Gaon, Saint, etc.) and even to detail his genealogy. One should record only his forename and surname, without honorifics or patronymics (unless the name is common and the addition is necessary for identification). If the author does not have a surname (or it does not appear on the title page), one should record his father's name or another identifying item (his location, his being a "Cohen" or "Levi", etc.). If the word "ben" appears on the title page only as part of a lengthy honorific (e.g., בהרה"ג [son of the Rabbi, the Gaon]) one can record instead the word "ben" in brackets. (translated)

According to this, Maher's example, "Mosheh b.la-a.a.m.ve-r. Naḥman" would be transcribed simply as "Mosheh [ben] Naḥman." Furthermore, while Maher would transcribe a patronymic appearing before a surname (Yitsḥak Dov ben Efrayim Fishel Feld), Adler-Shichor-Kedar does not require the patronymic (Yitsḥak Dov Feld), unless there are several authors by this name.

AACR1, rule 134E, states that when there are more than three authors, collaborators, etc. in the author statement of the item, only the first is recorded, the omission of the others being indicated by the phrase "and others" if the title page is in English, and by "et al." if in any other language with, however, four exceptions, two of which are for Hebraic transcription: ואחרים (ve-aḥerim = and others) for Hebrew and און אנדערע (un andere = and others) in Yiddish. AACR2-rev (rule 1.1F5) does away with "and others" in favor of "et al." in accordance with ISBD usage, however it indicates exception (without example) for nonroman scripts: "... add *et al.* (or its equivalent in a nonroman script) ...". The Yiddish און אנדערע does reappear in Appendix B12 (Hebrew Alphabet Abbreviations) where it has been reduced to its

---

[15]Paul Maher, *Hebraica Cataloging*, p. 36-37.

[16] Note that when the abbreviation is not pronounceable, only the consonants are romanized. For a recent list of LC practice in romanizing such abbreviations see: Joan Biella and Rachel Simon, "Hayah noten ba-hem simanim: Hebrew Abbreviations, Chiefly Rabbinic, and Their ALA/LC Romanization," *Judaica Librarianship* 9 (1-2) (Spring 1994-Winter 1995), 75-82.

initials: א״א. Library of Congress practice, since 1981, is not to use ואחרים but rather "et al." even at the expense of mixing alphabets and/or directions in the same line.[17] The Hebrew ואחרים form is standard in Israeli Hebrew cataloging (Adler-Shichor-Kedar, rule 7.5).

EDITION STATEMENT

Recording a Hebrew edition statement often involves transcription of a number given as a Hebrew word or represented by Hebrew-letter numerals. AACR2-rev rule 1.2B1 states: "Transcribe the edition statement as found on the item. Use abbreviations as instructed in appendix B and numerals as instructed in Appendix C." While Appendix B contains several vernacular Hebrew and Yiddish abbreviations for terms indicating "edition" (see section on abbreviations later in this chapter), rule C.5 of Appendix C stipulates that

> In cataloging Arabic alphabet, Far Eastern, Greek, Hebrew, Indic, etc. materials, substitute roman numerals or Western-style arabic numerals for numerals in the vernacular as instructed in the following rules. ... Use Western-style arabic numerals in the following areas and elements of the bibliographic description: 1) in an edition statement ... .

Hebrew vernacular transcription using this rule would produce such combinations as מהד׳ 1 for מהדורה ראשונה (first edition) or מהד׳ 15 for מהדורה ט״ו (15th edition, using Hebrew letter values 9+6). Israeli practice is to not only retain the letter values (מהד׳ ט״ו) but also to use them to substitute for the numeric word values (מהדורה ראשונה becoming מהד׳ א). The transcription of Hebrew letter-numbers is even more problematic in dealing with Jewish era dates, and will be further dealt with under that topic.

Another problem relating to Hebrew edition statements is the tendency of modern Israeli publishers to misuse the term *mahadurah* (edition) when, in fact, the item in hand is no more than a new printing and should more correctly have been labeled *hadpasah* (printing). In case of doubt, the cataloger must lean in favor of the more significant "edition" interpretation.[18] Maher has also noted that the term *mahadurah* is often found indicating the equivalent of a book club statement (e.g., *Mahadurat Yedi'ot aharonot*) and should then be given as a quoted note.[19]

---

[17] Personal communication from Paul Maher, Jan. 22, 1997.

[18] AACR2-rev, rule 1.2B3, Adler-Shichor-Kedar, rule 7.7, footnote 5.

[19] Paul Maher, *Hebraica Cataloging*, p. 37.

PLACE OF PUBLICATION

Both American and Israeli practice is to transcribe the place of publication as it appears on the piece being cataloged (AACR2-rev rule 1.4C1). A place which appears in Hebrew script will, therefore, be transcribed in Hebrew. There is, however, a difference in practice when the place is not named or is only probable. AACR2-rev rule 1.4C6 states: "If the place of publication, distribution, etc. is uncertain, supply the probable place in the language of the chief source of information, followed by a question mark". According to this, a supplied place of publication should, presumably, be in Hebrew script. Library of Congress practice, according to Maher, is different:

> LCRI 1.4C4 says that if the place of publication is not named in the item, or if the place of publication is only probable, it should be bracketed in its well-established English form if there is one. The roman form is given in both the vernacular and roman bibliographic records; cf. rule 1.0E.[20]

Rule 1.0E states that while transcribed publication area data should be given in the original language and script (whenever possible), interpolated information relating to "other forms of the place of publication" is an exception to this rule. The Library of Congress has interpreted this rather widely to cover any supplied place of publication. This is a change from AACR1 (rule 138D1): "If the imprint data are not found in the work itself, they may be supplied, the language of the title page being employed if the form in this language is available."

Israeli libraries will, of course, supply place of publication data in Hebrew since Hebrew is both the language of the item and of the "cataloging agency." While the Israeli cataloging rules do not discuss the question of supplied publication data in Yiddish cataloging, current policy of the Jewish National and University Library is to supply the place in its Hebrew form.

When no place of publication is available, however, both American and Israeli practice is to use the Hebrew abbreviated form [ח״מ] (= *ḥaser maḳom,* lacking place). This is in accordance with AACR2-rev rule 1.4C6 "If no place or probable place can be given, give *s.l.* (sine loco), or its equivalent in a nonroman script."

NAME OF PUBLISHER

Differences in practice in recording the name of the publisher parallel those for recording the place of publication. While Maher does not state so, presumably the same rule interpretation would apply. An unknown publisher is indicated by the Hebrew abbreviated form [חמו״ל] (= *ḥaser mo. l. (motsi la'or),* lacking publisher). In accordance with AACR2-rev rule 1.4D7, "If the name of the publisher, distributor, etc. is unknown, give *s.n.* (sine nomine), or its equivalent in a nonroman script."

---

[20]Paul Maher, *Hebraica Cataloging* , p. 37.

DATE OF PUBLICATION

Jewish era dates are commonly found in Hebrew publications, often as the sole date, occasionally in parallel with common (Christian) era dates. Their transcription in Hebrew cataloging is not simple, and the American rules have undergone several changes. The problems derive from the numbering scheme itself (the thousands digit is commonly omitted), the representation of the date using Hebrew letter numeric values (simple or chronograms), the desire to supply the parallel common era date, and the overlap between the Jewish and Christian years.

For example: the Jewish era year 5757 is represented in Hebrew as תשנ״ז - the number value of the letters (400+300+50+7) adding up to 757 (the thousands digit is understood - however in older Rabbinic publications it was occasionally included using the letter *heh* (=5) in the form: התשנ״ז). The Jewish era year 5757 corresponds with September 14, 1996 to October 1, 1997. Each Jewish era year overlaps two common era years: approximately one quarter being in one year and three quarters in the following year, with the Jewish New Year occurring during September or October (since the Jewish calendar is a lunar one, its dates relative to the solar calendar can vary somewhat). While occasionally indication of the month or even day of publication may appear on an item (or be inferable), in most cases it is impossible to know the exact single common era year of publication.

American Descriptive cataloging rules have always required both transcription of the Hebrew date and its conversion into a common era date. The way in which both of these are done has varied.

Rule 3:13C of the 1949 Library of Congress rules[21] states:

> *Dates not of the Christian era.* If the only imprint date on the title page is not of the Christian era it is given as it appears followed by the date of the Christian era.
>
> > Roma, anno xvii [1939]
>
> If the chronology does not coincide with the Christian year, and the month and date of publication are not known, the form 1881/82 is used.

According to this rule, the Hebrew date would be transcribed only if there is no common era date. Transcription of the date was in the original Hebrew form. Furthermore, the overlapping-year problem was indicated by entering both years with a slash between them. Library of Congress printed cards of this period show Hebrew dates in the form: תשט״ו [1955/56] .

---

[21]Library of Congress, *Rules for Descriptive Cataloging in the Library of Congress (Adopted by the American Library Association)* (Washington: Library of Congress, Descriptive Cataloging Division, 1949).

AACR1 (rule 141D) introduced changes both in the transcription and conversion of Hebrew dates:

> If the only imprint date on the title page is not a year of the Christian era it is given as it appears (except that Western-style Arabic numerals are substituted for oriental numerals in the cataloging of oriental materials—cf. Appendix IV F) ... If the precise year of the Christian era cannot be determined because the years in the two systems begin on different days and the month and day of publication are not known, the form 1881 or 2 is used.

This approach is also found in AACR2 (rule 1.4F1), however with both years recorded in full four-digit form:

> ... Give dates in Western-style arabic numerals. If the date found in the item is not of the Gregorian or Julian calendar, give the date as found and follow it with the year(s) of the Gregorian or Julian calendar.
>
> ...
>
> 5730 [1969 or 1970]
>
> ...

While the example given indicates a full Hebrew year (including the thousands digit), as mentioned previously, most Hebrew dates of publication omit the thousands and are therefore recorded in the form: **743 [1982 or 1983]**, which most users of the Hebraica catalog would have a hard time associating with the original Hebrew date.

Israeli practice in transcribing Hebrew dates has also gone through several changes. Oppenheimer's 1963 cataloging textbook indicates total supremacy of the Hebrew calendar. The Hebrew year is always transcribed. The common era year is to be transcribed only if its final digit is different from that of the Hebrew date (i.e., about the first quarter of each Jewish era year). It is not supplied if absent. She states that:

> This practice is a deviation from rule LC 3:13C according to which a Christian era date is added to a non-Christian era date and when the exact date cannot be ascertained, the two possible years are added. That rule is more accurate but is not common practice in Hebrew bibliography.[22]

This practice is recorded also in her 1974 edition, the only difference being in noting it as a deviation from AACR1 rules 141A and 141D.[23]

While it may be that common practice in Hebraica bibliography has been to record Hebrew dates alone, the use of common era dates in Israel is (and has been for some time) prevalent. Most non-Rabbinic current publications present either both or the common era year alone. While the majority of the Israeli public would know the

---

[22] Hana Oppenheimer, *Targilim be-ḳitlug* (Jerusalem [s.n.], 1963), 8.

[23] Hana Oppenheimer, *Targilim be-ḳitlug*, New ed., adapted to the Anglo-American Cataloging Rules, v. 2. (Jerusalem: [s.n.], 1974), 8.

current Hebrew year, many would be hard put to recognize the common era equivalent of a Hebrew year several decades earlier. In recognition of this, Adler-Shichor-Kedar rule 7.11 modifies Oppenheimer's approach somewhat. While recognizing the problem of conversion (and the clumsiness of the "1995 or 1996" form), this rule states that if both dates appear they should both be recorded, but if only the Hebrew date is found, it alone is transcribed. A footnote adds that "The cataloger may supply the common era year, bracketed, after the Hebrew year if he feels that the Hebrew year alone would be an impediment to library users." Of course, Israeli transcription of Hebrew dates retains the Hebrew form itself.[24]

An additional problem relating to Hebrew dates is the extensive use of chronograms (words or phrases whose numerical value adds up to the date of publication) in Rabbinic literature. AACR1 (rule 141E) states that:

> If the date occurs as a chronogram in the title or in the imprint it is transcribed as it appears. If the chronogram is lengthy or involved it is omitted. In either case the date is supplied in Arabic numerals in the imprint.

AACR2 does not mention chronograms at all and Maher indicates that only the numerical value of the letters and their common era equivalent are given. He adds that "Since this is a fairly common phenomenon in rabbinics, the Library of Congress does not ordinarily give an indication in the bibliographic records for Hebraica materials that the date is derived from a chronogram."[25]

Adler-Shichor-Kedar rule 7.11 states that the chronogram should be transcribed as is and then followed by its equivalent as a bracketed *Hebrew* date in the form: תברכו [ז״א תרכ״ח]. With regard to more complicated chronograms (those in which only selected, emphasized letters of a phrase are to be counted) Israeli practice is not uniform—some libraries simply add up the numbers and present the sum as a bracketed Hebrew date. Others attempt to transcribe the entire chronogram, using various diacritics to indicate the selected letters.

The calculation of a Hebrew chronogram is itself not a trivial task. The letter *heh* (=5) may represent the number five, or it may indicate five thousand. Often only specially marked or emphasized letters of a phrase are to be counted. Bella Weinberg has noted that "Even after all this calculation has been done, it is not uncommon to find the cataloger's note: 'Hebrew and common era dates do not correspond.' "

---

[24] In the Israeli ALEPH system the date field can be either Hebrew or roman. An internal four-digit filing year (FY) field is also required. If the cataloger does not supply one and the regular year field contains a Hebrew date, the system automatically creates the filing year by converting the Hebrew date to the common era date with the same final digit (i.e., that which three-quarters overlaps).

[25] Paul Maher, *Hebraica Cataloging*, 40.

PHYSICAL DESCRIPTION

The physical description is cataloger-supplied information, given in the "language and script of the cataloging agency" (AACR2-rev, rule 1.0E1). Accordingly, American cataloging will always convert Hebrew page numbering to regular numerals and use English abbreviations such as: *p.*, *v.*, *ill.*, and *cm*. Physical description in Israeli Hebrew cataloging is oriented right-to-left and will retain Hebrew numbering when found, and use equivalent Hebrew abbreviations (see section on Hebrew abbreviations at the end of this chapter).

NOTES

While notes are generally composed in the "language and script of the cataloging agency" (AACR2-rev, rule 1.0E1), notes can contain quotations or bibliographic information which should be transcribed in the language of the item. For example, AACR2-rev rule 1.7A3 ("Form of notes") states "When giving names or titles originally in nonroman scripts, use the original script whenever possible rather than a romanization." While this was previously Library of Congress practice, Maher indicates that "Since the implementation of TOSCA [Total-Online-Searching-for-Cataloging-Activities] in June of 1983, notes are usually given in romanized form only."[26]

In Israeli cataloging, Hebrew is, of course, the "language of the cataloging agency" and therefore all supplied notes will be in Hebrew. Quoted information or bibliographic data will be generally supplied in the language of the item (e.g., Yiddish).

MULTIPLE TITLE PAGES

Many recent (primarily 20th century) Hebrew books have additional, non-Hebrew (usually roman alphabet) title pages. These added title pages are presumably to aid librarians, book dealers, who might need to handle or identify these items without knowledge of Hebrew. When they have the appearance of title pages (not just a translation of author and title on the verso of the Hebrew title page), they are usually noted in the cataloging, e.g.,, "Added t.p. in English: Cataloging" or "Title on added t.p: ...). In Israeli Hebrew cataloging, since the language of cataloging is Hebrew. this would lead to a bilingual, bidirectional note, e.g.,:" Cataloging ‏"שער נוסף באנגלית:‏. Because of the difficulty in entering bidirectional text in manual cataloging (the need to type the roman section backwards), and the fact that it is usually not considered significant for retrieval, it is common in Israel to simply note the existence of the added title page (in Hebrew, as above) without citing its actual text. This has carried over to most automated Hebrew cataloging as well.

While this may suffice for Hebrew books with an additional title page, it is not sufficient for fully bilingual items such as dictionaries, Festschriften and community memorial books which often have entire sections in the second language or script, often beginning at the opposite end of the book with the final pages of both sections meeting in the middle of the volume. These items may likely be cited and sought under their non-Hebrew title page information as well. In American cataloging these are not significantly different from the first case: since the various access points are all given in roman alphabet form, an added entry for the additional title and an explanatory note regarding the text usually suffice.

In Israeli cataloging, with two separate catalogs for the Hebrew and roman alphabets, a more complicated solution had to be developed since many access points have to be given twice—in both Hebrew and the second script. Thus, for example, a bilingual Hebrew-English, English-Hebrew dictionary with both a Hebrew title page at one end and an English one at the other would have two author entries—one in Hebrew and one in roman script. This form of cataloging is known as "mixed" cataloging (*kitlug "ta'arovet"*). In manual cataloging two separate cards were created: one in Hebrew with a note indicating the second title page, and one in the second script with a note indicating the Hebrew title page. The tracing of each card included the main entry of the other.[27] Simply adding alternate script added entries to one card was considered confusing and would have created filing problems (e.g. arrangement of titles in different scripts under a heading). In current Israeli automated catalogs, however, this is exactly what is done—the item is cataloged according to one title page and additional, sometimes redundant added entries are given in the alternate script. In the RLIN system, vernacular added entries, when given, create the same effect.

ABBREVIATIONS

Appendix IIID of AACR1 contains 18 "Hebraic abbreviations" (7 Hebrew and 11 Yiddish). Appendix B.12 of AACR2 contains 20 (8 Hebrew and 12 Yiddish). Appendix D of Adler-Shichor-Kedar lists 10 Hebrew abbreviations only.[28] There are differences between all three lists.

AACR1 and AACR2 have five Hebrew terms in common:

גל׳	= גליון (*gilayon*, issue, sheet)
חוב׳	= חוברת (*ḥoveret*, issue)
ח״מ	= חסר מקום (*ḥaser maḳom*, lacking place, s.l.)
מהד׳	= מהדורה (*mahadurah*, edition)
מס׳	= מספר (*mispar*, number)

---

[27] For an example of this type of cataloging, see Adler-Shichor-Kedar, section 10.3.

[28] None of the Israeli cataloging manuals detail rules for cataloging of Yiddish materials. In practice, the AACR Yiddish abbreviations are used. Adler-Shichor-Kedar actually includes more Hebrew abbreviations than appear in the appendix.

AACR1 lists an additional abbreviation (הקדמה=) הקד׳ for introduction (*haḵdamah*) which was dropped from AACR2. AACR1 also has a Hebrew equivalent for i.e.: צ״ל (צריך להיות=) (*tsarikh lihyot*, literally "should be") which was changed in AACR2 to the more accurate (זאת אומרת=) ז״א (*zot omeret*, literally "that is to say"). In addition, AACR2 adds two new abbreviations, (חסר מוציא לאור=) חמו״ל (*ḥaser motsi la-or*, lacking publisher, s.n.), and (טעות דפוס=) ט״ד (*ṭa'ut defus*, printing error).

Adler-Shichor-Kedar recognizes all of the AACR2 abbreviations (except the "printing error"—preferring a simple "[!]"), as well as the AACR1 abbreviation for introduction. In addition it lists a series of collation abbreviations:

ד׳	= דף, דפים	(*daf, dapim*, leaf, leaves[29])
דק׳	= דקות	(*daḵot*, minutes)
כר׳	= כרך, כרכים	(*kerekh, kerakhim*, volume, volumes)
מ״מ	= מילימטרים	(*milimetrim*, millimeters)
ס״מ	= סנטימטרים	(*sentimetrim*, centimeters)
ע׳	= עמוד, עמודים	('*amud*, '*amudim*, page, pages)

Since, in American practice the collation is always recorded in English, there is no use for these abbreviations. AACR1 and AACR2 do have abbreviations for serial terms which may appear in the "Numeric and/or alphabetic designation" area where vernacular text abbreviations are used (see AACR1 rule 163A2.C and AACR2 rule 12.3B).

SUMMARY

We have seen that many of the differences between American and Israeli practices in bibliographic description derive from differences in basic orientation relating to the "language and script of the cataloging agency" that is used for cataloger-supplied information, and even transcription of numbers and dates. Some unique questions of Hebrew cataloging are related to transcription of Rabbinic title page information. Yet others are due to the technical limitations of manual (typewriter produced) Hebrew card production. Many of these can be solved in computerized cataloging, and some have been (e.g., vowel point capability in RLIN), however it remains to be seen whether catalogers will actually use the additional capabilities the computer allows.

---

[29]Israeli cataloging practice is to consider pages numbered on one side but printed on both to be leaves. Library of Congress practice is to consider "leaves" printed on both sides to be pages, recording the pagination in form: 37 [i.e. 74] p. (P. Maher, *Hebraica Cataloging*, p. 43).

7   Hebraica, Judaica, and Israelitica Subject Cataloging

Any discussion of classification schemes for Judaica must begin with a definition of the scope of a Judaica collection. The subject of the present book, strictly speaking, is the cataloging of Hebrew language material, not Judaica material. However, Hebraica and Judaica are so closely linked with regard to subject cataloging (unlike descriptive cataloging, where the distinction is clear and simple to define) that it was decided to include all three types of material—Hebraica, Judaica, and Israelitica—in the analysis of classification schemes and subject headings.

Bella Weinberg defines the scope of a Judaica collection as "material by and about Jews, and...including Hebraica, or material printed in the Hebrew alphabet. It is worth noting that Hebraica is not necessarily *by* Jews—it includes missionary publications and the works of Christian Hebraists. Thus, there is no subject that is outside the scope of Judaica."[1]

Furthermore, since subject headings are an integral part of subject cataloging with regard to many classification systems, the scope of these subject headings also needs to be determined. Defining the scope of a Judaica subject heading, it would seem, is even more problematic than defining the scope of a Judaica collection: "One would be hard pressed to come up with unambiguous criteria for the scope of a Judaica subject heading list, given the relationship of Judaism with Biblical Studies and with other religions, the relationship of Israel with the Middle East, the academic

---

[1] Bella Hass Weinberg, "Hebraica Cataloging and Classification," In *Cataloging and Classification of Non-Western Material: Concerns, Issues and Practices,* Edited by Mohammed M. Aman (Phoenix, AZ: Oryx Press, 1980), p. 339.

link between Hebrew and Near Eastern Studies, and the fact that just about any topic may be treated from a Jewish perspective."[2]

HEBREW JUDAICA, HEBREW NON-JUDAICA, JUDAIC NON-HEBRAICA: A Definition

In spite of these difficulties, define we must, not only the scope of a Judaica collection and a Judaica subject heading, but also the scope of the subject of this chapter: Hebraica, Judaica and Israelitica subject cataloging. We shall define Hebraica, therefore, as all materials in Hebrew; Judaica, as all materials about Jews and Judaism in any language; and Israelitica, as all materials published in or about the land of Israel (both pre- and post-state).

Once the scope of the various types of materials that are included in Judaica collections are defined and differentiated, the problematics of Judaica classification must be faced. The first question which arises is: what in the nature of Judaica made it necessary to develop Judaica classification systems in the first place? The second question which must be addressed is: given the existence of classification systems designed specifically to organize Judaica collections, what are the advantages and disadvantages of using such systems instead of fitting the Judaica into a general system?

Next, with regard to a general system such as DDC or LCC, one must consider what is the basis for its breakdown in classifying Judaica, that is whether it scatters Judaica and Hebraica through many subject classes or devotes a single class to them and subdivides that by disciplines. Finally, having determined the basis for its breakdown, one must ask whether the basis is logical, i.e., whether scattering Judaica or concentrating it best meets the needs of your Judaica library. For example, at one time the Library of Congress classified all materials in Yiddish under Yiddish literature (class PJ). The implicit implication was that these materials were not of interest for their *content*, but only for the fact that they were written in an obscure language. While this may be true for Yiddish works on science, for example, it is not true for Yiddish works on Jewish history. On the other hand, it is true that users often seek works on a subject or in a given literary form written in a certain language, in which case concentrating "exotic language" works by language could prove useful.

The problematics can best be analyzed by examining the various categories of classification systems for Hebraica, Judaica and Israelitica and the specific systems which fall within the definition of each category. Judaica scholars, both American

---

[2] Bella Hass Weinberg, "Compilations of Library of Congress Subject Headings for Judaica: Comparison, Evaluation, and Recommendations," *Judaica Librarianship* 5 (1) (Spring 1989-Winter 1990): 37.

and Israeli, have seen fit to devote time and knowledge to developing Judaica classification schemes both to organize specific collections and as a general tool to serve the needs of Judaica collections worldwide. The eminent scholar Harry Wolfson of Harvard developed a scheme for Harvard's Judaica collection which was in use until Harvard moved to LCC not so many years ago. In Jerusalem, the great Kabalah scholar Gershom Scholem created a system for classifying Judaica which is still in use in the Jewish National and University Library. Others, such as Miriam Leikind, Mae Weine and the David H. and Daniel J. Elazar sought to establish simpler but still comprehensive systems for the smaller libraries of American Hebrew schools, community centers and synagogues. We have divided subject cataloging systems into the categories: (1) systems for Judaica: American and Israeli; (2) Hebraica and Judaica subject cataloging in general classification systems: (2.1) Anglo-American systems, and (2.2) Israeli adaptations of Anglo-American systems; and (3) Israeli systems for Hebrew materials. Because of the large number of systems and multiple editions of the various schemes which will be discussed below, individual systems will not be footnoted within the chapter, but rather listed by author in the "Bibliography" at the end of this book.

SYSTEMS FOR JUDAICA: American and Israeli

American Systems for Judaica

The Dewey classification system forms the basis of several small Judaica schemes which are used primarily by synagogue libraries. These include the Leikind classification scheme, the Elazar classification and the Weine scheme.

Leikind

The simplest of the American schemes developed primarily to serve the needs of small synagogue libraries is the Leikind classification. Based on Dewey, it is limited by the Christian orientation which motivated other American Judaica classifiers, as we shall see, to radically alter the Dewey base or, in some cases, to abandon it altogether. Thus, in the Leikind system, Christianity (280) precedes Judaism (296).

Numbers 200-279 follow the arrangement in DDC rather closely, although in less detail. Religion starts at 200, Natural theology at 210 and Bible at 220, as in Dewey. The Bible is divided in the Christian way into the Old Testament and the New Testament, preserving also the Christian names for the books (e.g.,"Pentateuch," rather than "Torah," which DDC adds in parenthesis and Leikind does not!). Whereas in DDC 290 includes both comparative religion and religions other than Christianity, in Leikind 290 is comparative religion alone, and the numbers for other religions (292-295, 297, 299) are dropped. Judaism, 296, is expanded considerably beyond the Dewey numbers (e.g., 296.88 Rabbinate and institutions). The rest of the system consists of Dewey numbers or expansions which relate to Jewish or Israeli topics: a few numbers in the 300's (e.g., 383.956 Israeli postage stamps); Hebrew language (492.4+); a few numbers in the 700's (e.g., 709 Jewish art, history); Hebrew literature (892.4+); geography of Israel (915.69) and of Jerusalem (915.691); History of the Jews in Europe (940.5+); Jewish biography (9.22.96 and 922.96c for Collections); and History of the land of Israel, both pre- and post-state (956.9+).

The Leikind system, on the other hand, enjoys the advantages shared by other Judaica classification schemes based on DDC: (1) It has DDCs simplicity of notation—numbers only with decimal subdivision, and (2) it is generally compatible with DDC, so that a librarian can choose to synthesize new numbers by combining a basic number with an element from one of the tables.

Weinberg notes that "Leikind lags behind Dewey in that [recent] editions of the latter have moved Jewish history out of Jewish religion into the 900's....[while] Leikind classes Jewish history in 296.09, but places Holocaust in the 900's with Dewey's World War II schedule at 940.5405."[3]

Elazar

First published in 1968, the Elazar classification emphasizes the logical arrangement of a Judaica collection using Jewish principles to organize Jewish materials. It stresses the order of the main classes and enumerates many specific topics, such as Jewish political organizations and Israeli regional divisions.[4]

The Elazar system essentially allocates the entire 001-999 span to Judaica. It does include some other religions in 290-294 (Comparative Religion, Paganism, Christianity, Islam and Other Religions), the ancient Near East in 090, and ecumenical, patriotic and universal holidays and observances in 285-287 (it even includes George Washington's birthday: 286!). As for all other non-Jewish topics, you are presumably supposed to class them in a regular system such as DDC, resulting in two parallel sets of numbers. The suggestion of the authors is to "prefix the classification number with a star or some other symbol and shelve such marked material in a specially designated section of the library."[5]

---

[3] Bella Hass Weinberg, "Judaica Classification Schemes for Synagogue and School Libraries: A Structural Analysis," *Judaica Librarianship* 1 (1) (Fall 1983), 27.

[4] Bella Hass Weinberg, "Hebraica Cataloging and Classification," 8.

[5] David H. Elazar and Daniel J. Elazar, *A Classification Scheme for Libraries of Judaica*, Detroit: Wayne State University Libraries, 1968, 20.

On the plus side, as Marcia Posner enthusiastically notes, putting "The Bible" in 001-099 and the Talmudic period in 100-199,

> ...frees the 200's for all the books about the Jewish religion in exquisite detail and logical growth. It is beautiful! Comparative religion is assigned number 290, ecumenical holidays—285, and patriotic American holidays—286. Jewish holidays are from 235-282! What a difference! The 200's also contain provisions for Jewish religious movements, sermonic materials, customs and ceremonies, rites of passage, the Synagogue, Jewish home observances...and so on.[6]

The framework of the scheme is rather simple. It contains 10 classes: Bible and Biblical studies; Classical Judaica; Halakha and Midrash; Jewish observance and practice; Jewish education; Hebrew, Jewish languages and sciences; Jewish literature; the Jewish community; Society and the arts; Jewish history, geography and biography; Israel and Zionism; General works, structured as follows:.

001-099	Bible and Biblical Studies
100-199	Classical Judaica: Halakhah and Midrash
200-299	Jewish Observance and Practice
300-399	Jewish Education
400-499	Hebrew, Jewish Languages and Sciences
500-599	Jewish Literature
600-699	The Jewish Community: Society and the Arts
700-799	Jewish History, Geography, Biography
800-899	Israel and Zionism
900-999	General Works

The authors claim that their classification, its terminology and sequence, represent "the organization of Jewish library materials around Jewish principles." This is why Bible heads the list of divisions as the "Heart of hearts—the core of cores of the entire body of Jewish knowledge."[7] Further, they state that the use of classification schemes that are no more than variations of DDC or the LCC "either serves to scatter Judaica materials throughout a general collection or, in an exclusively Jewish library, creates a highly unsystematic and even confusing arrangement of books on the basis of numbers abstracted without reference to any meaningfully Jewish integrating principles."[8]

The subdivisions are detailed, and the authors offer them as options; in smaller collections many of these can be eliminated. In fact, the summary of the classification

---

[6] Marcia Posner, "At Last Elazar," *AJL Bulletin* 16 (1) (Spring 1981): 16.

[7] David H. Elazar and Daniel J. Elazar, *A Classification Scheme for Libraries of Judaica*, p. 3.

[8] David H. Elazar and Daniel J. Elazar, *A Classification Scheme for Libraries of Judaica*, p. 1.

contains only 103 sections against approximately 1,000 or more in the complete Dewey system.

In spite of its organization "on Jewish principles," Judaica librarians have given the Elazar classification system mixed reviews. Marcia Posner proclaims the "functional superiority" of the system, noting that in addition to its inherently Jewish organization, it allots an entire main class for Israel and Zionism, for instance.[9] Instead of lumping all Holocaust material in 940.4, "World War II and the Nazi Holocaust (1939-1945)" is ascribed the number 736, allowing more room for expansion:

736.01 Nazism and the related Anti-Semitic Movements
   .02 Genocide
   .1   Concentration Camps
   .2   Jewish Resistance
   .3   War Crimes, Punishments
   .4   Refugees
   .5
   .6   Memorials
   .7
   .8   Reparations

Bella Weinberg feels that the outline of classes is well thought out, that the authors graphically illustrate the links among the main classes in their lengthy introduction, and that it is a relatively easy system to classify from because of its detailed index and because it enumerates many specific topics, including names of organizations: "Thus, the classifier needn't agonize over the appropriate rubric for the *Bund*, e.g., the Elazars have told us that it belongs with the *Jewish Labor Movement* in 648."[10]

Criticisms range from conflicting personal preferences about where specific topics should be categorized to more serious warnings against adopting the system at all because of its defects. Posner would prefer a separate number for the Holocaust and a separate category for Women in Judaism, for example.[11] Weinberg states that in general, throughout the scheme, Israel, the U.S., and Great Britain are the only countries enumerated under specific topics, and that this Anglo-American bias limits the implementation of the Elazar scheme in Judaica libraries in Europe. Furthermore, she feels that the fact that form divisions are not introduced by zeros in Elazar will block the logical interpolation of new subjects in the scheme, since decimal subdivisions of whole numbers are used for such concepts as dictionaries and serials,

---

[9] Marcia Posner, "At Last Elazar": 15.

[10] Bella Hass Weinberg, "Judaica Classification Schemes for Synagogue and School Libraries": 10.

[11] Marcia Posner, "At Last Elazar": 16.

and that the system is inhospitable to general and non-Jewish material.[12] As noted above, the introduction to this scheme, as in the next scheme we will analyze, Weine, suggests classing these by another system.

Brunswick, reviewing the system, disagrees even with Weinberg's praise of the system's ease of use, stating categorically that while the classification scheme has been in use since 1952 at the Library of the United Hebrew Schools of Detroit, one of the reasons for its publication was to invite other Jewish libraries to consider its use, something he considers "would be a serious error, especially for small Jewish libraries such as synagogue libraries. Use of this classification scheme requires the services of a professional cataloguer and classifier, someone whom very few Jewish libraries actually employ."[13] He also criticizes the fact that although they have included a chapter to guide classifiers, they have not said a word about possible subject headings to be used together with the classification system, and recommends using LCC, with its nationally supplied classification numbers and subject headings instead.

In conclusion, and in spite of these criticisms, the Elazar scheme has been adopted in many Jewish school, center and synagogue libraries. In fact, several recent discussions in *Hasafran*, the Judaica librarianship listserv, demonstrate continuing interest in this scheme. In October 1995, Barbara Leff, Library Director of Stephen S. Wise Temple in Los Angeles, wrote the following to *Hasafran*:

> A small library's primary goal is to reach its audience--to make libraries accessible to users, especially browsers. That's what Elazar does for us and other synagogue libraries.... Elazar was created for Jewish educators, synagogues and schools; its numbering system....is in a logical sequence following the development of Judaism. Also, Elazar devotes all 000-999 numbers to Jewish topics, resulting in simpler call numbers— making it easier for use by children and non-academics....This is why Elazar is great for browsing—and browsing is what lots of adults and children as well as teachers do in our kind of library. Computers and online catalogs do not replace walking through a library and browsing the shelves.[14]

A 1996 posting mentioned that a computer database for the Elazar Classification System had been developed, a DOS program based in a licensed software product called Dataperfect.[15] In addition, according to information on the Elazar Web site, a 3rd edition of the printed Elazar classification scheme is scheduled for publication in

---

[12] Bella Hass Weinberg, "Judaica Classification Schemes for Synagogue and School Librar-ies": 27.

[13] Sheldon Brunswick, "Book Review" of Elazar, David H. and Elazar, Daniel J., *A Classification System for Libraries of Judaica, Jewish Social Studies* 32 (July 1970): 224.

[14] Posting in *Hasafran,* electronic Judaica librarianship discussion group, 12 October 1995.

[15] Posting in *Hasafran,* 22 February 1996.

the summer of 1997.[16] Like other schemes developed primarily for synagogue libraries, however, it has had little impact on academic and research libraries.

Weine

The Weine scheme is simpler than the Elazar scheme and, according to Bella Weinberg,[17] more widely used. Whereas Elazar uses only DDC-style notation, Weine uses many DDC numbers with the "Jewish" modifier understood.[18]

The Weine scheme is most similar to Leikind's, but it adheres to DDC's main numbers less than the Leikind scheme does. For example, Weine uses the entire Dewey Christianity series, 230-280, for Judaism and allots only one number, 296, to Christianity. In most other areas, Weine uses DDC numbers with the Jewish modifier understood and appropriates additional numbers from the history schedules for Israel, 950-958, instead of just 956.94, as allotted by DDC. Thus, in many cases the scheme is incompatible with DDC. Weinberg cites an example of this incompatibility in the area of materials on the Middle East. Because the DDC numbers have been preempted by the Weine numbers for Israel, there is no way a librarian can classify general materials on the Middle East using this scheme.[19] A solution suggested in the introduction to the Weine scheme is to class general materials by a separate scheme and assign the prefix "z" before the Weine class number to all Judaica items. Weinberg rejects this solution, noting that because many books of general scope contain Jewish material, for example, a general work on the Middle East is almost certain to treat Israel, and stating that what the scheme really needs is a notation that modulates from the general to the Jewish without an inordinate lengthening of the number for the Jewish topic.[20]

With regard to synthesis, Weine recommends using Dewey tables of standard subdivisions. For example, the Dewey geographic table would be compatible in most cases to further break down the local history of Jews in the United States.

The system actually consists of three parts: a classification scheme, a relative index and a subject heading list—the so-called Gratz College Subject Headings,

---

[16] David H. Elazar and Daniel J. Elazar, *A Classification System for Libraries of Judaica*, 3rd ed. [title page], Available: http://www.geocities.com/Athens/Acropolis/6527/classpg.htm.

[17] Bella Hass Weinberg, "Hebraica Cataloging and Classification," 340.

[18] In order to avoid copyright problems, each number is prefixed by a "z" in the printed schedules, a notational feature which, however, would be redundant for Judaica libraries to use.

[19] Bella Hass Weinberg, "Judaica Classification Schemes for Synagogue and School Libraries": 27.

[20] Bella Hass Weinberg, "Judaica Classification Schemes for Synagogue and School Libraries": 27.

compiled by the Jewish Library Association of Greater Philadelphia—with which it is intended to be used. The 1969 edition of the subject heading list cites several distinctive features of this list (features in which it differs from, e.g., LCSH), which it mentions explicitly is coordinated with the *Weine Classification System for an All-Jewish Library*, 5th edition. "The headings JEWS and JEWISH have been avoided for the most part, since it is taken for granted that all the books in a Judaica collection concern Jews. A book on Jewish music would be placed under MUSIC. O.T. for Old Testament has been omitted after BIBLE, since Jews consider the Old Testament to be the Bible, not part of it."[21]

Critics of the scheme fault it on several grounds. Marcia Posner claims that while it helped expand the DDC system, it is top-heavy in the 200's, and confused her because it was so similar to DDC, only intermittently changing subject headings—240 for DDC's 394 for Holidays, and 296 for Christianity instead of Judaism, for example.[22] Sandy Lepelstat, in her 1981 review of the 6th edition, states that after working with this system for two years it is her feeling that the disadvantages far outweigh the advantages. She feels that the major disadvantage is its inconsistency, with too many omissions and too many areas missing. When comparing the relative index and the subject headings, there are many instances in which a subject heading is mentioned in one place, but not in the other, or where the subject headings and classification scheme do not correspond. Furthermore she finds that the system does not allow room for adequate breakdowns within specific topics (ancient, medieval, modern), that Philosophy needs more breakdowns, that it pushes vital topics into too few numbers and leaves big gaps in other places, that the numbers are not equally distributed and that there are too many unused numbers, making very large gaps both on the shelves and in the filing system. Under Pure Science (500's), to illustrate, there are no breakdowns; Applied Sciences (600's) are underutilized; in the 400's, Language, there are no numbers between 400 and 461. But in categories such as Israel, Holocaust, and Philosophy, there is oversimplification of Jewish subjects: the 900s have to cover the entire history of the Jews, as well as all subjects dealing with Israel; under 250 Jewish Religion & Theology and Judaism all have to be fit in, with not enough breakdowns.[23]

Mae Weine states unequivocally in the preface to her classification scheme that it is intended primarily for a small Judaica library, such as one in a synagogue or school, and that "very large or very scholarly collections will probably find the Library of Congress classification more suited to their needs."[24] At the same time, as she also states here, the LC system suffers the drawback of being relatively unknown to most of the general public (at least as of 1975, when she wrote the preface to the

---

[21] Jewish Library Association of Greater Philadelphia. *Subject Headings for a Judaica Library,* 2d ed. (Philadelphia: Division of Community Services of Gratz College, 1969), p. ii.

[22] Marcia Posner, "At Last Elazar": 15.

[23] Sandy Lepelstat, "Weine Classification Scheme for Judaica Libraries: Pros and Cons": 7.

[24] Mae Weine, *Weine Classification Scheme for Judaica Libraries,* 6th ed., *Preface.*

6th edition), whereas the Dewey Decimal system is "familiar even to school children." Thus, she chose to base her system upon the Dewey system, drastically revising certain areas, most notably in the fields of religion, Jewish education and history. She was convinced that basing her scheme on a system used in public libraries would be a decided advantage in making the layman feel at home in the synagogue library. And, as Lepelstat concedes "in all fairness, in terms of simplicity, it is a fairly easy system for someone unschooled in this field."[25]

The scheme was revised in 1995 and the Relative Index in 1996.[26]

Freidus and Wolfson

The Judaica specialized classification schemes created by Abraham Freidus, of the Jewish Division of the New York Public Library, and Harry Wolfson, for Harvard's Judaica collection, differ from the previous American Judaica systems in several respects. Both of them were created for research collections, as opposed to small synagogue collections, and both of them were intended to be used only for the part of a large research collection which was strictly defined as its Judaica collection. In fact, however, while the Wolfson system was, in fact, used by one library only, Freidus was considered at one point by the JNUL (before they decided on Scholem) and was used by other American Judaica libraries as well, such as Hebrew Union College before they migrated to the LC system. The Freidus system was published in 1929 in the festschrift issued in his memory by Joshua Bloch.[27] The Wolfson system appeared in the 1972 Supplement to Harvard University Library's *Catalogue of Hebrew Books*.[28]

The Freidus system is described by Weinberg as "the first modern Judaica collection scheme."[29] Compiled by Abraham S. Freidus for the Jewish Division of the

---

[25] Sandy Lepelstat, "Weine Classification Scheme for Judaica Libraries: Pros and Cons": 7.

[26] Mae Weine, *Weine Classification Scheme for Judaica Libraries*, 8th ed., Revised by Judith S. Greenblatt, Rachel Glasser, Edythe Wolf, and Mae Weine (New York: AJL, 1995); *Relative Index to the Weine Classification Scheme for Judaica Libraries*, 3d ed., Revised by Judith S. Greenblatt, Toby Rossner, and Edythe Wolf (New York: AJL, 1996).

[27] Joshua Bloch, "The Classification of Jewish Literature in the New York Public Library," in *Studies in Jewish Bibliography and Related Subjects in Memory of Abraham Solomon Freidus* (New York: Alexander Kohut Memorial Foundation, 1929), L-LXXVII.

[28] Harvard University Library, *Catalogue of Hebrew Books* (Cambridge, MA: Harvard University Press, 1968), 6 vols.—Supplement I, 1972, 3 vols., *Appendix: Judaica in the Houghton Library* (in Supplement I, Vol. 1: Classified Listing).

[29] Bella Hass Weinberg, "Hebraica Cataloging and Classification," 339.

New York Public Library in 1897, it makes use of the symbol *P before its notation as a location symbol for the Jewish Division. Following that there is a two-letter sequence, which allows the scheme to distinguish 26 X 26, or 676 classes.

The main classes of the system are:

Manuscripts, Book Rarities. Works of Reference	*P
Bibliography. Literary History	*PA
General Works	*PB
Hebrew Language. Aramaic	*PC
Hebrew Bible	*PD
Archaeology	*PE
Pre-talmudical Literature and Sects	*PF
Christianity	*PG
Talmudical literature	*PH
Halacha	*PI
The Ritual	*PK
Homiletical Literature	*PL
Ethics	*PM
Doctrinal Theology	*PN
Post-talmudical Schisms and Dissensions	*PO
Philosophy	*PP
Kabbala. Chasidism	*PQ
Folk-lore	*PR
Belles-lettres	*PS
Dialects and their Literatures. Languages	*PT
Secular Sciences	*PV
Geography. General History. Biography	*PW
Jewish History	*PX
The Jewish race ethnologically and sociologically	*PY
Jews and Gentiles	*PZ[30]

The 1955 edition of the New York Public Library's *Classification Schedules for Printed, Microcopy and Phonorecord Materials in the Reference Department*[31] shows that a third letter had been added by then to some classes to allow the system to remain viable for its Jewish Division.

---

[30] Joshua Bloch, "The Classification of Jewish Literature in the New York Public Library," LX.

[31] *Classification Schedules for Printed, Microcopy and Phonorecord Materials in the Reference Department,* 2nd ed. (New York: The New York Public Library), 1955.

The alphabetic Freidus system is like Elazar both in that it was developed specifically for a Jewish collection and in its logical order of main classes. The "P" which begins the notation for each book, housed in the Jewish Division would be redundant for an independent Judaica library however. Broad topics are denoted by a single letter and subdivisions get a second letter, with a third letter, as mentioned, added in some cases in later editions. As Weinberg notes, because a letter base is larger than a number base as notation for a classification system (26 x 26 vs. 10 x 10), the Freidus scheme is able to get quite specific with two characters. On the minus side, however, it is incompatible with the major general systems and has no possibilities for synthesis; the classifier simply decides which is the general category to which the book belongs.[32] Assistance in this task, however, is available from the published catalogs of the Jewish Division.[33]

The principles of the Wolfson System, which was used for classifying Harvard's Judaica collection until its changeover in the 1970's to LC classification, are detailed in a "Note on the Classification" as consisting of three related classes—Heb, Y, and Jud with corresponding special classes for periodicals, Pheb, YP, and PJud—provide for Judaica. The Heb class contains all texts in Hebrew on any subject: translations of such texts and works about them in languages other than Hebrew are classed elsewhere. The Y class similarly contains all texts in Yiddish; it also includes works about Yiddish belles lettres written in the common European languages and translations of Yiddish belles lettres in the common European languages; but the translations of other Yiddish texts are classed elsewhere. The Jud class contains works written in the common European languages on Jewish history and civilization, Judaism, and Jewish literature, including translations of such works originally written in Hebrew; but belles lettres by Jewish authors who habitually write in one of the common European languages go in the appropriate literature class.[34]

The Israeli System for Judaica: The Scholem System

When the Jewish National and University Library was founded in the 1920s, no classification system seemed to have enough detail in the area of Judaica. It decided not to adopt the Freidus system for its collection, despite its theoretical excellence, for two reasons:

[32] Bella Hass Weinberg, "Judaica Classification Schemes for Synagogue and School Libraries":29.

[33] New York Public Library. Research Libraries. *Dictionary Catalog of the Research Libraries* (New York: NYPL, 1972-1981); New York Public Library. Research Libraries, *Hebrew -Character Title Catalog of the Jewish Collection* (Boston: G.K. Hall, 1981), 4 vols.

[34] Harvard University Library, *Catalogue of Hebrew Books* (Cambridge, MA: Harvard University Press, 1968), 6 vols.--Supplement I, 1972, 3 vols., *Appendix: Judaica in the Houghton Library* (in Supplement I, Vol. 1: Classified Listing), "Note on the Classification," [unnumbered prepages].

1. The library had decided to adopt the Dewey Decimal scheme for its general collection and did not want two notation systems.

2. Although the letter base is more powerful than a number base, the JNUL felt that Freidus had not provided a sufficient breakdown for its purposes.[35]

Therefore it commissioned an expansion of DDC to meet its detailed needs. What the new JNUL system did was to take the few numbers Dewey had provided for Jewish subjects and make a detailed breakdown of these numbers to enable close classification of the thousands of books on the *Bible,* Judaism, Jewish history, and Hebrew and Yiddish language and literature which the JNUL owned. The first edition of the system was published in 1927, and soon came to be known as the Scholem system, after Gershom Scholem, the Judaica department's director. An English translation was published of the second edition, a third Hebrew edition appeared in 1968 and a fourth edition in 1981.[36]

Expanding the Dewey system instead of inventing an entirely new, independent system enabled the JNUL to use a single classification system for its entire collection. The JNUL still uses this system, updating and republishing it periodically. Many other Israeli libraries followed the JNUL example and adopted the system as well. In addition, the Yeshiva University Gottesman Library of Judaica used Scholem until they migrated to LCC.

The approach which Scholem used in his system was

> ... to expand the areas of DDC allocated to Jewish topics, both by adding subdivisions to topics that were inadquately broken down, and by redefining the scope of topics to include more than DDC intended. For example, he added numerous subdivisions to 296 (Judaism) and 892.4 (Hebrew literature). Scholem's solution to the special problem of Jewish history, in which DDC recognized (until 1965) only the history of geographic entities, was to redefine and expand 933 to include Jewish history of all periods and geographic areas. (This creates an interesting anomaly, since material on modern Jewish history is found as part of class 930—history of the ancient world). He also moved such topics as Jewish art and music, Jewish law, and Jewish education to class 296 (Jewish religion), instead of leaving them with their specific disciplines. The geographic subdivision for Israel was abbreviated to a letter (E) and prefixed to general numbers (e.g., E550=Geology of Israel). In addition, various elements of the Universal

---

[35] Bella Hass Weinberg, "Hebraica Cataloging and Classification," p. 340.

[36] *Seder ha-miḳtsoʻot be-madaʼei ha-yahadut,* (Jerusalem: Hebrew University, Jewish National and University Library, 1927); *Classification for Judaica* (Jerusalem: Hebrew University, Jewish National and University Library, 1964); *Seder ha-miḳtsoʻot be-madaʼei ha-yahadut,* 3d ed. (Jerusalem: Hebrew University, Jewish National and University Library, 1968); *Seder ha-miḳtsoʻot be-madaʼei ha-yahadut,* 4th ed. (Jerusalem: Hebrew University, Jewish National and University Library, 1981).

Decimal Classification (UDC) were also used for further detail and subdivision.[37]

Citing the advantages and disadvantages of the system, Weinberg puts on the minus side the the fact that unless the abbreviations suggested are used, which make the sequence of classes unclear, the notation is quite long. On the plus side, the system is sound structurally—it takes advantage of Dewey general numbers, enumerates Jewish topics, and uses *Universal Decimal Classification (UDC)* symbols for synthesis of subjects and auxiliary concepts, e.g., 933.47 Holocaust, 933.47 (438) Holocaust in Poland. A certain amount of enumeration has been done in the schedules where synthesis would have been possible, but extensive revision is economically impractical. Its main advantage, however, is definitely its compatibility with DDC for general topics and tables. Weinberg adds that while some may argue that Scholem's complexity of structure and notation make the system unsuitable for small libraries, she feels on the contrary that a small synagogue or school library will probably never need such complex breakdowns and will simply be able to use the enumerated decimal numbers.[38] Even if they do not adopt the Scholem system, small synagogue libraries using DDC may find it useful as a reference work since it enumerates many classic works on Judaism in the schedules. A more serious disadvantage than its notational complexity for some librarians, of course, may be that except for the 1964 English edition, it is available only in Hebrew.

Interestingly, the Scholem system, created in Israel in Hebrew by and for Jews, has been criticized on theological grounds. Wunder[39] states that a religious library would find Scholem's viewpoint in his construction of the Judaism schedule unacceptable. For example, he places general works on Judaism after the Bible, instead of Mishnah and Talmud, which Wunder would prefer. Scholem's placement of the Kabalistic classic Zohar in a chronological position indicating its presumed medieval origin would also be highly offensive in a traditional religious library. In addition, Wunder finds Scholem's placement of Sabbateans between Kabbalah and Hasidism highly objectionable. He feels that Sabbateans should be placed in sects outside the mainstream of Judaism.

The Scholem system, furthermore, presents some problems even for Israeli libraries. It was designed for use in the JNUL—a library that naturally wished to emphasize the Jewish and Israeli facets of every subject. Not every library, even in Israel, wishes to segregate Jewish music, for example, from all other music or Israeli education from general education. In addition the complex UDC-style numbers,

---

[37] Elhanan Adler, "Judaica Cataloging: The Hebrew Bibliographic and Israeli Traditions," *Judaica Librarianship* 6 (1-2) (Spring 1991-Winter 1992): 10.

[38] Bella Hass Weinberg, "Judaica Classification Schemes for Synagogue and School Libraries": 29.

[39] Meir Wunder, ["Religious Libraries and Their Problems"], *Yad Lakore* 8 (March 1967): 73-79; in Hebrew.

which contain prefix letters, parentheses and other punctuation marks, are not particularly appropriate to open-shelf collections. (The JNUL collections are held in closed-shelf storerooms and must be ordered, except for the reference collections held in the various reading rooms). Furthermore, changes in the DDC itself have complicated the system in certain areas. Some Scholem numbers are based on general DDC numbers whose meaning has changed since the Scholem scheme was created, and in some areas, such as period subdivisions under Hebrew literature, DDC today is even more detailed than Scholem.

HEBRAICA AND JUDAICA SUBJECT CATALOGING IN GENERAL CLASSIFICATION SYSTEMS

Anglo-American Systems

The Dewey Decimal Classification System (DDC)

As mentioned above, the Scholem system was created to expand DDC in the areas dealing with Jewish subjects to enable a closer classification of the thousands of books owned by the JNUL in these areas. The JNUL opted, as all Israeli libraries after it have done, for classing Judaica as part of a general classification scheme rather than creating a separate one. This is particularly interesting in light of the fact that even with expansions and reallocations, both DDC and LCC, which are used by most of Israel's academic libraries, still retain a Christian orientation. In LCC Old Testament is put together with New Testament as part of Christianity and separate from Judaism. In DDC, through the 20th edition, this was also true. However, in the 21st edition, "an optional arrangement for books of the Bible as found in Jewish Bibles,"[40] was introduced. The preferred arrangement is at 222-224, in Bible, in the regular schedule, but Option B allows them to be placed at 296.11, in Judaism, which remains relegated to the miscellaneous religions section at the end of the 200 religion class.

Nonetheless, although Judaism remains subordinate to Comparative religion and religion other than Christianity, its schedule has been highly developed since early editions in which only the number 296 was available. Today, the Hebrew language can be subdivided to the same extent as English using a special table, although Yiddish, unfortunately, has been switched from 492.49, following Hebrew,

---

[40] Melvil Dewey, *Dewey Decimal Classification and Relative Index*, 21st ed. (Albany: Forest Press, A Division of OCLC Computer Library Center, Inc., 1996), vol. 4, Relative Index. Manual, p. 997.

to German dialects. Hebrew literature can be broken down by a quite detailed period table.

On the other hand, the classification of general and local Jewish history is both cumbersome and problematic in DDC because Jews are treated as an ethnic group rather than a geographic entity (using the -04 "special topics" standard subdivision). The base number for general Jewish history is 909.04924 to which additional period divisions can be added (909.0492407 = world history of Jews in the 18th century). Local Jewish history is to be classed with history of the country using the same ethnic group division (e.g. history of the Jews in England: 942.004924), thereby scattering much of Jewish history throughout general history. An alternate rule under 909 (world history) allows local history to be subdivided under the 909.04924 base (909.0492042 for Jews in England), in which case the period divisions of general Jewish history receive an extra zero (18th century Jewish history would now be: 909.04924007). In her 1983 article analyzing the usefulness of various classification systems for small Judaica libraries, Weinberg suggested that this problem might be soluble by using the Scholem schedule for Jewish history as it does not conflict with DDC but rather simply expands the scope of 933 from "History of Ancient Palestine" to "History of the people of Israel."[41] This schedule was incorporated into the Hebrew edition of the Universal Decimal Classification[42] and the Hebrew abridged edition of DDC published in Israel, both of which will be discussed later in this chapter.

Weinberg held that the 20th edition of DDC and the reprint of its religion class did not increase the appropriateness of DDC for small Judaica libraries. Its philosophical acceptablility was still low, too many topics enumerated in special Judaica classification schemes do not have their own numbers in DDC, and DDC's movement towards increased synthesis makes it more difficult to implement for untrained librarians.[43] An example cited by Weinberg of the Christian orientation that made for "low philosophical acceptability" was the fact that of all Jewish organizations, only "Young Men's Hebrew Associations" and "Young Women's Hebrew Associations" have their own numbers (296.673 and 296.675 respectively), in parallel to the numbers for the Young Men's Christian Associations and Young Women's Christian Associations (267.3 and 267.5). In the 21st edition, these two numbers have been discontinued and Young Mens's and Women's Hebrew Associations have been classed in 296.67, with the rest of Jewish organizations.

---

[41] Bella Hass Weinberg, "Judaica Classification Schemes for Synagogue and School Libraries": 28.

[42] International Federation for Documentation, *Miyun 'esroni universali,* Added t.p. Universal Decimal Classification (Tel Aviv: ha-Merkaz la-meda tekhnologi u mada'i, 1969); (International Federation for Documentation [FID] #445).

[43] Bella Hass Weinberg, "Deweineazar: *Dewey Decimal Classification. 200 Religion Class*" reprinted from Edition 20 of the Dewey Decimal Classification...with a revised and expanded index, and manual notes from Edition 20. Albany, NY: Forest Press, a division of OCLC, 1989. viii, 191 p. ISBN 0-910608-43-1. $15. LCCN 89-27221," *Judaica Librarianship* 6 (1-2) (Spring 1991-Winter 1992): 121.

The 20th edition did, however, enumerate some additional specific topics in Judaism, even if it did not radically restructure the Judaism class. For example, "Hasidism," which was only an example of the topics to be included under "Mystical Judaism" (296.833) in the 19th edition, was assigned its own number: 293.8332, in the 20th edition, and "Habad Lubavitch Hasidism" is allocated the number 296.83322. Some of the other peculiarities in the sequence of topics not corrected in the 20th edition in the schedule for the Jewish religion have been corrected in the 21st. For example, the order under reform movements was Conservative Judaism, Reconstructionist Judaism, and Reform Judaism. This is an alphabetical sequence, not an evolutionary sequence, which is preferable. In the 21st edition Reform Judaism has been relocated to 296.834.1, before Conservative Judaism.

In spite of some positive changes in the 21st edition, DDC's major philosophical problem was and remains that "the Judaism schedule is couched in Christian terms and divides up the universe of literature on Judaism on the basis of Christian constructs,"[44] e.g., "Doctrinal, moral, social theology." Its major advantage to Judaica libraries is the same advantage offered by the Library of Congress system: the availability of centrally-assigned class numbers in MARC and in CIP (Cataloging-in-Publication) data.

The Library of Congress Classification System (LCC)

Subject analysis is among the most complex elements of the cataloging process. Developing local subject cataloging systems, therefore, is both time consuming and expensive. For these reasons most Judaica research libraries, and a significant number of Jewish synagogue and school libraries as well, have opted to use both the Library of Congress Classification scheme (LCC) and Library of Congress Subject Headings (LCSH), since both are maintained and updated by the Library of Congress. Over the past twenty-five years or so most university Judaica libraries that used another scheme (e.g., theWolfson scheme at Harvard) have either reclassified their collections to LCC or started classifying all newly-acquired works according to what has become the de facto national standard in the United States and, to a growing extent, in Israel's university libraries as well.

The timing of the change in classification for many libraries coincided with the publication of AACR1 in 1967. Generally, Judaica research libraries that jumped on the LCC bandwagon that began rolling in the late 1960s, gave as their rationale for switching to the system the "adoption of national standards." In actuality, hardly any Judaica research libraries switched to LCC without making modifications. Furthermore, in spite of the massive switch for reasons of economics and national standards, "one would be hard pressed to find a Judaica librarian who considers LC Classification...a good one for Rabbinica, Jewish history, the Holocaust, or Jewish bibliography."[45]

---

[44] Bella Hass Weinberg, "Deweineazar: *Dewey Decimal Classification. 200 Religion Class*, 120.

[45] Bella Hass Weinberg, "From Copy Cataloging to Derived Bibliographic Records: Cataloging and Its Automation in American Judaica Research Libraries from the Sixties Through the Eighties," *Judaica Librarianship* 4 (2) (Spring 1988-Winter 1989), 119.

The problems with LCC for Judaica libraries focus primarily on two aspects of the system: (1) a basically Christian orientation mentioned above, and (2) limitations caused by the enumerative nature of the system.

With regard to the Christian orientation, all the attempts in both America and Israel to alter this (e.g., Hebrew University's 1982 modification of the scheme for Judaica[46]) have failed to eliminate it completely. On one hand, the Library of Congress has been successfully persuaded by the Association of Jewish Libraries (AJL) and American Judaica librarians to make changes in subject headings, such as the change to *Kibbutzim* replacing *Communistic settlements*. Persuading LC to undertake any basic reorganization of the classification schedules, however, is a much more difficult task. An example of a problem for Judaica libraries with the basic organization of the classification schedules is the Christian order of the books of the Bible. More serious is the fact that individual tractates of the Talmud, which are exclusively Jewish, are arranged alphabetically rather than within their traditional orders (*sedarim*). The alphabetical arrangement of liturgical works in class BM 675 by cutter number, e.g., .D3 *Daily Prayers* (i.e., Siddur), .H5 *High Holy Day prayers* (i.e., Mahzor), and .S3 *Sabbath Prayers* (i.e., Siddur for the Sabbath) constitutes another illogical sequence.[47]

An example of the latter problem—LCC's enumerative structure—can be found in DS 135, the number for the History of Jews outside of Palestine, which is followed by cutter numbers expressing the individual countries. Since the system does not allow synthesis in most cases (i.e., it does not permit combining numbers but only those class numbers it has established through literary warrant, when the number of materials in its collection on a given subject justified a new number), its assignment of chronological breakdowns to only a few countries in which Jews have lived limits the capability for close classification of materials in this area.

Judaica librarians should understand that LCC, unlike DDC, is inherently a nontamperable system. It is not coincidental that many of the small classification schemes for Jewish school and synagogue libraries have been based on DDC, but none have been based on LCC. One cannot effectively shorten an LCC number as one can in DDC. This is because LCC's notation does not, in most cases, increase in *length* as the specificity of a subject increases. A comparison of the classification numbers in DDC and LCC for the topics *History of Israel* and *History of Israel—Medieval Period* demonstrate the difference in the two systems nicely. DDC notation (956.94; 956.9403) expresses the greater specificity in the later concept, while LCC has the

---

[46] Hebrew University of Jerusalem, *Library of Congress Classification for Judaica* (Jerusalem: [s.n.], 1982).

[47] Bella Hass Weinberg, "Judaica and Hebraica Cataloging: Anglo-American Traditions," *Judaica Librarianship* 6 (1-2) (Spring 1991-Winter 1992), 17.

same number of characters in both class marks (DS117; DS124). The inability to shorten LC class marks is often given as the reason for its inappropriateness for synagogue and school libraries, even though LCC's letter base leads to shorter classification numbers than DDC's in most cases.

Another reason for LCC's lack of amenity to local modification is that its philosophical basis is the *literary warrant* of the Library of Congress collection. As mentioned above, new numbers are added when LC acquires extensive holdings on a subject. According to Weinberg, "it is therefore unfair to fault LCC for lack of specificity in cases where a Judaica library has a richer collection than LC does in a specialized area."[48]

DDC, on the other hand, comprises more of a theoretical division of knowledge than a practical classification scheme for a specific collection. It is a primarily *synthetic* classification scheme, building numbers for complex topics out of various elements within the system, rather than giving complete numbers for most of these topics, as in enumerative LCC. For example, the class number for "History of Jews in Poland" must be synthesized in DDC from a number in the basic history schedules, a standard subdivision and an ethnic concept in the tables, yielding 943.8004924, while LCC enumerates DS135.P6.[49]

In spite of LCC's "intamperability," the pages of *Judaica Librarianship* have often described both *examples* of LCC changes made at such centers for Judaica materials as Yeshiva University and the Jewish Theological Seminary,[50] and *methods* of tampering with LCC numbers found in actual practice in Judaica libraries. Weinberg's 1987 article on tampering with LCC numbers for Judaica,[51] in fact, both categorizes systematically the types (or levels) of tampering found in the field and suggests "tampering guidelines."

She breaks down types of tampering found in Judaica libraries into five categories: (1) independent assignment of class marks, (2) adopting official alternatives, (3) changing the meaning of LC class numbers, (4) modifying LC subject cutters and tables, and (5) modifying LCC base notation.

Category 1, *independent assignment of class marks,* is the assignment of a class mark to a work that LC either does not own or has not yet cataloged. Category 2, *adopting official alternatives*, involves using alternative class numbers which the Library of Congress has provided for certain categories, most notably bibliography.

---

[48] Bella Hass Weinberg, "Cutter J4: Tampering with the Library of Congress Classification for Judaica," *Judaica Librarianship* 3 (1-2) (1986-1987): 45.

[49] Bella Hass Weinberg, "Cutter J4: Tampering with the Library of Congress Classification for Judaica": 45.

[50] Pearl Berger, "Catalog Department," *Judaica Librarianship* 3 (1-2) (1986-1987):

[51] Bella Hass Weinberg, "Cutter J4: Tampering with the Library of Congress Classification for Judaica": 45-48.

The third category of tampering, *changing the meaning of LC class numbers*, is essentially what is done in the Dewey-based classification schemes for synagogue and school libraries, such as in the Weine system, in which the DDC number for music, 780, is assigned the meaning of *Jewish music*, with Weine's notation, z780, indicating that it is a non-standard DDC number. This sort of tampering is possible if the Judaica collection is held separately and has a special location symbol, and if the classification numbers are not interfiled (either manually or in an online file).

The fourth category, *modifying LC subject cutters and tables*, makes use of the primary synthetic devices or building blocks in the LC system as the basis for modification of its class numbers, while the fifth category, *modifying LCC base notation* makes changes in the notation in the main schedules. This last category is the most drastic type of tampering with LCC and most commonly involves the addition of integers where LC has not assigned a number or the interpolation of decimals to accommodate specific topics. An even more drastic type of change is the reordering of a series of class numbers to reflect a preferred order for a group of topics.

Another, less frequent, type of change within this fifth category involves modifications in the letter base of the scheme. Weinberg cites the example of the University of Haifa's employment of a letter unused by LC—X—to arrange its periodicals in broad categories (e.g., XP—linguistic periodicals) rather than classifying them specifically as LC does or arranging them alphabetically, as many other libraries do.[52] Under this modification, for example, XBM would group periodicals on Judaism and XPJ would gather serials on Semitic languages and literatures.

The implications of tampering with LCC fall into two categories: standardization and copy cataloging. Once a library begins implementing in-house modifications to LCC, it can no longer be regarded as using a standard classification system. Thus, one of the advantages of using a standard classfication system—that a user may expect to find a given bibliographic item in the same relative location in any academic or research library he or she visits without consulting the catalog—is lost. Additionally, standard classification numbers are helpful in interlibrary loan.

The second implication is that once a library begins to tamper with LCC, it lessens the economic advantages of copy cataloging, which is also one of the major advantages of using LCC, since it can no longer take advantage of complete, centrally-assigned class marks.

Summing up the advantages and disadvantages with regard to tampering with LCC, Weinberg gives the following guidelines to small Judaica libraries:

1. Given the cost of creating and maintaining local modifications to LCC, the first guideline is *avoid tampering unless LC's arrangement is totally unacceptable to*

---

[52]Bella Hass Weinberg, "Cutter J4: Tampering with the Library of Congress Classification for Judaica": 47.

your user community. The operable term here is *arrangement,* since if the *terminology* is less than optimal, it at least is not visible to patrons;

2. If the library's holdings in a specific class number are not unusually large, don't bother with detailed specification of subjects via the shelf classification, since it is frequently redundant with the subject headings; and

3. If the library finds it necessary to tamper with LCC, the most important guideline is to *maintain good documentation.*[53]

Summing up the reasons for a small Judaica library to use LCC, Weinberg cites four major advantages: (1) its specificity; (2) its integration of Judaic with non-Jewish topics, eliminating the need to use a second classification system; (3) the availability of complete class numbers including cutter numbers in centrally-provided LC cataloging records (as opposed to DDC numbers which do not include cutter numbers and which are usually unavailable for Hebrew materials); and the fact that it is the scheme maintained by the largest library in the United States, assuring that it will be kept up to date.[54]   Kaganoff cites as an additional benefit the combination of letters and numbers, which he feels reduces the chance of error in classifying, and actually prefers the fact that LCC is not a Jewish scheme. He holds that it "works to our advantage" that with the exception of subjects like Jewish religion (BM), Jewish history (DS) and Jewish literature (PJ), Jewish material is spread throughout the entire scheme (e.g., Jewish music goes with music and Jewish economics with economics), providing the classifier with a whole, wide range of numbers which can be used without any problem. Furthermore, he sees the class mark as nothing more than a location symbol,"marking and parking" the item, and therefore the basically Christian outlook of LCC is not really important, since "the major part of cataloging is not the classification, but the description."[55]

In 1969, the University of Haifa Library became the first major Israeli library to adopt LCC. Haifa was followed during the 1970s by the Hebrew University's Library of Social Sciences and Humanities, Ben Gurion University Library, and several others. While the reasons for converting to LCC had nothing to do with Judaica, they forced these libraries to review the LCC Judaica classification and make certain modifications. Although there has not been official coordination on adaption and changes, it is generally accepted in Israeli academic libraries that LCC for Judaica—primarily classes BM (Judaism), BS (Bible), DS (History), and PJ (Language and Literature)—is quite detailed and that only minimal changes should be made. Two examples of such changes are: (1) rearranging the BS table so that the

---

[53] Bella Hass Weinberg, "Cutter J4: Tampering with the Library of Congress Classification for Judaica": 48.

[54] Bella Hass Weinberg, "Judaica Classification Schemes for Synagogue and School Libraries," 27.

[55] Nathan M. Kaganoff, "LC Classification System," in *AJL Convention 5, New York, Proceedings* (New York: AJL, 1970), p. 34.

books of the Bible appear in Jewish rather than Christian order, and (2) the relocation of much of the Holocaust literature from D (general history) to DS (Jewish history).[56]

Library of Congress Subject Headings (LCSH)

Classification is not the only means of subject access to Judaica collections. There are also subject headings, which many, like Kaganoff, feel are the real keys to topical access, while the classification number is only for "marking and parking." Although many synagogue libraries use small specialized lists of Judaica subject headings, nearly all Judaica research libraries today are dependent on Library of Congress cataloging copy and therefore use LCSH. Sometimes these libraries modify some of these subject headings and compile lists of local headings as a supplementary cataloging tool.

In 1985 Bella Weinberg wrote that "in the Judaica library community as a whole, there is little exchange of information on in-house modification of LCSH, and therefore no coordination among libraries in this area."[57] Today, a little more than a decade later, this is no longer true. First, the advent of the Internet put catalogs of most major Judaica research libraries online even for those libraries which are not members of a bibliographic utility (such as the Israeli research libraries). This instant accessibility, coupled with the widespread participation among Judaica librarians all over the world in *Hasafran* has engendered an international forum for observation, discussion and coordination of LCSH changes and potential changes.

There have been significant changes (some welcome and some criticized) in subject headings for Judaica over the past few decades, many of which have been documented in the pages of *Judaica Librarianship*. Among these are the shifting of liturgical works from under the old descriptive heading *Jews. Liturgy and Ritual* to the subject heading *Judaism—Liturgy—Texts*.[58] The earlier change from *World War, 1939-1945—Jews* to *Holocaust, Jewish (1939-1945)* affected thousands of records. Generic posting for biography, e.g., entering Golda Meir under *Prime Ministers - Israel* and *Zionists*, is an LC practice that both violates the principle of specificity in subject headings and complicates the life of the cataloger. The change from direct to indirect geographic subdivison (Topic—Country—City) has affected thousands of entries for *Jews in [Place]*. Applying LC's rule that the latest form of a country's name be used has created anachronistic subject headings for memorial volumes (*yisker-bikher*) on *shtetlekh*, in that formerly Polish towns are defined as part of the Soviet Union. All of the current changes in Eastern Europe—above all, the demise of

---

[56] Elhanan Adler, "Judaica Cataloging: The Hebrew Bibliographic and Israeli Traditions": 10.

[57] Bella Hass Weinberg, "JEWS--DASH: Library of Congress Subject Headings for Judaica: a Methodology for Analysis," *Judaica Librarianship* 2(1-2) (Spring 1985): 20.

[58] Bella Hass Weinberg, "The Cataloging of Jewish Liturgy by the Library of Congress: A Critique," *Judaica Librarianship* 1 (2) (Spring 1984): 70-74.

the U.S.S.R.—have many implications for subject catalogers in general, and Judaica catalogers in particular.[59]

There have been a number of welcome changes in terminology, such as increases in specificity and precoordination, notably in Holocaust subdivisions. The changes in geographic subdivision and pattern headings have, however, wreaked havoc in Judaica catalogs. An example of the former is the modification of the direct subdivision (e.g., *Jews in Boston*) to indirect (e.g., *Jews—Massachusetts—Boston*). The abovementioned change in the handling of liturgical works has also brought with it unwelcome duplication in subject headings, requiring Judaica librarians to provide three unnecessary subject headings for every Haggadah cataloged: *Judaism— Liturgy—Texts; Seder—Liturgy—Texts*; and *Haggadot—Texts*.[60]

In the area of LCSH as in the area of LCC, it was Weinberg who organized and categorized the kinds of actions an individual library could take if it chose to tamper with objectionable subject headings. Stating here, as with regard to classification numbers, that the best policy is tampering as little as possible, she recognized that "while standardization is a lofty ideal, service to a library's user community is even more important, and one is reluctant to recommend that Judaica libraries cease all in-house tampering with LCSH in the interests of economy and uniformity."[61]

Having served up her disclaimer, she details five basic courses of action open to a Judaica library that objects to a subject heading:

1. **Accept LC.**

2. **Recommend Changes to LC.**

3. **Reject the Term.** (The decision may be made to omit the subject heading, and not to substitute any other for it.)

4. **Revise (one-to-one change).**

5. **Revise (one-to-many change).** (For subject headings that are not specific enough for Judaica library purposes, multiple headings may be recommended, either to supplement a heading, or to replace it.)[62]

---

[59] Bella Hass Weinberg, "Judaica and Hebraica Cataloging: Anglo-American Traditions": 17.

[60] Bella Hass Weinberg, "The Cataloging of Jewish Liturgy by the Library of Congress": 70-74.

[61] Bella Hass Weinberg, "JEWS--DASH: Library of Congress Subject Headings for Judaica": 21.

[62] Bella Hass Weinberg, "JEWS--DASH: Library of Congress Subject Headings for Judaica": 20.

The various problem areas in LCSH for Judaica libraries are then allotted a detailed discussion, a condensed version of that follows:

1. **Theologically Objectionable.** LC has often been accused....of "Christian Primacy." This means it assumed that Christianity is the standard, normal religion, and only nonstandard ones need be named in subject headings. Thus, in some cases, the Judaica headings *per se* may not be objectionable, but rather the unmodified heading which follows, such as *G-d* or *Angels*, which LC assumed included the Christian aspect....

2. **Politically Objectionable.** LC's use of the term *Palestine* for the Antiquities of the prestate period also appears to involve some bias, despite its literary warrant, because for historical materials on other countries, such as the Soviet Union, the latest name is used exclusively in subject headings. If LC is arguing that Palestine was the name of the country during the period discussed in historical works, it should add the heading *Judea* for works dealing with an even earlier period.

3. **Sociologically Objectionable.** In this category, we focus on terms that are offensive to the Jewish people, and that carry connotations of anti-Semitism.

4. **Obsolete Terminology.** The replacement of the heading *Amaurotic Family Idiocy* by the former cross reference *Tay-Sach's Disease* is a welcome change by LC.

5. **Transliteration vs. Translation.** There must be substantial literary warrant for transliterated forms in scholarly Judaic publications for them to be preferred over translations.

6. **Lack of Specificity.** This is the charge most frequently leveled at LCSH by librarians in many subject specialities, and it is the most frequent reason for the development of independent lists of subject headings.

7. **Insufficient Subdivision.**

8. **Redundancy of Headings.** (a) When the identical subject is expressed in two ways; (b) when the subject heading duplicates the information in the author-title catalog; and (c) when a broad heading is assigned in addition to a specific one.

9. **Inversion Desirable.** For the Judaica librarian, the preponderance of subject headings in our field that begin with the letter *J* is a disadvantage. In fact, the primary characteristic of local Judaica subject headings schemes is the elimination of the Jewish modifier.

10. **Inversion Undesirable.** One of the principles of American subject heading practice is that terms should be established in direct order. Headings like *Commandments, Ten* violate this principle.

11. **Inconsistent Pattern.**

12. **Unclear Scope.**

13. **Insufficient Cross References.**

14. **Inaccurate Cross-References.** *Judezmo* encompasses *Ladino* and other varieties of "Judeo-Spanish."[63]

Following the discussion of LCSH "problem areas" for Judaica collections is table 7.1, which summarizes the problem categories and giving examples of each. Since it is the most concise and well-organized presentation of this topic in the literature, it is reproduced below.[64]

---

[63]Bella Hass Weinberg, "JEWS--DASH: Library of Congress Subject Headings for Judaica": 21-25.

[64]Bella Hass Weinberg, "JEWS--DASH: Library of Congress Subject Headings for Judaica": 22

Table 7.1.

Problem Category	Example
1. Theologically Objectionable	*Bible. O.T.*
2. Politically Objectionable	*West Bank*
3. Sociologically Objectionable	*Jewish Question*
4. Obsolete Terminology	*Amaurotic Family Idiocy*
5. Transliteration vs. Translation	*Shabbat Shubah/ Sabbath*
6. Lack of Specificity	*Jews—History* for *Anshe Keneset Ha-Gedolah*
7. Insufficient Subdivision	*Holocaust, Jewish*
8. Redundancy of Headings	*Haggadah/ Haggadot—Texts*
9. Inversion Desirable	*Jews—; Jewish...*
10. Inversion Undesirable	*Commandments, Ten*
11. Inconsistent Pattern	*Jewish sermons; Sermons, Hebrew*
12. Unclear Scope	*Marriage (Jewish law) Marriage customs and rites, Jewish*
13. Insufficient Cross References	*Jewish criminals*
14. Inaccurate Cross References	*Ladino xJudesmo*

Since acquiring all the publications necessary to assign subject headings in accordance with LC's latest policies can consume a large percentage of a small Judaica library's budget, these libraries might consider one of several possible alternatives to using LC publications for subject headings. One alternative is to consult a compilation of LCSH designed specifically for the Judaica cataloger. Since 1982, Daniel Stuhlman has produced several editions of a booklet that purports to give the Judaica cataloger all relevant subject headings in a convenient format, reasonably priced.[65] Using the *Weekly Lists, Judaica Librarianship* has been monitoring additions and changes to subject headings for Judaica since its first issue in 1983 as a "current awareness" service to Judaica librarians.[66]

A number of Judaica subject heading lists patterned after, but not based exclusively on, LCSH are also available. The Association of Jewish Libraries (AJL), sells its own Judaica subject heading list intended primarily for synagogue, school, and center (SSC) libraries.[67] Another list designed for SSC libraries available from the Sinai Temple Library in Los Angeles is the *Central Cataloging Service Integrated Subject Headings List.*[68] This list includes AJL headings, LC headings, Sears headings, and local headings.[69]

These independent Judaica subject heading lists frequently delete the "Jewish" modifier in their headings. For example, in the heading *History*, the assumption is that *Jewish history* is understood. This deletion can lead to problems if the synagogue, school or center library acquires non-Jewish books.

Another option for Judaica libraries that want to use LCSH but do not wish to buy the entire set of subject heading tools is Joseph Galron-Goldschlaeger's *Library of Congress Subject Headings in Jewish Studies*, the first edition of which appeared in

---

[65] Daniel D. Stuhlman, *Library of Congress Subject Headings for Judaica* (Chicago: BYLS Press, 1982); Daniel D. Stuhlman, *Library of Congress Subject Headings for Judaica*, 3rd ed. (Chicago: BYLS Press, 1988).

[66] cf, Pearl Berger and Sharona R. Wachs, "Catalog Department," *Judaica Librarianship* 1 (2) (Spring 1984): 67-69.

[67] Mildred Kurland, and Mae Weine, *Subject Headings for a Judaica Library,* 4th ed. ([s.l.]: Distributed by Synagogue, School and Center Division of the Association of Jewish Libraries, 1982).

[68] *Central Cataloging Service Integrated Subject Headings List* (Los Angeles, CA: Sinai Temple Library, July 1989).

[69] Frischer, Rita C., Cover letter of Central Cataloging Service *Bulletin* No. 18 (Los Angeles, CA: Sinai Temple [Library], July 28, 1989) Section D.

1989, and has already been followed by several subsequent editions,[70] and which is now available free on the Web as well.[71]

The list includes headings only—no generally applicable subdivisions or geographic headings are included. Given that it is computer-produced, continual updating and expansion of the list is relatively easy. Furthermore, the fact that the compiler is affiliated with a research library that is committed to LC cataloging ensures continuous monitoring of changes in subject headings for Judaica and assures its place as an important reference tool for the Judaica librarian.[72] The Web site includes updates to the latest printed edition, marked as follows:

*	New Subject Heading
U	Update of an existing Subject Heading
C	Cancelation of a heading
UF	Use from
BT	Broader term
RT	Related term
NT	Narrower term[73]

LCSH in Israeli Libraries

Until the 1970s virtually all Israeli libraries had classified catalogs for subject access, rather than alphabetic subject headings. There are a number of reasons for this: the lack of an accepted list of subject headings, the lack of adequate Hebrew terminology in the formative years of the JNUL, and the fact that Israel has (even today) a highly multilingual population.

In 1969 it was decided to reorganize the book collection of the University of Haifa Library by LCC, as many university libraries in the United States had done.

In a 1974 article describing the implementation of the Library of Congress system in the first library in Israel to break with the JNUL tradition of using the

---

[70]Joseph Galron-Goldschlaeger, *Library of Congress Subject Headings in Jewish Studies,* 1st ed. ([s.l. :s.n.], 1989); 2nd enlarged and updated ed. (Bexley, Ohio: The author, 1991), 2 vols.; 3rd enlarged and updated ed. (New York: Association of Jewish Libraries, 1992), 2 vols.; 5th revised edition. (New York: AJL, 1996), 2 vols.

[71]Joseph Galron-Goldschlaeger, *Library of Congress Subject Headings in Jewish Studies,* Available: http://aleph.lib.ohio-state.edu/www/lcsh.html.

[72]Bella Hass Weinberg, "Compilations of Library of Congress Subject Headings for Judaica: Comparison, Evaluation, and Recommendations": 40.

[73] Joseph Galron-Goldschlaeger, *Library of Congress Subject Headings in Jewish Studies—1996,* Available: http://aleph.lib.ohio-state.edu/www/lcsh-new96.html.

classified catalog for subject access, Adler cites the following reasons for Haifa's decision to adopt the American system:

>   1. The University of Haifa Library has one central library which includes hundreds of thousands of books. The entire collection is available to the readers in open stacks. LCC is widely considered the best arrangement for large libraries with open stacks.

>   2. The U.S. Library of Congress catalogs and classifies much of the literature of the world in all languages. Using the LC system enables the library to utilize prepared cataloging and classification. This is especially important in areas in which the library has no subject specialist.[74]

The terms of the original LCSH are in English, a fact which poses a problem for the Israeli reader. While still in the planning stages and during the first year of setting up the catalog, the possibility was weighed of establishing a subject catalog with Hebrew terminology. This possibility would have required translating the Library of Congress terms into Hebrew and creating a sort of Hebrew-English "dictionary," which would enable the conversion of the English term into a Hebrew term. This possibility was rejected for several reasons:

>   1. A subject catalog in Hebrew is a serious departure from the LC system, which makes the work much more expensive, and which puts the entire economic feasibility of using the system in question.

>   2. A certain percentage of the terms that appear in the subject catalog (especially in the social sciences) are difficult to translate. It sometimes happens that the Hebrew term is not identical with the English term. It also happens frequently that the Hebrew term is found in dictionaries but not in the vocabulary of the readers (it seems that many of the faculty prefer to use the English term in their lectures).

>   3. There is no existing system of "see" and "see also" references from synonyms and related terms. This system is essential to all subject catalogs, and creating it would be expensive and would require a special team of librarian-linguists.

>   4. The assumption is that in a university library in which eighty percent of the books are in a language other than Hebrew, the reader must know the basic terminology of his profession in English. This assumption is of course invalid with regard to other types of libraries.[75]

---

[74] Elhanan Adler, ["Implementation of the Library of Congress System in the Library of the University of Haifa"], *Yad Lakore* 14 (November 1974): 16; in Hebrew.

[75] Elhanan Adler, ["Implementation of the Library of Congress System in the Library of the University of Haifa"]: 20.

To this day Israeli public libraries have generally followed the JNUL tradition of using classified catalogs for subject access. As this chapter was being written, the first set of subject headings for Israeli public libraries, compiled by the Center for Libraries in Israel (formerly the Center for Public Libraries in Israel), was about to go to press (more about these headings in the section on Israeli systems for Hebrew materials). Extensive use of alphabetic subject headings is found today primarily in the university libraries, particularly (but not exclusively) in those using LCC. These libraries use LCSH in English), relying on the fact that their reader communities supposedly have a working knowledge of English terminology. Here, also, minimal changes have been made to problematic headings. For example, the parallel use of *Palestine* (pre-1948) and *Israel* (post-1948) by the Library of Congress is clearly unacceptable (LC generally uses the current name of a country only, for example, *Iran* for *Persia*). In Israeli usage, the heading *Palestine* is used only for the publications of the British Mandatory authorities. Examples of other required changes are Hebrew rather than English terminology (*Pessah* rather than *Passover*) and uniform title headings.[76]

The publication of the Bar-Ilan *Hebrew Subject Headings*[77] a few years ago, however, changed the picture for Israeli (and non-Israeli) libraries that wanted to classify their Hebraica using LCC but wanted to use Hebrew subject headings. For the first time, since the appearance of this publication, Israeli academic libraries have the option of offering their readers Hebrew verbal subject access to Hebrew materials. So far only Bar Ilan University, among Israel's seven universities, has opted to move from English LCSH to the Hebrew headings, which will be analyzed in some depth below.

ISRAELI ADAPTATIONS OF ANGLO-AMERICAN SYSTEMS

The Abridged Hebrew DDC: The *"Taktsir"*

Most public libraries in Israel today use an abridged Hebrew edition of DDC[78] containing a simplified Judaica section (220-224, 296, 933, etc.) based on the Scholem expansion. In addition, the Scholem prefix "E" (= in Israel) was changed to the suffix "(9)", thereby causing materials to file by subject (geology of Israel = 550 (9)). Similarly, the Jewish facet represented by the Scholem prefix ayin (= 296.9...)

---

[76] Elhanan Adler, "Judaica Cataloging: The Hebrew Bibliographic and Israeli Traditions," 10.

[77] *Hebrew Subject Headings,* Developed by the Hebrew Classification and Cataloging Department, Wurzweiler Central Library, Bar-Ilan University: Shlomo Rotenberg, Shifra Liebman, Gita Hoffman, Sara Schacham, David Wilk (Ramat Gan: June 1992), 2 vols.

[78] Melvil Dewey, *Taktsir ha-miyun ha-'esroni,* 5th ed. (Jerusalem: Center for Public Libraries, 1983).

was changed to suffix (2) (Jewish music = 780 (2)). Geography and history of the land of Israel are exceptions to the 001-999 span of numbers and use the prefix (9), e.g. (9) 13 = archaeology of Israel. To date, five editions of this abridged DDC, known in Israel as *ha-Taḳtsir*, have appeared, and a sixth edition is in preparation.

Universal Decimal Classification

In the late 1960s an abridged Hebrew edition of the Universal Decimal Classification[79] was published to meet the needs of Israeli special (primarily technological) libraries. While these libraries have virtually no Judaica, the Judaism (296) and Jewish history (933) classes are based on the Scholem expansion.

ISRAELI SYSTEMS FOR HEBREW MATERIALS

Bilingual subject access in virtually all libraries in Israel was for many years provided through indexes to a classified catalog. Clara Hovne, writing in 1970 on the use of the classified catalog for subject access in the JNUL, indicated that suggestions which were made from time to time to abandon the classed catalog and to adopt a subject catalog in its place had always foundered on the obstacle of language. In spite of the adoption of LCC and LCSH by Haifa University a year before she wrote this article, Hovne states that "using English as the language for subject headings is not acceptable to a national Jewish library in Israel, and Hebrew, despite its rapidly expanding use in all fields of learning, is still not considered adequate to meet the needs of all scholars."[80] Thus the classified catalog, in all Israeli libraries until the 1970s, and in public libraries up to the present day, performed the task usually assigned to subject headings in American libraries. Hebrew subject headings entered the Israeli library scene very recently indeed, and subject headings for use in public libraries are about to be published for the first time at this writing.[81]

The primary advantage of the classified catalog is that it is *language-independent*, which a country of multilingual inhabitants, like Israel, may find it superior to the alphabetical subject catalog. LC makes no attempt to be language-free. Subject cutters such as *Subject bibliography—Jews—Religion—Special topics*, A-Z, e.g., C6- *Commandments* abound in the schedules.

---

[79] International Federation for Documentation, *Miyun 'esroni universali.* Added t.p. Universal Decimal Classification (Tel Aviv: ha-Merkaz la-meda tekhnologi u mada'i, 1969); (International Federation for Documentation [FID] #445).

[80] Clara Hovne, "Indexing a Classified Catalog," *Library Resources and Technical Services* 14 (Fall 1970): 547.

[81] Merkaz ha-hadrakhah le-sifriyot be-yisra'el, *Otsar munḥei miftuaḥ*, experimental ed., Rochelle Kedar, ed. (Jerusalem: ha-Merkaz, 1996).

Systems of cutter numbers for Hebraica for arranging materials on the shelf within the same class number, preceded the creation of Hebrew indexing and subject heading systems. A Hebrew author table was compiled by Tishbi[82] of the JNUL in 1958, and a Hebraica title table was published by Zafren[83] a year later, in 1959. A Yiddish author table has existed since 1921, when A. and P. Rozental compiled it in the Soviet Union.[84] While Hebraica Cutter numbers eliminate the problem of romanization, they do not eliminate the problem of variant orthography. For example, Zafren favors *ketiv haser,* so a library using *ketiv male* would find the distribution of numbers in his or her tables unsatisfactory.[85]

The use of Hebrew subject headings in Israeli catalogs, even today, is limited. A general list of Hebrew subject headings based on LCSH does not exist and is probably too expensive for the Israeli library community to undertake and maintain. The *Index to Hebrew Periodicals,*[86] which Haifa University Library has been producing in various formats for nearly two decades (and which is also a file in Israel's ALEPH network) is probably the closest thing to a general Hebrew subject heading list in existence. It contains some 40,000 generic terms (plus personal and corporate subjects), but it is limited to subjects covered in Hebrew articles.

The problems involved in creating a Hebrew subject heading list were described by Adler in two articles in the 1970s,[87] at the inception of the Haifa University indexing project. Some of the problems specific to the Hebrew language, such as distinguishing the intitial article letter "ה" from "ה" as the first letter of a word, have been solved as computer technology became more sophisticated (the initial article is indicated with computer-readable markers indicating the non-filing characters). Others, such as the problem of *ketiv ḥaser* vs. *ketiv male* are still handled on an individual basis: "The guiding rule has been to use the most widespread terminology, regardless of origin."[88]

---

[82]Tishbi, Peretz, ["Cutter Book Numbers Adapted to Hebrew Characters."], *Yad Lakore* 5 (January-March 1958): 20-36; in Hebrew.

[83]Zafren, Herbert C. , "Arranging Your Books," *Studies in Bibliography and Booklore* 4 (June 1959): 3-20.

[84]Rozental, Anna and P. Rozental, *Vi azoy darf men funandershteln bikher in di bibliotekn* (Kiev: Melukhe-Farlag, Yidsektsye, 1921); (Kultur-Lige. Populer-Visnshaft-likhe bibliothek. Bibliotek-visn, 1).

[85] Bella Hass Weinberg, "Hebraica Cataloging and Classification," p. 343.

[86]*Index to Hebrew Periodicals* (Haifa: University of Haifa Library, 1977-); in Hebrew.

[87]Elhanan Adler, ["Development of a Hebrew Thesaurus for Periodical Indexing"], *Alon ASMI* 63 (3) (February 1976): 65-68, 99; in Hebrew; "An On-Line Thesaurus for Information Retrieval," In *Proceedings of the International Conference on Literary and Linguistic Computing, Israel, April 22-27, 1979.* Ed. by Zvi Malachi (Tel Aviv: The Katz Research Institute for Hebrew Literature, Tel-Aviv University, 1979), p. 191-195.

[88]Elhanan Adler, "An On-Line Thesaurus for Information Retrieval," p. 194.

Israeli public libraries retained their classified catalog even after most of the university libraries switched to LCSH primarily because this approach has been followed by the catalog card service of the Israel Center for Libraries (formerly the Israel Center for Public Libraries), to which they subscribe. This is about to change, however, with the publication of a thesaurus of Hebrew terms[89] based on the thesaurus of indexing terms which serves the University of Haifa *Index to Hebrew Periodicals.* The editor, Rochelle Kedar, explains the 1994 decision of the Center to base the thesaurus of indexing terms for public libraries on the Haifa thesaurus as follows:

1. The development of a completely new thesaurus could take years, a circumstance which would be highly detrimental to the implementation of a future network of public libraries (similar to the ALEPH network of academic libraries).

2. The existing library management systems in Israeli public libraries had difficulty handling long, precoordinate subject headings, of the type found in LCSH and the Bar Ilan Judaica subject headings (which will be discussed in more detail below).

3. Many public libraries that were already independently indexing their collections used the Haifa University thesaurus because of the wide range of topics that it covered.[90]

There were elements of the Haifa thesaurus, however, that were not appropriate to a thesaurus for public libraries, such as its many precoordinated subject headings and highly specific terms which, though suitable for indexing of articles, are over-specific for the indexing of books. Therefore the University of Haifa allowed the Center access to their computer and opened a subdirectory for them in which the Center for Libraries, by way of the Internet, worked on a subset of the Haifa thesaurus, making changes as needed. The result was a thesaurus of indexing terms containing 12,087 descriptors and 5,534 nondescriptors[91] gleaned from the larger Haifa thesaurus and designed specifically for use in Israel's public libraries.

The Bar-Ilan Hebrew-language subject headings signify a different approach. Based on, although sometimes radically diverging from, LCSH, they provide Hebrew headings for Hebrew materials on the principle that there is no need for Hebrew terminology for topics on which there are no Hebrew publications. While this approach simplifies the situation somewhat at Bar Ilan University, it does have the disadvantage of dividing subject access for subjects that appear in both Hebrew and

---

[89] Merkaz ha-hadrakhah le-sifriyot be-yisra'el, *Otsar munḥei miftuaḥ.*

[90] Manuscript edition of English introduction to: Merkaz ha-hadrakhah le-sifriyot be-yisra'el, *Otsar munḥei miftuaḥ.*

[91] Manuscript edition of English introduction to: Merkaz ha-hadrakhah le-sifriyot be-yisra'el, *Otsar munḥei miftuaḥ.*

Roman scripts, since non-Hebrew materials are assigned subject headings using standard English LCSH.

LCSH-based Hebrew subject headings have their roots in a project that started more than three decades ago—in the early 1960s—in the Knesset. At that time the staff of the Knesset library began to assign and translate LCSH into Hebrew for use in cataloging their collection. Thus it was in a government library, rather than an academic library, that Hebrew LCSH made their first appearance. In fact, Hebrew LCSH preceded English LCSH in Israeli libraries. It was only in the late 1960s that librarians at both the University of Haifa and Ben Gurion University of the Negev began assigning LCSH in English to both English and Hebrew materials. The JNUL at Hebrew University's Givat Ram Campus had no subject headings but rather, as described above, assigned more than one classification number to most books and then used the classification numbers as the basis for subject searches in a classified catalog. At that time Tel Aviv University also assigned more than one classification number to each book and did not use subject headings either.

In 1970 the staff of the Bar-Ilan Law Faculty library began translating, on a small scale, LCSH into Hebrew for cataloging their Hebrew collection. Similarly, in the early 1970s a subcommittee of the Standing Committee of the National and University Libraries began planning the creation of a uniform set of Hebrew subject headings based on LCSH. Unfortunately, the necessary funding for this project (estimated at $100,000 per year for 6 to 7 years) was not forthcoming and the project was shelved.

In 1981, what was to become the ALEPH Israel Inter-University computer network began operating at Hebrew University's Mount Scopus library. Mount Scopus library staff began to assign LCSH in English to both Hebrew and English materials. That same year, the JNUL staff began providing subject index entries in English to their classified catalog, which they continue to do to this day.

Until 1983, Bar-Ilan used LCSH for its non-Hebrew materials, i.e., materials in the Roman, Cyrillic and Arabic alphabets, but its large Hebrew collection had no verbal subject access. Then, at the end of 1983, when it began computerizing its library, it decided to begin using Hebrew subject headings for Hebrew material.

Gita Hoffman and her colleagues, in their article describing the development and structure of the Bar-Ilan headings, summarizes the chronology of the application of subject headings to Hebrew materials in Israel in Table 7.2 below:[92]

---

[92] Gita Hoffman et. al, "Hebrew Subject Headings: Development and Implementation at Bar-Ilan University": 25.

Table 7.2. Chronology of the Assignment of Subject Headings to Hebrew Materials in Israel

	English Subject Headings	Hebrew Subject Headings
1960s		Knesset (LCSH)
1968	Haifa University (LCSH)	
1970		Bar-Ilan Law Faculty (LCSH)
1981	Hebrew University Mount Scopus Campus (LCSH)	
1983	Tel Aviv University (LCSH)	
1983	Jewish National and University Library (own system)	Bar-Ilan (LCSH expanded)

Hoffman explains the rationale for Hebrew subject headings as follows. Since the average Israeli student or library user's dominant language is Hebrew, asking them to use English subject headings requires a mastery of that foreign language to a level that most of them have not attained. (On the other hand, requiring them to search for a book by author or title in English is, in Hoffman's opinion, reasonable.) As for the rationale for choosing LCSH as the basis of the Hebrew list, there were several reasons. First, LCSH was already being used by Bar-Ilan's foreign-language cataloging department. Secondly, LCSH is an internationally accepted system of subject headings. The subject headings existed and were ready for use and translation. Finally, LCSH also provided an indexing vocabulary for online retrieval.[93]

There were disadvantages as well: LCSH were designed for the Library of Congress's own collection; they display both an American bias and sometimes a Christian bias; and they are not specific enough for a Judaica collection as large and varied as Bar Ilan's. Nonetheless, it was felt that the advantages outweighed the disadvantages, and it was upon LCSH that Bar-Ilan based its headings. When the required subject headings did not appear in LCSH, the Bar-Ilan staff consulted Israeli tools, such as the Haifa thesaurus and the thesaurus of index terms in social sciences and education of the Henrietta Szold Institute for the Social and Behavioral Sciences.

[93]Gita Hoffman et al, "Hebrew Subject Headings: Development and Implementation at Bar-Ilan University": 25.

In the field of Judaica they often created new subject headings in Hebrew, which they translated into English. Even newly-created subject headings, however, were combined with standard LCSH subdivisions, as in the following example:

> *Giyus baḥure yeshivah la-tsava—Hebitim kalkaliyim*
> (Draft of yeshiva students into the army—Economic aspects)[94]

Hoffman *et al* divide the problems they had to deal with in establishing subject headings for books in Hebrew characters (including Yiddish, Ladino and Judeo-Arabic publications) into six categories: (1) Linguistic problems, (2) Changes in LCSH to meet Israeli needs, (3) Jewish history, (4) Holocaust, Jewish (1939-1945), (5) Biases, and (6) Expanded Judaica headings.

The Bar-Ilan Hebrew subject headings, according to Weinberg[95], have potential applications in libraries with no plans to provide Hebrew subject access, although at first glance American and European Judaica librarians might consider this work irrelevant to their collections. First, Judaica librarians working with LCSH who cannot find appropriately specific headings for the works they need to catalog may find the Bar-Ilan list helpful in applying LCSH. Second, those who consider certain LCSH for Jewish topics theologically or politically objectionable may find models for revising these headings in the Bar-Ilan list. Finally, and perhaps most significant, there is interest among American Judaica librarians in standardizing parallel Hebrew access points in RLIN, not merely copying the Hebrew form of a name on a title page. The Bar-Ilan compilation provides uniform headings for Hebrew authors, which may save local authority work in standardizing parallel Hebrew points in these records.

LC has recently recognized the Bar-Ilan project. In a May 1996 posting in the *LC Cataloging Newsline* (Online Newsletter of the Cataloging Directorate, Library of Congress), the project is mentioned as one of three international cooperative programs involving LCSH (the others are in Lithuania and Pretoria, South Africa): "Wurzweiler Central Library of Bar Ilan University (Israel), a frequent correspondent with LC and the Cooperative Cataloging Team on subject usage, is translating LCSH into Hebrew."[96]

---

[94]Gita Hoffman et al, "Hebrew Subject Headings: Development and Implementation at Bar-Ilan University": 25.

[95] Bella Hass Weinberg, "*Hebrew Subject Headings*. Developed by the Hebrew Classification and Cataloging Department, Wurzweiler Central Library, Bar-Ilan University: Shlomo Rotenberg, Shifra Liebman, Gita Hoffman, Sara Schacham, David Wilk. Ramat Gan: June 1992. 2 vols. (798; 435 pp.) $400," *Judaica Librarianship* 7 (1-2) (Spring 1992-Winter 1993), 64-86.

[96] "International Cooperative Program Reaches Out to Three Continents," *Library of Congress Cataloging Newsline* <LCCN@loc.gov>, 30 May 1996.

CONCLUSION

More than a decade ago, before listservs and gophers and the World Wide Web, Bella Weinberg wrote with regard to different views on Jewish classification schemes that "in scanning the publications of the Association of Jewish Libraries (AJL), one finds a variety of opinions on classification schemes. These range from the 'marking and parking view'—it doesn't matter what class number you write on a book as it's just a label to define its place on the shelves—to the philosophical defense of organic Jewish schemes."[97] Today, Judaica librarians worldwide have the technological apparatus to express their opinions on every aspect of Judaica classification online—in such listservs as *Hasafran*, by individual e-mail to colleagues, through interactive utilization of the Web—and to receive responses in real time. The only thing that has not changed with the astonishing development of computer technology is the fact that one still finds a variety of opinions on classification schemes.

If one examines the reasons for choosing one classfication system over another, several principles come to light. First, it is the sequence of topics that determines the *philosophical acceptability* of a Judaica classification scheme, and not its use of letters or numbers.[98] In judging philosophical acceptability, the questions to be asked are whether it has a Christian bias and whether it juxtaposes topics in a way that is illogical or unacceptable to one's patrons. However, too much can be made of this issue. The patron is much less likely than the classifier to notice the sequence of the classes. Another factor that should be taken into account is the capability for *synthesis* or number-building within a system. Synthetic systems like DDC or Scholem allow close classification of highly specific topics but tend to produce longer class marks than does an enumerative system like LCC. In addition, synthetic classification is more difficult to apply, which might be a consideration against its use in a small synagogue, school or center library in which much of the work is done by volunteers or nonprofessional staff.

The small Judaica classification schemes that contain relatively few numbers can be difficult to apply because they fail to enumerate specific topics. For example, it could be argued that a small classification scheme that lists only broad fields such as *sociology, anthropology*, and *folklore* is more difficult to work with than a scheme that enumerates specific topics like *dress, manners,* and *food customs*. With the more specific scheme, the classifier can usually match title words of a bibliographic item to specific class numbers, whereas with the broader scheme, the classifier must determine the author's approach to the topic. However, small systems usually have simpler *notations*, composed of two to three numbers, which can be an advantage both

---

[97]Bella Hass Weinberg, "Judaica Classification Schemes for Synagogue and School Libraries: A Structural Analysis":26.

[98]Bella Hass Weinberg, "Judaica Classification Schemes for Synagogue and School Libraries: A Structural Analysis":26.

for patrons and for shelvers. In general, it should be remembered that there is a tradeoff between *specificity* and *complexity* of notation.

Another consideration is the *expandability* of a system. Small Judaica libraries may become medium- or large-sized libraries if the synagogue, for example, expands to serve a school or community center. If the classification system is small and not readily expandable, large-scale reclassification may become necessary. Similarly, the system's *compability* with general classification schemes should be considered. Compability allows borrowing of class numbers for marginal topics not included in the Judaica classification scheme rather than making them up. Nearly any topic can have a "Jewish" angle and that "we cannot expect a Judaica classification scheme designed for a small library to predict the creation of works on Jewish crime, philately, papercuts, etc."[99] Weinberg feels that because every library has different collection strengths, merging elements from various compatible classification schemes is preferable to tampering with a single system and creating *ad hoc* numbers.[100] Use of a hybrid system of this sort however does require excellent documentation in a manual or a classified authority file.

Redundancy is another factor to be considered in choosing a Judaica subject cataloging system. If the classifier uses specific subject headings for retrieval, a broad classification system may be sufficient for arranging a small collection on the shelves. Complex, narrow classification schemes and subject headings are often redundant, i.e., represent identical topics, and in the case of a small collection, their use may simply make unnecessary work for the classifier.

In her 1983 article comparing Judaica classification schemes for synagogues and school libraries, Weinberg constructed a table comparing many of the above features for seven schemes, encompassing large schemes and small schemes, schemes exclusively for Judaica and general schemes, American schemes and Israeli schemes. It is the only table of its kind which we found in the literature, and it warrants duplication here:

---

[99] Bella Hass Weinberg, "Judaica Classification Schemes for Synagogue and School Libraries: A Structural Analysis":26.

[100] Bella Hass Weinberg, "Judaica Classification Schemes for Synagogue and School Libraries: A Structural Analysis":28.

Table 7.3. Structural Analysis of Judaica Classification Schemes[101]

Features	Philosophical Acceptability	Specificity	Notation	Compatibility with general systems	Possibilties of Synthesis	Availability of class numbers	Updating frequency
Schemes							
LEIKIND	Low	Low	Simple	High	Medium	None	Infrequent
WEINE	Medium	Medium	Simple	Medium	Medium	None	Medium
ELAZAR	High	High	Mainly decimal, some mixed	None	Medium	None	Medium
SCHOLEM	Medium	High	Complex	High	High	Retrospective, Microfiche	Medium
DEWEY	Low	Medium	Simple	High	High	High	Frequent
FREIDUS	High	Medium	Simple	None	None	Retrospective, Published	Infrequent
LC	Low	High	Complex	High	Medium	Very High	Frequent

What is obvious is that there is no one best Judaica classification scheme for all purposes. For example, a Judaica library would probably find a general scheme that scattered materials by subject more suitable than one that lumped all Judaica in one class, but a general library would probably find that the former type of scheme would make it difficult to identify material of interest to its Jewish studies patrons. Further, since all Judaica libraries include at least some general reference works, if a Judaica classification scheme cannot juxtapose them and requires the use of a second scheme to classify the general material in the collection, this is a significant disadvantage—so significant that it might be worth selecting a less philosophically acceptable scheme which allowed greater compatibility with general classification systems.

Using LCC and LCSH in the online, networked environment has the advantage of allowing the library potential compatibility with Hebrew-enriched records in RLIN, although even in RLIN, while stringent requirements have been established for uniformity in descriptive cataloging and LCSH is the standard for subject headings, the choice of a classification scheme is up to the individual library. Accepting LCSH, however, without tampering with them to make them more appropriate for an individual library, has a distinct economic advantage for RLIN members. Local modifications of LCSH are considered non-standard in RLIN, and a

---

[101]Bella Hass Weinberg, "Judaica Classification Schemes for Synagogue and School Libraries: A Structural Analysis":29.

charge is incurred for creating records that include such non-standard headings. In the end, each librarian must decide what is the relative importance of each factor in evaluating Judaica classification and subject heading systems for his or her library. For some, the monetary advantages of ready-made class numbers may outweigh the philosophical acceptability of another. For others, philosophical considerations may take precedence.

Part II: Hebraica Library Automation

8 Hebrew Character Sets: Development and State of the Art

Uniform computer representation of Hebrew characters is a major factor in any attempt at inter-system searching or exchange of data. Unfortunately there has been an appalling lack of standardization—not only between Israeli and non-Israeli systems but even within Israel itself. In addition, as will be seen, there is not even worldwide agreement as to how many and which characters are actually needed for Hebrew character bibliographic records.[1]

The basic Hebrew alphabet consists of twenty-two consonants, five of which have alternate forms when they appear at the end of words, for a total of twenty-seven consonant characters.[2] In addition to the basic consonants, a full-function Hebrew character set would require characters for vowel points, diacritics (such as the *dagesh*), digraphs (two letters as a single character) and even cantillation marks (for Biblical texts). In the context of bibliographic records, the character set commonly used is significantly smaller—vowel points and diacritics are not transcribed, even when appearing on the title page[3] and even at the expense of creating ambiguity in the reading of a text[4]. While the reasons behind this practice may well derive from the

---

[1]For a discussion of the various Hebrew character sets, particularly as they relate to international standards see: John Clews, "Coded Character Sets in Hebrew Library Automation," in *Hebrew Studies: Papers presented at a colloquium on Resources for Hebraica in Europe ...* , edited by Diana Rowland Smith and Peter Shmuel Salinger (London: The British Library, 1991), pp. 220-231.

[2]In Arabic script applications (in Arabic speaking countries) it is becoming common to represent each letter by a single character value, determining its display form via an algorithm based on its location in the word and proximity to other letters. In Hebrew this would be extremely difficult--while final forms virtually never appear in mid-word (a rare exception: לסרבה in *Isaiah* 9,6) non-final forms at the end of words are much more common, both in abbreviations (e.g. בע״מ) and in Hebraized foreign words when the final form cannot be aspirated ?? (e.g. ג׳יפ = jeep; writing the word with the final form: ג׳יף would cause it to be pronounced "jeef").

[3] The omission of existing diacritics and vowels is common practice in Hebrew cataloging, even though it may be contrary to cataloging rules (for further discussion of this point see the section on title transcription in chapter 6).

[4] Non-voweled Hebrew texts occasionally contain a few vowel points to resolve ambiguous forms where there may be two possible (and even logical) vocalizations of the consonants.

limited number of characters on Hebrew typewriters (and the problems of superimposing the vowels and diacritics over, above and within the characters), use of consonants alone has generally simplified the problems of coding Hebrew bibliographic data.

ISRAELI HEBREW CHARACTER SETS

While Hebrew character coding in international practice has been part of the general task of coding nonroman scripts, requiring a solution for hundreds of different characters (and for many years not a matter of high priority for the computer industries of the United States and Europe), the Israeli computer community has had to find its own local solution for Hebrew from the start. The Israeli approach has been to superimpose the basic 27 consonantal characters within the commonly used character sets (EBCDIC and both 7 and 8-bit ASCII), in place of (and at the expense of) existing characters. This, of course, meant that hardware and software would have to be adapted to display the Hebrew characters rather than the displaced ones. In the early days of computers, this was done by replacing the chip containing the character set in imported terminals and printers with one containing the Hebrew substitutions. In recent times such chips often contain multiple, selectable, character sets which already include Hebrew. In addition, in many systems today, fonts are maintained in software and displayed via graphic interfaces that eliminate the need for "hard-wired," permanent character sets.

The positions chosen for the Hebrew characters in the modified sets have, unfortunately, not been standard. Within the original 7-bit 128 character ASCII character set a common approach was to replace spacing grave accent (ASCII 6/0, decimal 96) and lower case roman (26 characters, ASCII 6/1-7/10, decimal 97-122) with the Hebrew consonants (27 characters, ASCII 6/0-7/10, decimal 96-122). For the Israeli data processing community this was a convenient solution—the addition of Hebrew was considered worth the loss of lower case roman. This solution came to be known as "old code" Hebrew when superseded by "new code" 8-bit Hebrew.

With the advent of 8-bit 256 character sets, Hebrew could be better moved to the upper 128, returning lower case roman to its rightful, standard place. Hebrew would still displace other characters but these were considered less crucial ones—special European language characters and graphic symbols. Unfortunately, here two separate standards evolved. The first, generally associated with the advent of the IBM PC to Israel (and commonly known as "PC Hebrew" or "DOS Hebrew"), was to put the Hebrew alphabet at the very beginning of the upper 128, at positions 128-154 (8/0-9/10). This was an arbitrary decision of IBM-Israel and has been recognized by the Israel Standards Institute as a de-facto code.[5] The second approach was to put Hebrew towards the end of the character set at positions 224-250 (14/0-15/10)—the "old code" 7-bit locations + 128. This system of coding was originally known in Israel as "Digital

---

[5]Yehavi Bourvine and Hank Nussbacher (1993, May 3), Hebrew Support Requirements for use in TCP/IP networks, V9, March 1993, *ILAN-H Discussion in and about Hebrew in the Network* [Online]. Much of the historical information regarding Hebrew character sets is based on this paper.

Hebrew," or "VT220/320/420 Hebrew" since its first widely used implementation was on Digital Equipment Corporation terminals and printers. This code is now more commonly (and correctly) known in Israel as "ISO Hebrew" since it is an International Standard, ISO/IEC 8859-8.[6] It is gradually becoming the dominant Israeli standard and is used in Israel not only in UNIX and Digital VMS systems, but has been adopted by Microsoft for Hebrew Windows based applications.[7] The Standards Institute of Israel has also proposed a much fuller 8-bit character set which uses most of the upper 128 codes and includes vowel points, accents and cantillation marks, while retaining the consonants in the same positions as in ISO/IEC 8859-8.

Example of ASCII based Hebrew code tables

	"Oldcode" 7-bit	"DOS" 8-bit	"ISO" 8-bit
alef	96 (6/0)	128 (8/0)	224 (14/0)
bet	97 (6/1)	129 (8/1)	225 (14/1)
gimel	98 (6/2)	130 (8/2)	226 (14/2)
...	...	...	...
final mem[8]	109 (6/13)	141 (8/13)	237 (14/13)
mem	110 (6/14)	142 (8/14)	238 (14/14)
...	...	...	...
shin	121 (7/9)	153 (9/9)	249 (15/9)
taf	122 (7/10)	154 (9/10)	250 (15/10)

In addition to the above three ASCII based substitutions, there are Hebrew code substitutions for the EBCDIC coding system which is private to many IBM systems (but not the PC, which uses the ASCII system). There are no current Israeli Hebrew bibliographic applications running on equipment where a Hebrew form of EBCDIC would be used.

The existence of several different systems for Hebrew coding, all based on replacing existing characters from standard character sets, creates a rather chaotic situation for transferring Hebrew texts between computers of different manufacture and with different operating systems. While transfer of a Hebrew-text file between two computers or systems with preidentified character sets requires fairly simple code conversion (shifting 27 characters from one code value to another), there may be some character confusion if the source file uses a larger character set than the target system

---

[6]International Organization for Standardization, *Information Processing--8-bit Single-Byte Coded Graphic Character Sets, Part 8: Latin/Hebrew Alphabet*, ISO 8859-8, 1988.

[7]Adopting this standard for Microsoft Windows has created a situation in which the same PC may have DOS applications which use the "PC Hebrew" code and Windows applications which use the "ISO Hebrew" code. The Hebrew edition of Microsoft WORD-6 has a special option for converting texts imported from Hebrew "DOS code" word processors.

[8]Note that the final forms precede the regular forms since, in filing, these forms indicate the end of a word (followed by a space, punctuation or end of line character) and therefore would always precede any continuing word, e.g. אם would always precede any word beginning את.

(for example, converting a file containing 8-bit Hebrew and lower case roman text to 7-bit Hebrew would leave both the lower case and the Hebrew using the same coding—in effect changing all the lower case text to Hebrew-character gibberish).[9] This problem is much more acute when the Hebrew code used by one system is not necessarily known to the other, as in electronic mail. While MIME (Multipurpose Internet Mail Extensions) compliant e-mail systems can recognize the character set of the text sent, not all e-mail systems support MIME or Hebrew character sets. As a result, in Israel today, most electronic mail messages are still sent in English, unless both sender and receiver know they are using compatible mail systems that support Hebrew.

The practical implication of the Israeli approach of character substitution is that the non-Hebrew character set is more limited than that available in roman-only character sets.[10] In the context of bibliographic records, this means that some characters may have to be omitted or changed. The most extreme example of this is that the use of 7-bit "old code" Hebrew completely precludes the use of lowercase roman. While all current Israeli systems use the 8-bit codings, much of the Israeli university Hebrew cataloging was entered in the past using 7-bit coding and as a result, the roman character data was entered entirely in upper case. Even today, while the ALEPH system can support both upper and lower case roman, most Israeli university libraries continue to enter roman character data in upper case in order to maintain consistency in authority files (*SHAKESPEARE* and *Shakespeare* would be separate entries). While some of the Israeli ALEPH libraries currently catalog using lower case, only one (the Jewish National and University Library) makes use of the additional European language characters of the extended (code 128+) ASCII-based character set. The other libraries ignore the accents, umlauts, etc. and transcribe the letters without them—umlaut-a becoming simply *a*. Even within the ALEPH system today, technical limitations preclude entering lower case roman and Hebrew within the same field and any roman text in a Hebrew field must be entered in upper case only.

The Israeli ALEPH system today supports several additional scripts (Arabic,[11] Greek, Cyrillic) however these all follow the same pattern of substitution for other characters in the extended ASCII code table. As a result, only one nonroman script can appear in a given field (although multiple nonroman scripts, in different fields, may occur in an individual record).

---

[9]A related problem exists for Israeli users of the World Wide Web. When displaying text containing special European characters (French accented characters, German umlauts, etc.) using Israeli Windows fonts, Hebrew characters appear instead of the special characters.

[10] This limitation is true for other 8-bit national character sets such as Cyrillic and Arabic, as well. The extreme limitation of the Hebrew 7-bit "old code" seems to be unique.

[11] The ALEPH approach to Arabic is proprietary and non-standard and mimics the Israeli approach to Hebrew, i.e., all forms of each character have specific codings. In the context of Arabic, when some characters can have 3 or more different forms this requires 87 different codings. The more common approach to Arabic today is to code each character once only and determine its display form at the time of display, based on the adjacent characters (all forms must, of course, be available in the display font). ALEPH is planning to change to this methodology in the future.

In summing up the state of the art in Israel in 1989, Elhanan Adler wrote:

> Israeli libraries have, therefore, followed the general data processing approach to Hebrew character representation. This has been done primarily for the pragmatic reason that this is what was available and the Israeli library market is too small to justify major hardware adaptations. Israeli libraries could live with this approach since Hebrew was the only additional language with which they felt the need to cope. Additional alphabets would be either Romanized (e.g., Cyrillic) or Hebraised (e.g., Arabic).[12]

Although Israeli systems have developed to allow display of both Arabic and Cyrillic characters (Cyrillic becoming particularly important since the recent mass emigration from the former Soviet Union to Israel), Hebrew representation still follows the industrywide standards.

THE RLIN/USMARC CHARACTER SET

While Israeli libraries could simply adopt the standard, national conventions for entering, processing and displaying Hebrew text, the American library community had no such crutch upon which to lean. Writing on the state of the art of Hebrew word processing in the United States in 1986, Aaron Wolfe Kuperman commented:

> Anyone trying to work with Hebrew text on a personal computer tends to be envious of colleagues whose computing is limited to the Roman alphabet ... No "off the shelf" computer will willingly display Hebrew characters or write right-to-left ... There is currently no "standard" system for recording Hebrew characters in machine (computer)-readable format, meaning that files produced for one system are probably unintelligible on any other system.[13]

The desire of most major American Judaica libraries not to automate without Hebrew script capability kept them for many years waiting on the side for the necessary hardware, software and standards to process nonroman scripts.[14] This challenge was taken up in the 1980s by the Research Libraries Group (RLG) which undertook to add major nonroman script capability to its Research Libraries Information Network (RLIN), starting with Chinese, Japanese and Korean (CJK)

---

[12]Elhanan Adler, "The State of the Art in Hebraica Library Automation: American and Israeli Standards and Practices," in *Hebrew Studies: Papers presented at a colloquium on Resources for Hebraica in Europe ...* , edited by Diana Rowland Smith and Peter Shmuel Salinger (London: The British Library, 1991), p. 212.

[13]Aaron Wolf Kuperman, "Hebrew Word Processing," *Judaica Librarianship* 3 (1-2) (1986-1987): 17.

[14]For a general introduction to the problematics of nonroman scripts in bibliographic records, see: Joan M. Aliprand, "Nonroman Scripts in the Bibliographic Environment," *Encyclopedia of Library and Information Science* (New York: Marcel Dekker), vol. 56, supplement 19, pp. 260-283.

released in 1983, followed by Cyrillic and Hebrew[15] and more recently, Arabic. With such a broad goal, it is obvious that substitution within a standard character set was out of the question and the best solution would be separate character sets for each script, using an "escape" sequence (as defined by the International Standard ISO 2022) to shift from one character set to the other. The ISO 2022 technique allows for up to 188 unique graphic characters in an 8-bit set, more than enough for Hebrew. It also allows multiple nonroman character sets in one data field (which could not be done using the approach chosen by ALEPH).

RLG commissioned Bella Weinberg to prepare a proposal for a Hebraic character set. In the introduction to her 1985 proposal she states:

> While this proposal features a full set of vowel points and diacritics, it is not intended that cataloging be corrective in any way (even though AACR2 calls for insertion of missing diacritics according to standard usage in the language). These special characters are included in the proposal to enable the cataloger to record them when they occur in the work being cataloged...

> Digraphs are enumerated as special characters because it is believed that the RLIN Hebraic character set will be designed on a grid with each letter and diacritic in fixed position. Since context-sensitive display is not expected to be a feature of the system, it is necessary to precoordinate certain letters and letter-vowel combinations to ensure their correct positioning. Some "precoordinated" characters are included because of their frequency and/or importance in Romanization.[16]

Weinberg's initial proposal listed 77 characters including not only the basic consonants and vowel points but also some marked and unmarked consonants (e.g., both kaf and khaf), consonant + vowel combinations (e.g., alef + patah, hataf-patah), digraphs (e.g., Yiddish double vav, Judeo-Arabic alef-lamed), and various other diacritics.[17] This proposal was submitted to the RLG Advisory Group on Hebrew which excluded many of the composite characters—particularly those which could be coded using two overlaying characters (alef+patah, khaf+dagesh, patah+shva).

Particular attention was given to the special needs of Yiddish orthography. Joan Aliprand of RLG, analyst for the RLIN Hebrew project, explains:

> Most members of the Advisory Group felt that the digraphs *tsvey vovn* (double vav), *tsvey yudn* (double yod) and *vov yud* were necessary for correct Yiddish orthography.... As a very large number of publications within Hebraica are in the Yiddish language, it is important that a character set

---

[15] Joan M. Aliprand, "Hebrew on RLIN," *Judaica Librarianship* 3 (1-2) (1986-1987), 5.

[16] Bella Hass Weinberg, Proposed Hebraic Character Set for the Research Libraries Information Network (March 1985), typescript.

[17] For a figure showing Weinberg's original proposed character set, see Joan M. Aliprand, "Hebrew on RLIN," *Judaica Librarianship* 3 (1-2) (1986-1987): 7

designed for cataloging purposes accommodate the special orthographic features of this language. The Yiddish digraphs are unique graphic symbols ...

In sum, a Hebrew character set consisting only of the 22 consonants is inadequate for Yiddish, because its use distorts the standard orthography of the language.[18]

Despite the above, the use of the Yiddish digraphs was, and still is, a subject of some dispute. Aliprand cites correspondence from the Library of Congress indicating that they would not use the three Yiddish digraphs but rather key these characters as separates.[19] Today this is still Library of Congress practice as well as that of many RLIN Hebraica libraries. For indexing and searching in RLIN, the Yiddish digraphs are normalized to their component letters, so either can be used in a search request.

The preliminary RLIN Hebrew character set was pruned down from Weinberg's initial 77 to 48 characters.[20] It included 30 consonants (the standard 22+5 Hebrew consonants and the three Yiddish digraphs mentioned above) and 18 Hebrew and Yiddish vowel characters and special diacritic marks. Subsequently this set was changed somewhat as a result of ISO assessment and Israeli comments: 4 diacritics were dropped, the three composite *hataf* vowels were added, and some character codes were changed.[21] The final character set, now a USMARC specification,[22] contains 47 Hebrew characters.

From Weinberg's introduction to her proposal it is clear that she expected libraries using the RLIN Hebrew capability to enter vowel points, at least when appearing on the title page. Despite this, and her championing the need for the Yiddish digraphs, most RLIN Hebrew and Yiddish cataloging uses the basic 27 consonants only.

HEBREW IN THE UNICODE™ STANDARD

Most current character sets (with the notable exception of East Asian scripts) are based upon using a single 8-bit byte for character representation, limiting the set to 256 different characters. The various 8-bit standards for multiple scripts all require some kind of additional indication as to which character set is in effect when multiple

---

[18]Joan M. Aliprand, "Hebrew on RLIN," *Judaica Librarianship* 3 (1-2) (1986-1987): 6

[19]Joan M. Aliprand, "Hebrew on RLIN," *Judaica Librarianship* 3 (1-2) (1986-1987): 15

[20]These are the unique Hebrew characters only. The RLIN Hebrew character set also includes 10 digits (0-9) as well as 21 standard punctuation marks.

[21]Joan M. Aliprand, "Hebrew on RLIN--an Update," *Judaica Librarianship* 5 (1989-1991): 12-13.

[22]*USMARC Specifications for Record Structure, Character Sets and Exchange Media*, prepared by Network Development and MARC Standards Office, 1994 ed. (Washington, D.C., Cataloging Distribution Service, Library of Congress, 1994).

character sets may be in use. The Unicode Standard[23] resolves this problem by using a 16-bit code which provides 65,536 unique values—more than enough for all modern scripts. This standard was developed by the Unicode Consortium, a group of information processing and computer companies with active participation of the Research Libraries Group, insuring that library requirements would be fully addressed.

The Unicode Hebrew character block contain 82 characters including the 27 standard Hebrew consonants, the three Yiddish digraphs, vowels and diacritics plus the cantillation marks (added in Version 2.0). The Unicode set also includes 45 additional "presentation forms" which include such compound characters as "alef with patah," "bet with dagesh," "shin with dagesh and shin dot," and "bet with rafe" as well as alternate forms of some characters (such as the varika, which is considered to be a variant of the rafe). Compatibility characters exist merely to provide support for existing implementations.

The first major software product to utilize Unicode was Windows NT, released by Microsoft in 1993. Since then, other products which use Unicode have been released, including Sun's Java, IBM's AIX, Novell's NetWare 4.0, and Apple's QuickDraw GX. Unicode based library systems, however, are only now beginning to appear. In 1995, Joan Aliprand of RLG, who is also secretary of the Unicode Consortium, summed up the situation for library systems:

> It is too early for the Unicode standard ... to be fully utilized in library systems. Many of the members of the Unicode Consortium are building Unicode-based software, which will, in due course, underpin software for library applications. At the present, however, the implementation of nonroman scripts entails the use of script-specific character sets.[24]

At the present time (late 1996), some US library vendors have developed library applications which run on platforms which are Unicode-based to some degree. However, neither USMARC nor UNIMARC allow for the exchange of Unicode data at this time, so all cataloging transferred using these standards must still be based on 8-bit codes. Work is underway within the American Library Association to extend USMARC to allow Unicode data to be used.[25] A similar project for UNIMARC (managed by the British Library) is underway in Europe.[26] Certainly no Hebrew cataloging is currently being input, stored or transferred using Unicode, although one

---

[23] Unicode Consortium, *The Unicode Standard*, Version 2.0. (Reading, MA, Addison-Wesley Developers Press, 1996).

[24] Joan M. Aliprand, "Nonroman Scripts in the Bibliographic Environment," p. 268

[25] *Proposal 96-10: USMARC Character Set Issues and Mapping to Unicode/UCS*, Dated May 24, 1996, revised: July 22, 1996. Document and appendix are available from the Library of Congress server: URL: gopher://marvel.loc.gov:70/00/.listarch/usmarc/96-10.doc and URL: gopher://marvel.loc.gov:70/00/.listarch/usmarc/96-10.app

[26] Computerized Bibliographic Record Actions (CoBRA). *Research and Development for Libraries in Europe*. March 1995. (Its Fact Sheet 1).

recent client application (DRA's FIND running under Windows NT) uses Unicode to display Hebrew sent by the server in USMARC character sets.

BIDIRECTIONALITY

USMARC data is always in logical order, first to last. Display software, upon encountering an ISO 2022 escape sequence (switch to alternate character set) must be able to determine whether the following data should be displayed from left to right or right to left. It is therefore possible to encode a data field containing not only multiple character sets but in which the display flow of the text may zigzag back and forth. For example, a multiscript title such as:

Maimonides' סיכובנ הרומ with commentary [logical order]

would display as:

Maimonides' מורה נבוכים with commentary [word display order 1,3,2,4,5; the character logically following position 12 (space) being the rightmost Hebrew character (mem) at display position 24!]

The tasks of reversing the necessary text, handling line breaks in right-to-left text, etc. would be the responsibility of the software. Inputting and editing bidirectional data can be even more complicated and confusing since some character sets will "push" existing data to the left and others to the right and the cursor positioning may be confusing. In presenting the RLIN software approach to this problem, Aliprand notes that:

> Insertion and deletion are on a strictly logical basis. This sometimes causes the cursor to reposition itself at the end of a line, when insertion or deletion occurs at a directional boundary ... This may be disconcerting at first, but it is entirely logical: the logical approach is the only way to achieve consistent behavior in bi-directional character manipulation.[27]

Apparently this was found to be too confusing, and in her subsequent update article on Hebrew in RLIN, she describes an "internal order key" which had been introduced, allowing the cataloger to toggle back and forth between the logical and display formats (as above) to simplify insertion and deletion in bidirectional fields.[28]

The ALEPH approach to bidirectionality is much more limited. Each ALEPH field can use one character set only, and its directionality is determined by that character set. The Maimonides example above (Hebrew words in a roman field) could not be entered in ALEPH since nonroman characters are not available in an ALEPH roman field. Roman characters can be entered in a Hebrew or Arabic field, however

---

[27]Joan M. Aliprand, "Hebrew on RLIN," *Judaica Librarianship* 3 (1-2) (1986-1987): 8

[28]Joan M. Aliprand, "Hebrew on RLIN--an Update," *Judaica Librarianship* 5 (1989-1991): 13

they are limited to upper case only (this is not a character set limitation but one of the inputting software). Roman characters in Hebrew or Arabic fields in ALEPH are stored in display order rather than logical order—the index-creation algorithm does the inversion to logical character (but not word) order.

SUMMARY

Israeli libraries have followed the various local industry standards for coding the basic 27 consonant characters of the Hebrew alphabet by substituting them for other, less important characters in the 7- or 8-bit (128 or 256 character) code sets. The American RLIN/USMARC approach allows for a separate, extended Hebrew character set which includes vowels, diacritics and digraphs as well. In actual practice, most RLIN libraries have not made use of the extended set and have also made do with the basic 27 consonant characters. Variant Hebrew coding is therefore not as great an impediment to sharing of bibliographic data as it might have been. In the future, Unicode based systems may bring Israeli and American systems to a common character set as well.

The major impediment to the sharing of bibliographic data between the US and Israel is not the character sets, but differences in how multiple scripts are implemented (the use of ISO 2022 escape sequences in USMARC versus field level definition of scripts in ALEPH) and differences in levels of coding. These will be further discussed in chapter 11.

9 The American Scene: Hebrew in RLIN

In chapter 2 ("Hebraica Descriptive Cataloging: Segregated or Integrated?") we discussed the various alternatives that were used for cataloging Hebrew publications before the onset of automated cataloging: partial or full romanization—the Anglo-Saxon tradition—and separate Hebrew and non-Hebrew catalogs—the Israeli tradition. In a recent article, RLG's John Eilts categorizes the options for cataloging nonroman scripts materials in North America prior to automation into four models: Model 1: native script was used for the entire cataloging record (i.e., what we referred to as "the Israeli tradition"); Model 2: the entire record was romanized in Latin letters representing either the closest possible pronunciation for an English speaker or an attempt to represent the written characters; Model 3: the record used a mixture of scripts; and Model 4: bibliographic information was translated from the native script (used only by libraries with small collections in nonroman scripts).[1]

Early American automated systems (both local and network) could offer no more than an extended Latin character set and therefore full romanization was the only practical option available to libraries which wished to follow American standards. Even when multi-script capability was added to the USMARC standard, it was always clear that it was to be used in addition to romanization—not instead of romanization. The rationale behind this was simple: every USMARC bibliographic record should be searchable and displayable without the need for special graphic equipment or capabilities (using the proverbial "dumb terminal"). Even in the future, when Unicode-based graphic user interfaces may become the norm, it should still be possible for a searcher without knowledge of a nonroman script to be able to search and display a nonroman record (e.g., interlibrary loan staff). This requires not only intermixing scripts in a bibliographic record in a format which would make each clearly identifiable, but also the software capability to manipulate each script

---

[1] Eilts, John, "Non-Roman Script Materials in North American Libraries: Automation and International Exchange," in *61st IFLA General Conference - Conference Proceedings - August 20-25, 1995,* available: http://www.nlc-bnc.ca/ifla/IV/ifla61/61-eilj.htm.

according to its own requirements. The format for this was defined by USMARC; the primary implementation of the multi-script capability was, and still is, RLIN.

THE USMARC BIBLIOGRAPHIC FORMAT FOR NONROMAN SCRIPTS

The principles for intermixing scripts in computer-encoded data which USMARC uses were set forth in the standard called *American National Standard Code Extension Techniques for Use with the 7-Bit Coded Character Set of American National Standard Code for Information Interchange (ANSI X3.41-1974).*[2] Following this standard, modifications were made in the USMARC Format for Bibliographic Description to enable the inclusion of nonroman scripts in MARC records (and subsequently in the RLIN nonroman implementation).

The modifications included three parts, which remain constant for all nonroman scripts:

1. Identification of the character sets present in the record.
2. Association of alternate representations (in romanization and in the original).
3. Allowable mixing of roman and nonroman scripts (one or more) in a single data element.[3]

Extensions to the USMARC format provided for a new 066 field (Character Sets Present) that identifies in subfield c (in repeating occurrences) any nonroman character sets included in the record and defines them as singlebyte or multibyte. The original scripts themselves appear in multiple occurrences of the USMARC 880 field (Alternate Graphic Representation).

The default directionality of USMARC is left-to-right. When a field's directionality is declared right-to-left, the right-to-left field directionality marker, /r, is inserted at the end of the linkage subfield 6. A cataloger will make a field right-to-left when its contents are entirely or predominantly in Hebrew. (In RLIN, the directionality marker itself is not shown; its presence is manifested as field contents presented on the screen from right-to-left.) This *nonroman linking subfield* (‡6) was defined to link 880 fields and those fields in the range 0XX through 8XX which may have an alternate graphic representation.

Each romanized field with an alternate graphic representation has an occurrence of linking subfield 6 containing tag 880 (for the "alternate graphic representation") and an occurrence number. In the 880 field which corresponds to that romanized field, linking subfield 6 contains the tag of the romanized field, the same occurrence number, and the second and third characters of the escape sequence of the

---

[2]Joan M. Aliprand, "Hebrew on RLIN," *Judaica Librarianship* 3 (1-2) (1986-1987): 6.

[3]Joan M. Aliprand, "Nonroman Scripts in the Bibliographic Environment," In: *Encyclopedia of Library and Information Science*, v. 56 (New York: Marcel Dekker, 1995), p. 270.

first non-Latin character set in the 880 field. If the 880 field is declared to have right-to-left directionality, "/r" will also be in subfield 6, at the end. For example, a Hebrew title field might be coded:

245 10‡6880-01‡aParashat ha-melekh ...

while its vernacular equivalent would be coded as:

880 10‡6245-01/r‡aפרשת תשרלמה‎ ... [Hebrew text in logical order]

In this example, the title field is the first "pair" of such fields (occurrence number 01) and the two fields are linked by the ‡6 subfields (field 245 pointing to field 880-01 and the corresponding 880 field containing reference to 245-01). In this way, clear linkage is maintained between the fields even when there may be multiple pairs with the same MARC tag. In the RLIN implementation, the cataloger never sees the actual USMARC 880 and ‡6 coding (which might have the romanized title near the top of the record and its vernacular equivalent far below) but rather a second 245 field would be shown immediately below the first, without the linking apparatus. This is, of course, a display convenience only and the records are stored in the standard USMARC format.

Alternate graphic representation fields that do not have a romanized equivalent always have an occurrence number of *"00."* Thus, when the record does not contain a romanized field to which an alternate graphic representation can be linked, subfield 6 of the 880 field contains the tag of a romanized field *which does not exist in the record.* The occurrence number *"00"* in subfield 6 of the 880 field indicates that the corresponding romanized field is hypothetical. For example, a library might opt to enter a contents note in Hebrew alone, rather than romanize it as well.[4] An additional and problematic use of the "00" can occur with roman and vernacular fields with the same content, but sufficiently different not to be linked (see discussion of RLG policy on parallel fields later in this chapter). In RLIN, a nonroman field that does not have a romanized equivalent must begin with "‡6."

In addition to the use of additional, parallel fields, the USMARC standard defines techniques for escape sequences, imbedded codes which specify the character set which follows. This technique allows unlimited switching between character sets within a single data field. Correct display of these characters and correct directional layout are dependent on the software implementation.

HEBREW IN RLIN

The first major implementation of nonroman cataloging was by the Research Libraries Group (RLG) for its RLIN system. The demand for this capability came from libraries with major collections in these scripts, particularly the so-called JACKPHY languages (Japanese, Arabic, Chinese, Korean, Persian, Hebrew and Yiddish). The need for vernacular capability in these scripts was considered crucial because their romanization either obliterates the semantic differences among homonyms or necessitates an interpretation of the pronunciation which may not be

---

[4]The question whether romanized equivalents for all fields are required or not will be addressed under the discussion of the RLIN "core fields" concept later in this chapter.

correct, or both. To answer this need, (and for Cyrillic script as well—termed JACKPHY-Plus) RLG introduced, between 1983 and 1991, enhancements to its RLIN system to accommodate these scripts.[5]

The RLIN system has pioneered the use of nonroman scripts in cataloging and in setting their standards. For Hebrew, it is still the only network system available and all American local system applications which currently support Hebrew (currently DRA, VTLS and three American ALEPH sites) primarily download and display Hebrew data cataloged via RLIN. The RLIN Hebrew script capability has also, finally, brought most of the major American Hebraica collections into the computer age— making their data accessible to other research libraries world-wide.[6] The RLIN implementation of Hebrew (over and above the USMARC standards) has also become the American de-facto standard for Hebrew cataloging, used by the Library of Congress in-house as well.

The RLIN Hebrew implementation is based on the USMARC standards previously discussed. It adds the software mechanism to input, edit, display and search in Hebrew. Some of these are part of the general RLIN nonroman capability and some are unique to the problems of Hebrew data. In the following pages we will discuss the RLIN Hebrew enhancements and nonroman enhancements as they apply to Hebrew.

CORE FIELDS AND "DOUBLE KEYING"

While the USMARC format mandates a primarily romanized record and contains the mechanism for additional, nonroman data fields, it does not indicate which fields must (or should) appear in each script. The RLIN system requires that romanized equivalent fields (i.e., vernacular fields) must be entered for four "core" fields. These fields are 245[7] [Title statement], 250 [Edition statement], 260 [Publication, distribution, etc. (Imprint)] and 4xx [Series statement]. Vernacular fields are optional for other fields—including the main entry (1xx) and added entry (7xx) fields. The lack of mandatory 1xx and 7xx vernacular fields has important implications for searching as it is possible that a Hebrew author search might not

---

[5]Karen Smith-Yoshimura, "Sidebar 9: RLIN'S JACKPHY-Plus Script Development," in Michalko, James and John Haeger, "The Research Libraries Group," *Library Hi-Tech* 12 (2) (1994): 25.

[6]For a comprehensive presentation of the various options considered by American Hebraica libraries, and the reasons why most opted for RLIN, see: Elizabeth Vernon, *Decision -making for Automation: Hebrew and Arabic Script Materials in the Automated Library*, Occasional Papers, no. 205 (Urbana: University of Illinois, Graduate School of Library and Information Science, 1996).

[7]While there is no question that the title proper (subfield a) should be entered in both romanized and vernacular forms, here are differences of practice amongst RLIN Hebraica libraries as to the need to romanize subtitles (subfield b) and author statements (subfield c). See: various articles under: "Modification of RLIN Hebraica Records: a Cataloging Workshop," 8 (1-2) (1993-1994): 25-35.

retrieve a Hebrew title which is actually in the data base but has only a romanized author entry.[8]

One of the arguments voiced against the RLIN Hebrew implementation has been the need for "double keying," or entering the same data twice, in both romanized and vernacular form. Vernon quotes Charles Berlin, explaining Harvard's policy of romanized-only Hebrew cataloging because, "The need for increased cataloging productivity mitiates against adding nonroman script data to the romanized record."[9] In her original 1986 article, Aliprand addresses this problem with the following ameliorating arguments:

1. Double keying is unnecessary if the Hebrew record for the title being cataloged is already in the RLIN database (copying can be done by a single command). Only if the title is not in the database, or if the only record is completely romanized according to an unacceptable scheme, do all fields have to be keyed.

2. The RLIN system requires "double keying" only for the "core" fields, stipulating that the inclusion of all other paired romanized and nonroman fields is at the cataloger's option, and vernacular headings are *not* mandatory.

3. Two of the four core fields—edition statement and series note(s)—do not occur in every record, with edition statements occurring in 15% of all RLIN records and series notes in 30% only.[10]

Actual experience with RLIN seems to indicate that the fears of "double keying" may be overblown. Reardon-Anderson reported that the productivity of cataloguers in the C. V. Starr East Asian Library at Columbia University was increased through the use of RLIN CJK.[11] The input of Chinese characters (at that time, as a series of components) was far more time-consuming than typing Hebrew letters. Lerner has recently reported that at Stanford "Since it was found that approximately two-thirds of Hebraica with available copy in RLIN was already enhanced with Hebrew script fields, the impact on the copy catalog department of adding Hebrew script to the remaining records would not be too great."[12]

---

[8]Under the RLIN clustering method (see later in this chapter) all records for a specific item will be retrieved in a Hebrew search if the access field appears in Hebrew in <u>one</u> of them. If, however, none of the records contain a vernacular form of the search term , none can be retrieved. If a work is not retrieved by a vernacular search, the romanized form could be tried.

[9] Elizabeth Vernon, *Decision-Making for Automation:* 41.

[10] Joan M. Aliprand, "Hebrew on RLIN": 12.

[11] J. Reardon-Anderson, "RLIN/CJK: The First Year," New York: C. V. Starr East Asian Library, Columbia University, March 1985. (Unpublished paper, available from Distribution Services Center, RLG).

[12] Heidi G. Lerner, "Current Practices and Standards of Cataloging in RLIN," 8 (1-2) (1993-1994): 26.

PARALLEL FIELDS

The USMARC standard for handling "alternate graphic representation" fields provides the mechanism for linking vernacular fields with their roman equivalents but does not specify the definition of when fields are to be considered equal: are they equal only if there is exact, character-by-character equivalence (i.e., systematic romanization) or even if they contain the same information in a different formulation. RLG has taken the first, more conservative approach and fields which are not exact, systematic romanization equivalents are not linked—not only will their 880 field have an occurrence number "00" (no link to the romanized heading), but the vernacular field must be considered a local, nonstandard one. While romanized titles and series notes will usually be systematic representation of their vernacular equivalents, this policy has serious implications for many of the access fields (main entry, most added entries, subject headings). While these are not core fields, and not mandatory in RLIN records, most Hebraica libraries would want them to be part of their bibliographic records.

For example, under this policy the personal heading *Maimonides, Moses* would not be matched with its Hebrew equivalent משה בן מימון (= *mosheh ben maimon*). Not only would it not display immediately under it (RLIN display practice for linked fields), but it would have to be coded with a local data tag.

Entering vernacular headings as local data has another, far more significant implication. The purpose of special local data fields is specifically to allow libraries to input their own private data which is not wanted by or relevant to other libraries (local call numbers, notes relating to specific copies, private access points, etc.) Bibliographic utilities are programmed to automatically drop such local fields when duplicating records for other libraries. Coding many vernacular Hebrew fields as local ones would undermine much of the rationale for using RLIN for Hebraica cataloging, as each library using such a record would have to rekey many of the Hebrew fields, making the cataloging process much more expensive. As Vernon has noted in this context: "Having to rekey data defeats the purpose of copy cataloging—i.e., which is to avoid having to do cataloging work which another library has already done."[13]

In view of the above, Aliprand argued for pairing of any nonroman heading with its AACR2 equivalent—regardless of by what method the AACR2 form was established (i.e., *Maimonides, Moses* and the Hebrew *Mosheh ben Maimon* are semantically one and the same, and therefore linkable). She also notes that the Library of Congress is in effect doing this already to prevent its own system from eliminating many vernacular fields from its own USMARC subscription tapes.[14] Since the RLIN system has no way of enforcing this policy, a library which chooses to link semantically equivalent headings can do so. In addition to the Library of Congress, several

---

[13] Elizabeth Vernon, *Decision-Making for Automation:* 67.

[14] Joan M. Aliprand, "Hebrew on RLIN--An Update," *Judaica Librarianship* 5 (1990): 18.

other major Hebraica libraries also ignore the official RLIN policy and link these fields to make them available to other libraries.[15] An alternative solution might be to allow transfer of local fields in copy cataloging. Vernon quotes a 1995 personal communication from John Eilts stating that a change request which will allow the X9X fields to carry over [with the DERive command] in copy cataloging is being processed since users have requested this.[16]

INPUT AND DISPLAY

The RLIN software has been programmed to respond to various "escape sequences" indicating change of character set. When the key sequence to invoke a script is entered, not only will the character value of many of the keyboard keys change to that character set, but the software is able to accommodate change of direction (right to left display) for Hebrew and Arabic as well. This character set will be maintained until another escape sequence is entered, or the field is completed. The data itself, is stored in first-to-last, logical order. Using this mechanism it is possible to enter and properly display several different character sets, some with text which displays in opposite directions, in the same data field (for a more detailed description of the problems of displaying and editing bidirectional text, see chapter 11).

RLIN has chosen to display the parallel "880" fields under their equivalent tags (and indeed to hide the entire linkage apparatus from the viewer). Using our previous example, the pair of fields internally coded and stored in USMARC as:

245 10‡6880-01‡aParashat ha-melekh ...
880 10‡6245-01/r‡aפ‎רשת תשמה‎ ...

with many other fields between them, would display together simply as:

245 10 Parashat ha-melekh ...
245 10   ... פרשת המלך

with the Hebrew data both reversed and right-justified. RLIN supports several different display formats, as well as printing of screen displays (but not catalog cards).[17] The RLIN Hebrew implementation requires use of the special RLIN terminal software (available for Windows 3.1 or Windows 95). The reader-oriented RLIN service "Eureka" does not support nonroman scripts. The RLIN Z39.50

---

[15] See Claire Dienstag, "Modifications Made by the New York Public Library to RLIN Hebraica Records," *Judaica Librarianship* 8 (1-2) (1993-1994), 27, and Rosalie E. Katchen, "Use or Non-Use of Parallel Linking Fields in RLIN for Hebrew-Script Access Points," *Judaica Librarianship* 8 (1-2) (1993-1994), 31-32.

[16] Elizabeth Vernon, *Decision-Making for Automation:* 67.

[17] Joan M. Aliprand, "Hebrew on Rlin": 12. For an example of a special local program for printing Hebrew cards from RLIN, see: Laurel S. Wolfson, "Hebrew Card Production from RLIN Records at the Klau Library," *Judaica Librarianship* 8 (1-2) (1993-1994): 36-39.

standard server Zephyr can deliver nonroman script data, but its display is dependent on the receiving client program having multiscript capability.

CLUSTERING AND INDEXING HEBREW

The RLIN bibliographic database contains clusters of individual records from specific libraries, rather than master records with holdings. A cluster represents a "bibliographic entity," that is, the same bibliographic manifestation of a work. All records in a cluster share their access points.

Clustering (gathering together records for the same bibliographic edition of a work) is based on the romanized fields of records. Therefore two records for a Hebrew-Japanese dictionary, for example, with Hebrew script in one and Japanese script in the other, will cluster together as long as the *romanized* fields used for clustering match.

Because all records in a cluster share their access points, a Hebrew search will often retrieve completely romanized records which are in the cluster with one or more records containing Hebrew script. In the case of the Hebrew-Japanese dictionary, a search on either of the nonroman scripts will retrieve both records (although only one of the nonroman scripts will be displayed, because it is not yet possible to use CJK and other nonroman scripts simultaneously on RLIN).

Nonroman fields in RLIN records are indexed as fully as their romanized equivalents, and may be searched using all the search features applicable to roman alphabet fields, i.e., searches on names, words or phrases, or identifying numbers (such as ISBN), Boolean searches, and searches on truncated words or phrases. At a minimum, Hebrew records can be searched by Hebrew phrases or words from the title proper and subtitle and from any series note the record might include, since these are core fields, for which RLIN requires parallel romanized and nonroman forms. In addition, if Hebrew personal names, corporate bodies or subjects have been included in a record as optional nonroman access points, they can also be searched.[18]

When the RLIN indexing methodology was evaluated to determine its effect on Hebrew data, the following linguistic features of Hebrew were identified as affecting indexing: medial versus final forms of letters, vocalization and diacritical marks, and prefixed particles. The following decisions were taken with regard to these features:

1. The medial and final forms of letters (e.g., *nun* and *nun sofit*) are not differentiated in indexing, although they are differentiated in input and display.

2. Vowel points and diacritical marks are ignored in indexing.

---

[18] Joan M. Aliprand, "Hebrew on RLIN": 10.

3. Both vocalized and unvocalized Hebrew are retrieved, whether the search uses vocalized or unvocalized spelling. However, RLIN does not automatically merge *ketiv ḥaser* and *ketiv male* (*plene* or defective Hebrew spelling), just as it does not merge British and American spelling.

The first decision, to treat medial and final forms of Hebrew consonants which have these dual forms as one, is based on a technique known as *normalization.* When access points are normalized, procedures such as ignoring nonessential punctuation and not differentiating between different forms of the same letter—i.e., upper and lower case letters or, as in the case of Hebrew, medial and final forms of the same letter—are applied in indexing in order to enable the retrieval of records whose access points are identical in all significant aspects except for one of these slight spelling differences, as Aliprand notes in a Yiddish normalization example:

> Because of normalization, a search on the Yiddish word *oyf* will retrieve titles containing the Soviet form using medial *fey* in final position. (In the search argument, the word may be spelled with either a medial or a final *fey.*) Normalization is also applied to the Yiddish digraphs, since there is no way for the researcher to know whether the catalogers keyed them as digraphs or as the component letters.[19]

Aliprand predicted that the second decision, the dropping of vowel points and diacritics, would have particular significance for searching in Yiddish: "The dropping of diacritics will cause 'false drops' in Yiddish, since different letters will be normalized to the same unmarked letter in indexing."[20] ('Diacritics,' in this context, clearly refers to the 'points' that distinguish pasekh alef from kamatz alef, and fey from pey.) This has not proven to be the case. Most RLIN Hebraica users (including the Library of Congress) do not transcribe any points appearing on the source of information.[21]

The romanizations of the Hebrew definite article *ha-* and *he-* are ignored in title word indexing. In the parallel Hebrew script title, while initial definite articles attached to the first word of a title can be dropped via the second indicator (Nonfiling characters) of the title field, there is no provision for distinguishing between *he/ha* indicating a definite article and *he/ha* in a subsequent initial word in the field. Furthermore, there is not even an indicator for nonfiling characters to eliminate definite articles of corporate bodies in main entry and added entry Hebrew script parallel fields.

In her two papers on Hebrew on RLIN, Aliprand describes a number of strategies for "particle detection" which RLG considered. ("Particle detection" is the

---

[19] Joan M. Aliprand, "Hebrew on RLIN": 10.

[20] Joan M. Aliprand, "Hebrew on RLIN": 10.

[21] Based on a 1996 survey by the authors via the elctronic discussion group *Hasafran.* For details, see chapter 11.

removal of prefixed particles as part of the word indexing of vernacular text.) This indexing enhancement has not been implemented because users have not reported problems in searching.

AUTHORITY CONTROL FOR HEBREW RECORDS

Authority control for Hebrew names has long been a concern for Hebraica catalogers[22]. This problem has become even more acute now as the RLIN system enables the inputting of vernacular access points, but not their control. The problems of Hebrew authority control can be broken down into three aspects: (1) authority control issues common to all bibliographic records; (2) authority control issues common to all bibliographic records containing nonroman scripts; and (3) authority control issues unique to records containing Hebrew script.

Since the first problem is out of the scope of the present work, we will start by addressing the second problem: issues common to bibliographic records containing any nonroman script. The primary problem common to all nonroman cataloging records involves the approach used for collating all the works of an author who may have works published in several languages in several scripts. As Vernon puts it, "will they all be collated under one form of the name or will a single database contain an English book under 'Maimonides, Moses,' a Hebrew book under 'Mosheh ben Maimon,' and an Arabic book under 'Musa ibn Maymun?' "[23] A decision must be made on how to handle name entries (normalized access points), as opposed to title and series entries (transcribed access points in RLIN libraries (and other libraries following AACR2), although not in Israeli academic libraries).

One solution is to maintain name headings in one script and link script name headings in the other script(s) via cross-references in a multi-script authority file. This solution allows a single author search to retrieve all materials for an author regardless of the language. ALEPH, for example, has the capability to include both nonroman and roman scripts in one authority record, which is linked to the cataloging record.[24] Another approach is to establish separate authorized forms, and therefore separate authority records, for each script, but again, with a single author search retrieving all materials regardless of script. Vernon cites an example of this model at the Institut du Monde Arabe (IMA).[25]

---

[22] For a comprehensive discussion of the problematics of Hebrew authorities, see Bella Hass Weinberg, "Hebraic Authorities: A Historical-Theoretical Perspective," *Judaica Librarianship* 8 (1-2) (1993-1994), 45-55.

[23] Elizabeth Vernon, *Decision-Making for Automation*: 61.

[24] Susan S. Lazinger, "ALEPH: Israel's Research Library Network: Background, Evolution, and Implications for Networking in a Small Country," *Information Technology & Libraries* 10 (4) (December 1991): 275-291.

[25] Elizabeth Vernon, *Decision-Making for Automation,* 62.

Bella Weinberg observed recently that "cataloging of non-Roman scripts is inextricably linked with technology," and that "the lack of availability of non-Roman scripts in the Library of Congress's local library system is the reason that we do not have original alphabet data in the authority records today, even though there is a USMARC format for this, noting also that a recent survey by RLG indicated that a change in this situation may soon occur and that nonroman headings and references may soon be input into RLIN'S authority file."[26] Actual implementation will, however, be possible only after the Library of Congress implements its new integrated library system with multi-script possibility.[27]

In the meantime, with mixed-script authority records not yet available in RLIN, the same author may appear in the RLIN database under different forms of the name in the nonroman script. Because RLIN has a clustered database structure, records describing the same bibliographic entity share access points. If variant forms of name in the nonroman script occurred in records in the cluster, a search on any of the variant forms would retrieve all the records in the cluster (including completely romanized records.)   If, however, the different forms of name were in different clusters, only the cluster with an access point matching the search term would be retrieved. Because almost all RLIN records will have AACR2 access points, the greatest number of hits will result from a search using a controlled, romanized heading rather than uncontrolled nonroman headings. The critical missing piece is cataloging rules for Hebrew access points approved by the U.S. library community.

The need for nonroman script authority control—both to prevent multiple nonroman forms of the same name and to link roman and nonroman forms of the same name—is clear. With regard to the third problem—authority control issues unique to records containing Hebrew script—the need is even more urgent because of the problem of *ketiv ḥaser* and *ketiv male*.

Returning to the example of Maimonides, Moses/Mosheh ben Maimon/Musa ibn Maymun (for Latin, Hebrew and Arabic books), there is still another problem in establishing the correct heading in Hebrew, even if we discount the possibility of totally different forms like "Rambam" and "Mosheh ben Maimon." Because of variant orthography in Hebrew (see Chapter 4), the Hebrew heading for "Mosheh ben Maimon" could be spelled with a double yod in some records and a single yod in others, causing a search under one of these headings to retrieve only some of the author's works. Like other problems of variant forms this could be solved by cross references within a multi-script or Hebrew script authority record, or it could be solved through the Israeli approach of normalizing Hebrew headings to standard form. The normalization solution, however, is not an easy one since "correct *ketiv male* is as much of an intellectual effort as Romanisation."[28] In addition, decisions must be

---

[26] Bella Hass Weinberg, "Non-Roman Scripts in The Library of the Future," 37.

[27] Personal Communication from Linda Lerman, *RLG*, 23 May 1997.

[28] Elhanan Adler, "The State of the Art in Hebraica Library Automation: American and Israeli Standards and Practices," in *Hebrew Studies: Papers presented at a colloquium on resources for*

taken regarding Yiddish headings whose orthography can have several forms all of which do not interfile well with Hebrew. Whatever the solution decided upon, variant Hebrew orthography is a problem which American libraries must face, as Israeli libraries have, if there is ever to be adequate Hebrew authority control in RLIN, or in any Hebraica catalog.

Romanized form Hebraica authority control in RLIN took a significant step forward in October 1994, with the implementation of one of the most significant cooperative cataloging projects related to Judaica librarianship. Between October 2 and October 7, catalogers from nine major Judaica libraries[29] met in New York at the Jewish Theological Seminary and the New York Public Library for formal NACO (National Coordinated Cataloging Operations) training. During these five days the participants learned how to create and revise name authority records in order to contribute them to the National Authority File (NAF), and how to submit proposals for new and revised LC subject headings to the Subject Authority File. Furthermore, the training dealt with other areas of Hebraica cataloging, in addition to USMARC authority format, such as romanization issues. The group called itself the "NACO Hebraica Funnel" and as such submitted its first Funnel record on October 11th, 4 days after the close of the training workshop.[30] Since then there has been a steady stream of contributed headings, substantially adding to the number of Hebraica names in the NAF.[31] The Hebrew Funnel Project was the catalyst for creating the Heb-NACO listserv. This listserv serves as a discussion group for all issues pertaining to Hebraica cataloging, but was specifically designated to discuss Hebraic authority issues. At present subscription to the Heb-NACO listserv is restricted to participants in the NACO project, but plans are underway to open it eventually to other Hebraica/Judaica catalogers worldwide.

SUMMARY

The USMARC standards for nonroman cataloging supply a very sophisticated framework for the coding of various scripts in the same record or even field, as well as for linking parallel fields containing the same content in different scripts. The RLIN implementation of this standard as it applies to Hebrew has enabled Hebraica libraries to finally automate their bibliographic records while retaining Hebrew search and

---

Hebraica in Europe held at the School of Oriental and African Studies, University of London, 11-13 September 1989/11-13 Elul 5749, edited by Diana Rowlands Smith and Peter Shmuel Salinger, British Library Occasional Papers 13 (London: The British Library, 1991), pp. 217.

[29] The Library of Congress; The Center for Jewish Studies; Gratz College; the Jewish Theological Seminary; the New York Public Library, Jewish Division; Stanford University; University of Toronto; Yeshiva University; YIVO.

[30] NACO Hebrew authority records were already being submitted by individual libraries prior to the creation of the "Hebrew Funnel". See, for example, Rachel Simon, "Contributing Hebrew Name Headings to NACO: a Participant's View," *Judaica Librarianship* 8 (1-2) (1993-1994): 61-68.

[31] R. Katchen (1994, October 31), Naco Hebraica Funnel, *Hasafran* [Online], available: e-mail: hasafran@lists.acs.ohio-state.edu.

display capability. Underlying the USMARC/RLIN approach is the supremacy of a "core" of romanized data which is both required and used (in RLIN) to identify and "cluster" identical records. Hebrew data fields are, at this point, without automated authority control which is a major challenge for the future.

10 The Israeli Scene: Hebrew in ALEPH

At the First International Conference of Judaica and Israeli Librarians in Jerusalem in July of 1990, Adler remarked that "while automation has led to greater standardization and uniformity within Israel, it has created a new area of difference between Israeli and non-Israeli bibliographic data."[1] In chapter 9 the RLIN standard for nonroman bibliographic data, which mandates a full romanized record to which parallel vernacular fields may be appended, was described. Based on the USMARC Bibliographic Format for Nonroman Scripts, RLIN's Hebrew capability became operative only in early 1988. Israeli libraries could not afford to wait until the late 1980s to see how the international bibliographic community decided to handle Hebrew. Concerned with developing a system that would connect its research libraries into a network and, as the only country in the world in which Hebrew is the official language, unable to accept the romanization-plus-Hebrew approach, the Israeli academic library community realized by the late 1970s that it would have to develop its own software.[2]

It was clear from the outset that Israel's native system would have to be able to handle both the Hebrew alphabet and the roman alphabet. Thus, from its inception in 1981, ALEPH was fully operative in both Hebrew and roman mode, the "first implementation of nonroman scripts in automated library systems."[3] Initially developed at the Hebrew University of Jerusalem, later developed and maintained by ALEPH-Yissum Ltd., a company owned by Hebrew University, ALEPH-Yissum merged as of January 1, 1996 with Ex Libris, the Tel Aviv-based marketing company for the ALEPH software both in Israel and abroad to become Ex Libris Ltd. (EXL). In spite of the merger and name change, however, the name "ALEPH" persists as the popular designation of (1) the software, (2) the company, and (3) the Israeli university

---

[1] Elhanan Adler, "Judaica Cataloging: The Hebrew Bibliographic and Israeli Traditions," *Judaica Librarianship* 6 (1-2) (Spring 1991-Winter 1992): 11.

[2] For an a more detailed history of library automation in Israel and the circumstances surrounding the development and implementation of the ALEPH system, see Susan S. Lazinger, "ALEPH: Israel's Research Library Network: Background, Evolution, and Implications for Networking in a Small Country," *Information Technology & Libraries* 10 (4) (1991): 275-291.

[3] Joan M. Aliprand, "Nonroman Scripts in the Bibliographic Enviroment," *Information Technology & Libraries* 11 (2) (1992): 105.

181

library network, one of its first implementations. The ALEPH system—originally designed to serve the automation needs of a single small country, and now installed in 29 countries, using 17 different "languages of conversation" and 5 character sets[4]—has from its beginnings presented a striking contrast to the RLIN approach to Hebrew in virtually every aspect of its development: character sets, software/hardware implementations, format, text storage, and authority file structure. Since character sets were discussed in chapter 8, we shall begin with the two different multiscript implementations developed and used concurrently in ALEPH—the hardware (chip) approach and the software (Soft Font) approach.

NONROMAN SCRIPTS IN ALEPH: Hard Chips and Soft Fonts

Nonroman script support in ALEPH has gone through a number of permutations. Since manual Hebrew cataloging in Israel had always made do with the twenty-seven characters of the Hebrew alphabet (twenty-two letters and five final forma), omitting the marking of vowel sounds (*nikud*) and stress marks (*dagesh*), it was assumed that they were sufficient for automated Hebrew cataloging as well. Because Israel could not begin automating its libraries until it had a system that was fully bi-lingual and bi-directional, it initially opted for the simplest solution—substituting the Hebrew alphabet for lowercase roman (see chapter 8: Hebrew Character Sets). As mentioned above, with this character set, roman characters could be input only in uppercase, the shift-down being used to input Hebrew. In the next permutation, two full character sets were supported, allowing roman fields which used both upper and lowercase letters and Hebrew fields which contained Hebrew and uppercase roman letters (requiring a control-sequence to shift the keyboard from lower case to Hebrew). Both these implementations required a Hebrew chip or "hard font." When Arabic-script capability was added a few years later using a microcomputer-based terminal with a graphics card, ALEPH was on the way to being a multiscript, rather than a bi-script system. However, this hardware-based solution meant that Arabic script could only be entered and read as Arabic from a special workstation (Arabic records retrieved at a regular Hebrew/Roman terminal by a non-Arabic search, such as by subject heading were "hebraized" in display).

In order to convert ALEPH into a truly multiscript system, ALEPH-Yissum began concentrating its efforts in the mid-1980s on the development of a software solution to multiscript data. ALEPH felt no urgent demand to develop a capability for handling the East Asian (CJK) scripts, which it left to RLIN to implement in 1983. However, because Israel's research libraries had large collections in Cyrillic, as well as Arabic, it was decided to focus on a new and unique approach to allow the input of these materials into the ALEPH system. The solution that ALEPH-Yissum developed was "soft fonts," software in the library system rather than the hardware-based solution used in all systems with nonroman capabilities up to this time.

---

[4] "EXL Profile," Available at: http://www.aleph.co.il/prof.html#networks.

Terminal soft fonts are sets of characters that are resident in the computer as software as opposed to character sets that are derived from a chip installed in the terminal. In a soft font the characters are downloaded from the remote computer to the terminal. ALEPH supports soft fonts for a series of DEC-standard terminals and for their PC emulations (if the emulation software supports soft fonts—not all do). Soft fonts are available in ALEPH for Arabic, Hebrew, Cyrillic and Greek character sets, bring the total number of character sets that ALEPH supports, including latin/roman, to five.

The software approach to nonroman scripts brought to an online library system for the first time the possibility of combining scripts not only within records but also in the language with which the user communicates with the system, what ALEPH-Yissum termed the "language of conversation." Just as ALEPH was the first library system to implement nonroman scripts, with the introduction of soft fonts it became the first library system to allow different scripts to be input and viewed simultaneously both in bibliographic records and in the character script in which the user inputs data or commands.

Languages and character scripts in ALEPH are divided into two sets of codes, ALPHA codes and LANGUAGE codes. "ALPHA" refers to the character script of each field, each of which is accessed by a code as follows:

ALPHA codes

Arabic	=	A
Hebrew	=	H
Latin	=	L
Greek	=	R
Slavic	=	S

A-K are scripts that are written from right to left, and L-Z are scripts that are written from left to right. Character scripts are used for groups of languages; for example, the Hebrew character script is used for Hebrew and Yiddish. Each of these scripts (actually multilingual code tables) is limited to 256 characters (one standard 8-bit byte).

Languages, as opposed to fonts or character scripts, have separate codes, as in the following examples:

Languages			ALPHA
Arabic	=	ara	A
English	=	eng	L
Spanish	=	spa	L
Greek	=	gre	R
Hebrew	=	heb	H
Russian	=	cyr	S[5]

---

[5] Susan S. Lazinger and Judith Levi, "Multiple Non-Roman Scripts in ALEPH--Israel's Research Library Network," *Library Hi Tech* 14 (1) (1996): 114.

Thus, languages are designated in ALEPH by the first three letters of the English name of the language, each unique, while ALPHAs are single-letter codes for scripts which may include any number of languages that ALPHA L, that includes such languages as Spanish (spa), Italian (ita), French (fre), and German (ger). Each ALPHA has a default language which the system records in the bibliographic record's field for language (LN) unless instructed otherwise, such as English (eng) for ALPHA L and Hebrew (heb) for ALPHA H. The language code designates the language of the item cataloged—not necessarily the language of any or all of the data fields.

Screens in ALEPH can be in any of 17 currently available languages, with the possibilities for tailoring to other languages potentially limitless. The "language of conversation" (i.e., the language in which the system communicates with the user via screens and messages) is implemented with the "?" or DIALOG command (e.g., ?/SPA). The character script in which the user inputs data or commands is determined by the "ALPHA/alpha code" command (e.g., ALPHA/A = switch to Arabic). The languages of conversations available in the system are defined in a local specification table and in various screen and command table files. However, the character set of the language of conversation can be Latin, for example, while the character set being used for inputting commands or data is in a soft font. For example, the language of the screens may be English while commands may be entered in Arabic. Screens can also be created using the soft font characters, although in practice most users have preferred to use the soft font primarily for input of data and commands.

Finally, there is a distinction between *input* of data using soft fonts and *display* of data. Individual data fields can be input in any or all of the five ALPHA character sets, but the display on the screen is limited at any one time to one soft font plus the character script that comes as a hard font.[6] In the Israeli ALEPH context, this means that both basic Roman (7-bit ASCII) and Hebrew are supported by hardware and an additional character set such as Arabic or Cyrillic (but not both simultaneously) can be displayed at the same time. Switching from an Arabic to a Cyrillic record (nonsimultaneos display) involves a slight delay while the replacement soft font characters are downloaded to the terminal.

These unique ALEPH solutions to multiscript processing have the disadvantage of being nonstandard. It is even theoretically possible for a library or group of libraries to create their own private soft font character set within ALEPH. As we will see further, ALEPH's enormous flexibility has always been both its greatest strength and most dangerous weakness.

---

[6] Susan S. Lazinger and Judith Levi, "Multiple Non-Roman Scripts in ALEPH—Israel's Research Library Network," 114-15. For more detail on the soft font package components, display priorities, fallback display languages, etc., see pages 113-16.

ALEPH FORMAT FOR NONROMAN SCRIPTS:
The "Single Script" Vernacular Record

Perhaps the most striking example of ALEPH's flexibility, with all its strengths and its weaknesses, is the non-MARC format in which Israeli universities catalog their Hebrew (and non-Hebrew) materials. Writing in 1991 on the history of ALEPH's development in order to provide an automated library system for an Israeli research library network, Lazinger points out both the rationale behind and the high opportunity cost of Israel's decision to opt for a non-MARC format:

> It was clear both at the outset and in retrospect that trying to solve the problems of Hebrew cataloging within the MARC format would have set the automation of Israel's university libraries back a number of years and required long-term participation in international committees, which Israel could ill afford either financially or practically. There is no question that these goals, as stated, have been carried out. However, it is clear to all involved that the cost to Israel with regard to international exchange of data...was high.[7]

Today, as Ex Libris Ltd. points out in its Web site profile, although ALEPH software is fully MARC-compatible, allowing for the import and/or export of data in MARC format, with parameter tables that allow for conversion between different MARC standards (e.g.,USMARC to UNIMARC), "a library can opt to use a mixture of MARC codes for the cataloging of standard items, and non-MARC codes for the cataloging of special, non-standard items."[8] In practice, Israeli libraries do not as of this writing use MARC format, but rather ALEPH's initial system of mostly two-letter mnemonic field codes (e.g., **TL** for the MARC **245** title field for Latin script records and כת, the mnemonic code for כותר (title) in Hebrew script records). Discussing the storage of right-to-left text in RLIN and ALEPH, Adler describes in a 1991 article the RLIN solution to the this problem in cataloging Hebrew in MARC format and compares it to the approach which ALEPH, which was not bound by MARC standards, utilized:

> MARC format cataloguing in Hebrew raises several unique problems which have been addressed and solved at RLIN. These include display and input of right-to-left text within a left-to-right framework and correct display and input of bi-directional text within the cataloguing data itself. In both cases the logical order of the text differs from the way it is manipulated for display purposes (for details see Aliprand, 1986-1987).

> ALEPH uses a different approach, coding each line of text as either Roman (left-to-right) or Hebrew (right-to-left). The coding apparatus

---

[7]Susan S. Lazinger and Judith Levi, "Multiple Non-Roman Scripts in ALEPH--Israel's Research Library Network": 283.

[8]"EXL Profile."

itself follows the same direction. Within a given field, text is stored in the display order rather than in logical order; however, the index form derived from such a field will have the text in correct logical order. ALEPH also includes provisions for inserting special non-displaying symbols to handle sorting problems such as non-filing characters in access fields. MARC coding does not adequately solve all such problems.[9]

The nondisplaying symbols to which Adler refers here are inserted before and after the text which the cataloger wishes to suppress as nonfiling characters. Unlike ALEPH's optional filing stop list which automatically eliminates initial articles in access fields in various languages written in Latin script (e.g., the French "Le," the German "Die" and the English "The"), ALEPH's system for designating Hebrew script nonfiling characters is not automatic. Instead, the problem of differentiating between, for example, the initial ה used as an article in words like המורה (the teacher) and initial ה which is the first letter of the word, as in המון (a great many) is delegated to the cataloger, as in MARC, which uses indicators in certain (but not all!) access fields to designate non-filing characters. In the example above, the word המורה would be coded מורה>>ה<< causing it to file as מורה. In addition, unlike the MARC indicators for non-filing characters, the ALEPH suppression symbols are not limited to initial characters, but can be used anywhere in a field, for example: ישראל. >>ה<<משרד לקליטת העליה. >>ה<<אגף לקליטה חברתית.

The format of ALEPH records in Israeli universities today, as described above, is non-MARC, mnemonically coded rather than numerically coded as in MARC, and varying somewhat from library to library. Some ten years after its inception, the Israeli university network added a rudimentary "Union List of Monographs" to its databases, a file which, in reality, is neither a Union List nor exclusively monographs, but a sort of index of holdings in member libraries with pointers to the full records each library stores in its own file in the node of the network on its own campus.[10] In spite of this highly imperfect finding aid added to the network as an afterthought, the network remains both highly decentralized and idiosyncratic, due at least in part to the parametric nature of the ALEPH system, which allows each institution to determine the fields, their codes, how they are displayed, and how they are edited.

Although the ALEPH system provides a default format option that the user library can adopt in full or in part, each user library has the option of adding, subtracting, and altering fields according to its own local needs, i.e., of determining the parameters of its records. The library defines the descriptive information it wants in its cataloging records, the tag and name for each field and the order in which it

---

[9]Elhanan Adler, "The State of the Art in Hebraica Library Automation: American and Israeli Standards and Practices," In *Hebrew Studies: Papers presented at a colloquium on resources for Hebraica in Europe held at the School of Oriental and African Studies, University of London, 11-13 September 1989/11-13 Elul 5749*, Edited by Diana Rowlands Smith and Peter Shmuel Salinger, British Library Occasional Papers 13 (London: The British Library, 1991), p. 217-218.

[10] For a more detailed description of the function of the Union List of Monographs (ULM) in Israel's highly distributed university library network, see Susan Lazinger, "To Merge and Not to Merge: Israel's Union List of Monographs," *Information Technology and Libraries*.

wants the fields to appear in the display format. In addition the user library determines whether a given field will be an index field, opening an authority record for each occurrence of the field in a record, and if so, in what sort of file (e.g., whether all authority records will be held in one dictionary arrangement or whether there will be separate alphabetic indexes for authors, titles, subjects, etc.).[11] In theory Israeli libraries have agreed upon a standard set of field codes in order to be able to exchange cataloging data among themselves, but in spite of fact that TL can more or less be counted on to define a title field and AU to define a personal main entry field, little else *can* be counted on a network-wide basis. For example, AU in some libraries defines both personal and corporate main entries (in Hebrew מח), and in others, only personal main entries, with code CB (in Hebrew חא), defining corporate body main entries. Furthermore, not only does coding for the same field vary among libraries in the network, the definition of the fields themselves vary. In some libraries, for example, the PP (עמ) field includes both pages and illustrations, while in other libraries, this information is distributed in two fields, usually coded as PP and CO (אג). Many libraries have defined unique fields for local data as well, and when records are copied from one library to another within the network, these unique fields, along with other fields which the copying library has coded differently from the source library, are transmitted as erroneously-coded fields for the copying library to sort out afterward.

The character set in ALEPH is determined, as mentioned, at the field level. If the field is a roman character field, Hebrew cannot be inserted into the same field. Thus, for example, a roman character record cannot have a note which states that there is a parallel title in Hebrew and then gives the title in Hebrew. A Hebrew notes field can do this, since depressing the SHIFT key when inputting in Hebrew will allow upper case latin/roman letters to be input, but the order of the input will remain the right-to-left order of a Hebrew field, so the roman character title must be input backwards.

In addition to differences in format and storage of bi-directional text in RLIN and ALEPH, probably the most significant difference between the Hebrew bibliographic record in American RLIN libraries and in Israeli ALEPH libraries is that the Israeli Hebrew record is fully vernacular—"single script"—whereas the American record is multiscript, combining a fully romanized record with parallel Hebrew fields. Hebrew alphabet materials in all Israeli libraries are cataloged entirely in Hebrew, with only LC Subject Headings (in the libraries which use them), LC classification numbers (again, where used), and parallel titles in roman alphabet fields. Several of the fields which the system adds as a default if the cataloger does not input them are also roman alphabet fields: LN, the field which designates the language of the item, is a three-letter code composed of the first three letters of the language in English, with a default of "eng" if the record is cataloged in roman letters and a default of "heb" if it is in Hebrew. Both Dewey and LC classification number fields are left-to-right roman alphabet fields, as is the MT or material type field.

---

[11]Susan S. Lazinger, "ALEPH: Israel's Research Library Network: Background, Evolution, and Implications for Networking in a Small Country": 283.

While the direction and script are determined at the field level in ALEPH, the language of conversation establishes both the direction and the alphabet in which records will be input and displayed. For example, if the system is in Hebrew mode, with commands and help in Hebrew, the cataloging screens will be in Hebrew, right-to-left and with the cataloging codes both displayed and input in Hebrew. Inputting data into a roman alphabet field, such as the SH, subject heading, field, requires switching to a roman alphabet language of conversation (English, in Israeli libraries), either by using a programmed control key (such as F7 for Hebrew and F6 for English) or a somewhat more complicated built-in command (alpha/h, alpha/l). Codes and commands are then switched to English, and the roman alphabet fields can be input in their natural left-to-right order within the basically right-to-left Hebrew record. When the finished record is displayed, Hebrew fields will appear on the screen from right-to-left, with the field names in Hebrew, and roman fields will appear from left-to-right, with the field names in English.

AUTHORITY CONTROL IN ALEPH

In her 1991 description of authority control in the ALEPH system and the Israeli academic library network, Lazinger wrote:

> In discussing authority control in the ALEPH network, one cannot help thinking of the opening line to the series of jokes that start, "I've got good news and bad news." The good news is that ALEPH can claim.... authority files fully linked to its cataloging records. The bad new is that, on a network-wide level, there is no authority control.[12]

Both these characteristics of authority control in ALEPH and the Israeli network are still valid as a description of the situation today, nearly six years later, although things may be about to change. In October 1996, for the first time, the Israeli academic library network came under the auspices of a network coordinator. Among the projects planned for the network are unification of network menus and commands and tightening up of authority control. It seems clear that the entire set of standards upon which the Israeli academic library network has been based—including its non-MARC format—will have to be radically changed in the next few years to a more MARC based standard. This will probably come with the implementation of the next major ALEPH software implementation, planned for about the turn of the century, which will have a GUI (Graphic User Interface) and pull-down menus to help catalogers with minimal knowledge of MARC formatting, code their records. Considerable effort will also have to be expended to convert the Israeli libraries considerable ALEPH databases of Hebrew bibliographic records to the new format. Israeli libraries will also need to develop their own version of MARC to accomodate the Israeli full-vernacular-record approach at precisely at the moment in library

---

[12]Susan S. Lazinger, "ALEPH: Israel's Research Library Network: Background, Evolution, and Implications for Networking in a Small Country": 284.

automation history when efforts are being focused on unifying all the various MARC formats worldwide into a single MARC format for all countries.

To return to the "good news," the authority file software itself, the ALEPH authority control module was released, nearly in its present form, with the earliest version of the system. Its capabilities then were far beyond any other software on the market, and even today it is impressive in the way it handles both multiscript linkage and global corrections. ALEPH authority files can be created for any type of field. These files provide for global change of any heading in all linked cataloging records. Furthermore, the cross reference structure automatically switches nonpreferred terms to the preferred term when a global change is made.[13] Users can create as many authority files as necessary. The files are defined in a parameter table of ALEPH. The authority database may be a central database (e.g., uploaded from the Library of Congress) used for reference and extraction. In addition a library can create a local database of authority headings which reflect the bibliographic records linked to each heading. As new records are cataloged and added to the database, the system automatically extracts the fields that build each authority list and opens authority records accordingly. As mentioned above, different filing procedures are available for different authority files. For a list of roman alphabet titles, for example, initial text can be suppressed by a stopword list defined in a sub-table. In addition, users may exclude part of a heading (in any alphabet) when determining its filing sequence by using the nondisplaying symbols which mark off nonfiling characters. Authority control includes cross references and defining phrases, and relationships can be "see," "related term," "broader term," and "narrower term." Cross references can be built between terms in different alphabets and languages. This gives the user the ability to search the database using a term in any defined language (e.g., English). The system retrieves all document records linked to the requested term, independent of the language or character set of the document and the language or character set of the search term.(i.e., all documents in Hebrew or English containing the search term in Hebrew script[14] or roman script).

The "bad news" is perhaps not as bad as it might be, or even as bad as it is likely to become in RLIN databases of records containing Hebrew script if problems of variant orthography (*ketiv male* and *ketiv ḥaser*) are not worked out fully, but as of this writing, authority control in the Israeli academic library network is still decentralized. In theory, rules have been established (e.g., *ketiv ḥaser* exclusively in all headings), but in practice there is inconsistency among Israel's academic libraries in their Hebrew authority records. *Ketiv ḥaser* is not always the orthography in which headings are established, both because of the difficulty of determining when to delete a *yod* or a *vav* in certain words, even for an educated native speaker of Hebrew, and because of the preference for cataloging using spellings that are familiar to the Israeli public, which spells more and more in *ketiv male*, providing as many vowels as possible to make the pronunciation of written words less a matter of guesswork.

---

[13]Susan S. Lazinger, "ALEPH: Israel's Research Library Network: Background, Evolution, and Implications for Networking in a Small Country": 285.

[14]"EXL Profile," Available at: http://www.aleph.co.il/prof.html#networks.

Elizabeth Vernon, discussing the approach to problems of Hebrew variant orthography and its implications for authority control of Hebrew script headings in sites using ALEPH software in America, notes that,

> At the ALEPH sites in the United States, the Israeli solution to the problem of Hebrew orthography by normalization to *ketiv haser* of bibliographic data was not implemented. For example, at the Jewish Theological Seminary (JTS), the spelling that appears on the item is used.... At the Ohio State University Library, according to Joseph Galron, Jewish Studies librarian, the first (and sometimes the second) word of the title is normalized to *ketiv ḥaser* with occasional cross-references from *ketiv male* to *ketiv ḥaser* as considered appropriate.[15]

The "Israeli solution," as we discussed in chapter 4: Variant Orthography is, like most of the solutions to the implementation of Hebrew in online bibliographic records in ALEPH, an attempt to institutionalize local practices which have grown up in the cataloging community of the only country in the world in which Hebrew is the national language. At the time of ALEPH's development, there already existed a large body of manual Hebrew vernacular records in its older university libraries in *ketiv ḥaser*, and so it was decided to continue the normalization of headings to this form in their automated catalogs. As the language has moved toward *ketiv male* in its written form in Israel, the opposing standard in its online catalogs has led to problems both in searching, for users who are not aware of this policy of normalization, for example, and for catalogers, who have to adhere to standards which may vary from library to library. For example, libraries treat titles differently, some of them allowing access via the normative form only and others making both forms searchable. Again, the lack of a central authority to enforce standards has led to a looseness in authority control in Israel's online catalogs which would never be tolerated in RLIN or OCLC. In the early 1980s, when Israel was trying, with limited resources, to establish an academic library network, it opted for flexibility, rather than control, leaving authority control to the discretion of individual member libraries, in order to establish a functioning network as quickly as possible. The choice of flexibility over control worked: the software was developed; ALEPH-Yissum not only continued to enhance and revise the software developed for this network, but developed into EX Libris, a company with a worldwide market; the network database continue to grow and expand; new databases are added periodically in a wide variety of disciplines, making the network not only a link between the nation's academic libraries, but also a rich resource of material in all disciplines, and especially in areas of Hebrew bibliography (e.g., Kiryat Sefer, the Index of Articles in Jewish Studies (RAMBI), and the Index to Hebrew Periodicals). While there has been some discussion of the need to create a standard file of Hebrew name authority records, little has been done so far aside from lists of Judaica uniform titles and political parties.

---

[15]Elizabeth Vernon, *Decision-Making forAutomation: Hebrew and Arabic Script Materials in the Automated Library*, Occasional Papers, no. 205 (Urbana: University of Illinois, Graduate School of Library and Information Science, 1996), p. 58.

11 Automation and Cooperation: Exchanging Machine-Readable Hebrew Cataloging, or Synthesizing the Traditions

INTRODUCTION

In the previous chapters we have presented the differences between American and Israeli cataloging practices, both manual and automated. In this chapter we will discuss the possibility to bridge the gap and exchange machine readable bibliographic records for use in the systems of both countries.

For many years Israeli libraries have made use of roman alphabet, American USMARC cataloging data from a variety of sources (LC CD-ROM products, the Israeli copy of current USMARC data, online searching abroad, etc.). Downloading (and downgrading) USMARC data to the simpler ALEPH standard used by the Israeli libraries is a relatively simple procedure. Even upgrading and converting Israeli roman character data to the standards followed by American libraries is significantly more difficult. The transfer of Hebrew data adds several levels of complexity.

In our context of Hebrew cataloging, it would appear that this exchange would be primarily a one-way arrangement, with American libraries taking advantage of Hebrew bibliographic data originating in Israel. Israel is today the place of publication of the vast majority of current Hebraica, its research libraries purchase and catalog virtually every current item of research value, and Hebraica bibliographic skills are far less of a rarity in Israel than outside Israel. Israeli libraries would also have little use for romanized or partially romanized American Hebrew bibliographic records. While Israeli academic libraries make extensive use of Library of Congress cataloging data, here has never been any interest in subscribing to the LC MARC Hebrew cataloging service, available since 1989.

Unfortunately, for reasons that were justifiable in the past, but problematic today, Israeli machine readable cataloging developed its own unique standards, which are both less specific and contain less information than the prevailing international standards. The differences are many but not insurmountable. Adler's 1987 proposal for converting data in Israel to American standards[1] did not lead to serious discussion between American and Israeli libraries (as the author had hoped) and virtually nothing has been published on the topic since. During the period 1990-1994 there was some correspondence between the Jewish National and University Library (JNUL) and the Research Libraries Group (RLG) about the possibility of uploading JNUL records into the Research Libraries Information Network (RLIN). This correspondence never got to the stage of detailed analysis of the problems involved.

There are several levels of difference which have to be overcome in order to freely exchange Israeli and American cataloging data: differences in cataloging rules, levels of detail, character sets, and treatment of bidirectional text. We will examine each of these in detail. This comparison relates to *current* Israeli practice using ALEPH version 3. The next generation version of ALEPH (ALEPH-500) which will probably be implemented in Israel in a few years is much more MARC-oriented and will have important implications which we will discuss later in this chapter.

DIFFERENCES IN CATALOGING RULES

Throughout this book we have presented the differences between American and Israeli cataloging practices. Many differences in descriptive cataloging derive from the basic "language of the cataloging agency" orientation. It is now generally accepted that international exchange of bibliographic records means that using cataloging records from different countries may carry over a certain degree of local practice and language orientation (local abbreviations, language of cataloger-supplied notes, etc.). With regard to headings, however, the situation is more complex. No American library would use an Italian record with a heading *Venezia* ... when its own headings for the same city remain *Venice*... Such differences can be overcome with an adequate authority control system which would automatically change such headings.

Hebrew headings are more problematic than non-English roman headings. Israeli records with Hebrew-only headings will never be usable as-is in American libraries which require romanized headings (although local agencies would wish to retain the Hebrew headings as additional access points). Israeli libraries are highly unlikely to add romanized access points which serve no domestic purpose. In addition, Israeli Hebrew access points are all normalized to a standard orthography (in on-access transcription, the original orthography is retained). American practice has avoided the standard orthography option, at the expense of scattering the same words with varying spellings. Creation of a multiscript (not just multilingual) authority capability would be a major step towards adapting Israeli headings to their American counterparts—both in uniformity of the Hebrew headings and in addition of the romanized forms. This would apply, of course, only to name and uniform title

---

[1] Elhanan Adler, "The Use of Israeli Machine Readable Cataloging by American Libraries: A Proposal," *Judaica Librarianship* 4 (1) (1987-1988), 23-26. This chapter is based to a large degree on the ideas appearing in this article.

headings—romanization of other, uncontrolled access points (such as titles) would still require manual intervention.

LEVEL OF DETAIL

American libraries follow the level of detail set down within the USMARC format. While some may begrudge the fine distinctions between types of similar-purpose fields (which often make no practical difference in catalog use), adherence to the standard has enforced an overwhelming degree of uniformity in American libraries.

With the inherent flexibility of the current ALEPH system, Israeli catalogers tended to think of the elements of bibliographic records in terms of their immediate use and significance and avoid what, to them, seemed to be pointless levels of detail and distinction. Standard Israeli cataloging records use field tags, but not indicators or subfield codes (other than ISBD punctuation). For example, many Israeli libraries use field code AU (=author) for the entire 1xx range of MARC tags. There are no indications of levels of detail within a field (such as the presence of a surname in an author name coded 100) or subfield codes. Mapping such a record into full MARC-level coding would require at least some manual human intervention.

Standard Israeli coding does not include all the details normally found in the preliminary fields of a standard USMARC[2] records, such as the myriad items coded in the fixed length 008 field. Some of this data is recorded elsewhere (language of the publication, four-digit publication year) but most of this information is missing from Israeli records.

CHARACTER SETS AND BIDIRECTIONAL TEXT

While the RLIN character set for Hebrew is much richer than the standard Israeli one (see chapter 8), many, if not most American RLIN Hebrew records make do with the same basic 27 characters (22 regular consonants and 5 final forms). Conversion of these characters on a one-to-one basis is a simple procedure. ALEPH, however, is also limited in the number of character sets available in a given field. A Hebrew field can contain only roman upper-case, and a roman-oriented field cannot contain Hebrew at all (compare with RLIN's ability to use multiple character sets in a single field).

Treatment of bidirectional text is even more problematic. We have shown the sophisticated procedures instituted in RLIN to allow recording bidirectional text in

---

[2]Our comparisons are made between Israeli cataloging practice and USMARC both because Israeli non-Hebrew cataloging has traditionally followed American practice and because of the extensive use of LC cataloging data in Israel. Converting Israeli data to an alternate MARC format such as UNIMARC would not be easier and would only complicate the US-Israel coordination.

logical order while displaying in correct visual order. ALEPH's bidirectional capability is much more limited and conversion of data would require some effort.

EXAMPLE

An average Israeli university ALEPH-3 cataloging record as described by Adler,[3] might consist of:

Main entry (Normalized Hebrew)
Uniform title (Normalized Hebrew)
Title, parallel title, subtitle, author statement (Exact Hebrew, separate fields)
Edition statement (Exact Hebrew)
Place, publisher, date (Exact Hebrew or roman—depending on data, separate fields)
Collation (Normalized Hebrew, divided with ISBD punctuation)
Series traced (Exact Hebrew, divided with ISBD punctuation)
Series untraced (Exact Hebrew, divided with ISBD punctuation)
Note (Hebrew, exact or normalized)
Added entry (Normalized Hebrew)
Added title (Normalized Hebrew)
Added series (Normalized Hebrew)
Personal name as subject (Normalized Hebrew or English)
Topical subject: English (LCSH, with minor changes in Judaica)
Classification (LC, with minor changes in Judaica)
ISBN (becoming more frequent in Israeli publications)
Local data

An attempt to "map" such a record into standard USMARC format would encounter the following problems:

Character set: Changing the minimal Israeli 27 character character set from one coding scheme to another should present no problems.

MARC Tags: For some fields (LC classification, ISBN, title, imprint, etc.) there is one-to-one equivalency. For others, however, the level of detail in the Israeli records is much lower. MARC distinguishes between several types of main entry, note, etc. There would have to be some manual intervention. If the transfer of data were routed through an "expert system" key words in fields could be used to make an "intelligent guess" as to the exact field type).

MARC Indicators: Many of the field indicators are unchangeable or determinable (e.g. title traced). Some would have to be manually set. Here also, it should be possible to provide computer-aided assignment in most cases.

---

[3] Elhanan Adler, "The Use of Israeli Machine Readable Cataloging by American Libraries: A Proposal."

MARC Subfield codes: The subfields of MARC tags 245 (title) and 260 (imprint) are separate fields in ALEPH and should be simple to add. Also subfield codes of fields 300 (imprint) and 4xx (series) should be reconstructable from the ISBD punctuation. Some subfield codes would have to be manually set (e.g., subdivisions under subject headings), again with computer assistance in many cases.

MARC Fixed length data fields (particularly field 008): Some of the data required can be derived from the record (e.g., language, place of publication), some can be deduced (manually) from the record (intellectual level, government publication, fiction, etc.).

Miscellaneous MARC 0xx fields: 039, 040, etc. The data required in these fields should usually be obtainable automatically.

Many of the MARC related differences will be resolved when Israeli machine-readable cataloging evolves (as we believe it must) to an Israeli MARC format. Even then, however, the following differences will still remain:

Romanization: All vernacular fields must become secondary fields (field 880) to be replaced by either systematic romanization or established English-language form. ALA/LC romanization, which requires addition of vowels, cannot by any stretch of the imagination be performed automatically by computer.

Authority control: In order for a romanized Israeli record to be used freely by American libraries, it must go through some kind of authority validation, preferably by checking against LC name authorities. Given time, it should be possible to create a Hebrew-English authority file which could also handle much of the romanization of personal and corporate access points, solving part of the previous problem.

Different practices: Within the vernacular fields themselves there are differences between American and Israeli practice, e.g. in the method of recording Jewish-era dates. These will generally have to be handled manually. In addition, a preference for title-page orthography where Israeli libraries are using normalized Hebrew may cause the need for changes within the vernacular access-point fields (straight title-page form in fields where Israeli libraries are using normalized Hebrew may often require reference to the work itself).

A standard Israeli Hebrew record would require, therefore, extensive upgrading and editing in order to make it usable to the American library community. The questions remaining are who should do this upgrading, how, and at what cost.

POSSIBLE SOLUTIONS

1. On-demand conversion: The Hebrew cataloging of major Israeli Hebraica libraries could be made available to American libraries via a suitable online interface. The American library would search the Israeli library's catalog and retrieve the desired

record via an interface which would do the mechanical conversion as far as possible. The cataloger would then add the required conversion decisions (those which could not be machine made) and add all the romanized fields needed.

2. Load all the Hebrew cataloging of these libraries (the JNUL and others) into a central American file. The data would remain vernacular only, but would be format-converted as far as possible. Libraries would be able to retrieve and enrich these records as above, the difference being that the conversion stage (and perhaps some of the "intelligent" conversion decisions) would be made centrally, in advance.

3. Totally convert such data to USMARC standard, including the addition of romanized fields. The data could then be easily uploaded into a bibliographic utility such as RLIN. The conversion and upgrading could be assisted by an authority file with references from Hebrew (character) names to their Library of Congress Name Authority (LCNA) equivalents. Such a project would require significant investment in professional staff and could only be undertaken at the national level. The logical place to do this upgrading would be in Israel, but Israeli libraries would be hard pressed to justify the expenditure in adding bibliographic data which is foreign or not needed by their users. The resultant record would be in full USMARC format, usable by American libraries as "copy cataloging" via one or more of the American cataloging utilities, no different from an original cataloging record input by an American participating library. The effort involved (most of which is not needed from an internal Israeli standpoint) would have to be justified by external funding (at least at the initial stage). Ultimately it should be seen as the price of Israel's participation in the international bibliographic community.

SUMMARY

Israeli Hebrew cataloging could and should be available to American libraries. The problems of computer encoding differences will become less as Israeli libraries migrate from their unique ALEPH format to a format closer to international MARC standards. Minor differences in cataloging practice can perhaps be ignored or overlooked, however the need for romanized access points in American Hebrew cataloging will require both bilingual authority files and manual intervention.

12 Hebrew Cataloging Online: Present Innovations, Future Implications

In the conclusion to the 1996 report on her survey of Hebrew and Arabic cataloging in the United States, Vernon summarizes the options which have been chosen by libraries both in the United States and other countries with regard to automation of records for these materials:

1. The major library installations providing local access to Hebrew in their original script without parallel romanization are in the Middle East. For these institutions, the provision of data in Hebrew or Arabic script was an absolute requirement, which overrode both development costs of customized library systems and ease in international data sharing (although local data sharing was significantly enhanced in Israel by the uniform acceptance of ALEPH, with its non-MARC format).

2. Outside the Middle East, there are only a few institutions providing access to Hebrew or Arabic collections in the original script without parallel romanized data. Examples of institutions which provide such access to Hebrew collections are the Jewish Public Library of Montreal, two ALEPH installations in Spain, and the automated British Library Catalogue. The first is not just a research library, but also a public library, where specialized knowledge, such as that of romanization rules, cannot always be expected of patrons. Furthermore, the Jewish Public Library of Montreal specifically chose to implement nonroman script-only cataloging in order to avoid having to input romanized data in addition to Hebrew script data, and the British Library material with Hebrew script access was implemented only for retrospective conversion of the the main catalog, and not for retrospective conversion either of the Hebrew catalog or for current Hebrew cataloging, which still is done manually.

3. Most automated research libraries outside of the Middle East have online catalogs that provide access only in romanized form, which allows these libraries to

provide access to Hebrew bibiliographic data within the framework of their general library automation infrastructure.

4. Only a handful of libraries within the United States doing Hebrew cataloging currently have Hebrew script support available in the online catalog for both display and searching (Jewish Theological Seminary of America, University of Pennsylvania's Center for Judaic Studies, Ohio State University's Jewish and Middle East Studies Libraries, Yeshiva University) or for display only (Brandeis University). At the University of Pennsylvania and Ohio State University, ALEPH catalogs are provided in parallel to the main university OPACs which do not yet support Hebrew script.[1]

The conclusions she reaches with regard to the implications of the Hebrew cataloging options chosen by the institutions she surveyed are as follows:

1. Since a high percentage of libraries doing combination romanized/Hebrew script cataloging in the United States are located in institutions of higher Jewish learning, one might infer that the motivation to provide local access to Hebrew bibliographic data derives from institutional cultures, where a priority has been placed on providing local access in Hebrew script because Hebrew collections and the Hebrew script are central to the educational mission of the institution.

2. A few other university and research libraries in the United States do combination romanized/nonroman script cataloging in RLIN for some or all of their Hebrew materials but provide only the romanized data in their online catalogs (e.g., Library of Congress, New York Public Library, New York University, Stanford University, Universityof Michigan, and Yale University). The implication of this choice is that these institutions have decided that the projected future benefits of the nonroman data being added to their records outweigh the present additional cataloging costs.

3. Although much combination romanized/nonroman script cataloging has been carried out in the past decade for Hebrew, the vast majority of patron search transactions in online catalogs in the Western world continue to be done in roman script because of the small number of libraries with online catalogs that support the Hebrew scripts for searching.[2]

With regard to the potential effects of the implementation of Unicode in USMARC on future Hebrew cataloging choices by American libraries, there are several factors to keep in mind. First, there are four options for implementating Unicode in USMARC: no implementation; full implementation, replacing the entire USMARC character set with Unicode; partial implementation, which would involve

---

[1] Elizabeth Vernon, *Decision-Making for Automation: Hebrew and Arabic Script Materials in the Automated Library,* Occasional Papers, no. 205 (Urbana: University of Illinois, Graduate School of Library and Information Science, 1996), p. 71-73.

[2] Elizabeth Vernon, *Decision-Making for Automation: Hebrew and Arabic Script Materials in the Automated Library,* p. 73.

continuing the ALA extended character set for roman script data and use Unicode only for nonroman script data; and parallel implementation, by mapping USMARC data to both the ALA and the Unicode character sets and allowing the USMARC record to be output as either of the two. However, as Vernon points out, the effect of Unicode implementation on Hebrew cataloging decisions in the United States may be less far-reaching than proponents of nonroman script cataloging would wish:

> The implementation of Unicode would only resolve the technical issues of hardware and software vis-a-vis the Arabic and Hebrew (and other nonroman) scripts. While Unicode represents an important step forward in multiscript automation, it will not solve all of the problems of the automation of nonroman script bibliographic data. In particular, unless there is a change in the USMARC requirements of romanized data for core fields, catalogers will still have to key some fields more than once, as this is unrelated to the character set used.[3]

Double keying, in the opinion of some of the central figures involved in nonroman cataloging in the United States today, is not really the major problem for catalogers of Hebrew materials. RLIN's Joan Aliprand, for example, pointed out that the *real* difficulty for American catalogers of Hebrew is not the double keying necessitated by adding the Hebrew fields, which, after all, are copied from the title page of the item in hand, but rather the romanization they need to do for the parallel romanized fields.[4] As discussed in chapter 3, even with the implementation of a single system of romanization throughout the United States, and in spite of LC's best efforts to codify and clarify romanization using ALA/LC tables, the very nature of Hebrew makes romanization an inexact and difficult exercise. The lack of expressed vowels, the shifts in pronunciation of the same word with various prefixed articles and after certain consonants demands a level of familiarity with the fine points of Hebrew grammar that is not reasonable to expect of a Hebrew cataloger in the United States.

Furthermore, in spite of implementation of Hebrew in RLIN and in several local systems in America, the underlying reason that romanization is almost certainly destined to stay a part of the American Hebrew cataloging scene is that the structure of USMARC requires it. The Alternate Graphic Representation is just that, an alternate way to present the required romanized data defined in USMARC, and since the dominant language of the United States is English, it is highly unlikely that anyone in America is ever likely to press for a restructuring of USMARC to accomodate an entirely Hebrew record. Even in the unlikely event that such a restructuring of USMARC ever occurred, no USMARC field will ever be "entirely" Hebrew (unlike fields in ALEPH, in which even the field codes are in Hebrew in Hebrew records) as there will always be USMARC tags and subfield pairs in ASCII.

Prophesy is always a risky undertaking, but in summing up the present state of Hebrew cataloging in the two centers—Israel and the United States—the authors

---

[3]Elizabeth Vernon, *Decision-Making for Automation: Hebrew and Arabic Script Materials in the Automated Library,* p. 70.

[4]Joan Aliprand, Private Communication, 26 January, 1997.

would like to present a scenario of a possible future. Two diametrically opposed trends appear to be increasingly dominating the growing global information network of which Hebrew cataloging records are a subset. On one hand, there seems to be a visible trend toward unification of standards worldwide. Unicode is one example. The increasing use of LC/ALA romanization of Hebrew, even in countries in which English is not the official language, such as Israel (in most of the country's university libraries, for records requiring romanization, for instance, for Israeli corporate bodies, such as Universitah ha-Ivrit bi-Yerushalayim, in non-Hebrew publications), is another. Efforts are underway to move toward unification of all the national MARC formats, and even maverick Israel is probably heading toward eventual conversion of its eccentric alphabetic ALEPH field codes to numeric, universally-recognized MARC codes (although the full vernacular Hebrew record—which is just as certain to remain a part of the Israeli landscape because it represents the national language as romanization is certain to remain a part of the American landscape for the same reason—will always require a customized, Israeli version of MARC).

At the same time, the spectacular and snowballing growth of the Internet, and particularly the World Wide Web, as the vehicle which brings together all the popular information and an increasingly large segment of the scholarly, controlled information of the world into a single, universally accessible global network, has been made possible by communication protocols which override differences in standards. Library catalogs from a wide variety of countries, programmed in a wide variety of software using equally widely varied cataloging standards, have been made accessible and searchable with a unified set of commands. This has been done by interfacing them with theTCP/IP and Z39.50 protocols of the WWW. For example, the experimental Web-accessible catalogs of the University of Haifa and the Bloomfield Library of the Humanities and Social Sciences of The Hebrew University of Jerusalem (the only two catalogs of the ILAN ALEPH-based Israeli Academic Library Network accessible on the Web at the time of this writing), are composed of records cataloged in the 3.2 non-graphic version of ALEPH and then run through a program which renders them viewable using the graphic interface to the Web.

Another example of technology used in a somewhat unorthodox way to override a lack of standardization, this time in end-user search terms, can be seen in cross-reference structures in some of the files in the Ilan network. A recent search by one of the authors of this book on the subject term "Israel" in one of the university catalogs turned up an astonishing array of "see from" references in its linked authority file, including terms such as "Holy Land," "Erez Israel," and even the common misspelling of the country's name, "Isreal." The only explanation for such a bewildering list of "see from" references, many of which had never been used in any publication anywhere except as a typographical error, was a rather touching attempt to link the correct term to any possible incorrect term an inexperienced user might come up with when trying to locate documents about Israel. Perhaps a similar approach to alleviating user confusion about spelling of romanized headings in a global network— i.e., adding every conceivable form, from alternate romanization systems and likely user misspellings alike, to linked authority records, which would then retrieve all the records with correctly-romanized headings no matter which of the incorrect romanizations the user input—may be worth considering in the future.

Finally, side by side with the seemingly opposed trends toward increasing worldwide standardization on the one hand and technological advances which provide access to materials in non-standarized formats and software on the other, is the refusal of small, specialized classification systems of Hebraica and Judaica to "wither away." Both Weine and Elazar have recently been published in new, revised editions, for example, indicating (as do the many requests for information about these systems on the listserv *Hasafran*) that there still is a considerable demand for them in synagogue and parochial school Judaica libraries, in spite of the virtually universal adoption of LC classification in America's academic libraries.

There can be no doubt that Judaica librarianship, which after all is a part of the larger library community, will be swept up with all its special problems and considerations into the tide of change which is moving the world toward a Global Information Infrastructure. The need for exchanging machine-readable Hebrew cataloging within this infrastructure has already moved the two centers of Hebrew cataloging toward synthesizing the traditions. Hebrew capability is part of the American bibliographic network reality, and MARC will most likely become part of the Israeli bibliographic network scene by the end of the century. Library of Congress Subject Headings are used today in most Israeli academic libraries and the ALEPH database of Hebrew Uniform Headings is available to any American Judaica library that cares to telnet to it. Israeli and American catalogers of Hebrew materials share opinions, argue about issues, and exchange information informally and daily in *Hasafran*, and formally in print in *Judaica Librarianship*. Differences remain, problems persist, but networking, both of the formal and informal variety, has given the practitioners of the two traditions free access to each other and has changed both traditions in the process. Wherever Judaica librarianship is heading, whatever the ultimate solutions to the technical and philosophical problems of cataloging Hebrew materials, the online environment has joined the two centers irrevocably, and it is together they will move forward into the next century.

BIBLIOGRAPHY

Adler, Elhanan. "An On-Line Thesaurus for Information Retrieval." In *Proceedings of the International Conference on Literary and Linguistic Computing, Israel, April 22-27, 1979.* Ed. by Zvi Malachi. Tel Aviv: The Katz Research Institute for Hebrew Literature, Tel-Aviv University, 1979, 191-95.

Adler, Elhanan, editor. ["Cataloging Decisions and Rule Changes in Israeli University Libraries."] *Yad Lakore* 25 (January 1991), 69-74; in Hebrew.

Adler, Elhanan. ["Development of a Hebrew Thesaurus for Periodical Indexing."] *Alon ASMI* 63 (3) (February 1976), 65-68, 99.

Adler, Elhanan. "Hebrew Cataloging and the Computer—The View from Israel." *Information Technology and Libraries* (September 1982), 238-45.

Adler, Elhanan. ["Implementation of the Library of Congress System in the Library of the University of Haifa."] *Yad Lakore* 14 (November 1974), 64-86; in Hebrew.

Adler, Elhanan. "Judaica Cataloging: The Hebrew and Bibliographic and Israeli Traditions." *Judaica Librarianship* 6 (1-2) (Spring 1991-Winter 1992): 8-12.

Adler, Elhanan. "The State of the Art in Hebraica Library Automation: American and Israeli Standards and Practices." In *Hebrew Studies: Papers Presented at a Colloquium on Resources for Hebraica in Europe Held at the School of Oriental and African Studies, University of London, 11-13 September 1989/11-13 Elul 5749.* Edited by Diana Rowlands Smith and Peter Shmuel Salinger. British Library Occasional Papers 13. London: The British Library, 1991, 210-19.

Adler, Elhanan, "The Use of Israeli Machine Readable Cataloging by American Libraries: A Proposal." *Judaica Librarianship* 4 (1) (1987-1988), 23-26.

Adler, Elhanan, and Aviva Shichor. *Ha-ḳitlug: sefer ʻeḳronot ye-kelalim.* Jerusalem: Center for Public Libraries in Israel, 1978.

Adler, Elhanan, and Aviva Shichor. *Ha-kitlug: sefer ʻeḳronot ye-kelalim.* 2d ed. expanded and adapted to AACR2. Jerusalem: Center for Public Libraries in Israel, 1984.

Adler, Elhanan, Aviva Shichor, and Rochelle Kedar. *Ha-kitlug: sefer'ekronot ve-kelalim.* 3d ed., expanded and adapted to AACR II], 2d rev. (1988). Jerusalem: Center for Libraries in Israel, 1995.

"Ha-Aḳademiyah la-lashon ha-'ivrit." *Kelalei ha-ta'atik mi-ketav' ivri li-ketav latini.* (offprint from *Zikhronot ha-Akademiyah* III-IV). Jerusalem: ha-Aḳademiyah, 1957.

"Ha-Aḳademiyah la-lashon ha-'ivrit." ["Rules For the Unpointed Script."] *Leshon-enu la-'am*, maḥzor 21, kuntres 6 (1969); in Hebrew.

Aliprand, Joan M. "Hebrew on RLIN." *Judaica Librarianship* 3 (1-2) (1986-1987), 5-16.

Aliprand, Joan M. "Hebrew on RLIN—An Update." *Judaica Librarianship* 5 (Spring 1989-Winter 1990), 12-20.

Aliprand, Joan M. "Linkage in USMARC Bibliographic Records." *Cataloging & Classification Quarterly* 16 (1) (1993), 5-37.

Aliprand, Joan M. "Linking of Alternate Graphic Representation in USMARC Authority Records." *Cataloging & Classification Quarterly* 18 (1) (1993), 27-62.

Aliprand, Joan M. "Nonroman Scripts in the Bibliographic Environment." *Encyclopedia of Library and Information Science*, v. 56. New York: Marcel Dekker, 1995, 260-83.

Aliprand, Joan M. "Nonroman Scripts in the Bibliographic Environment." *Information Technology and Libraries* 11 (2) (June 1992), 105-119.

American Library Association. *A.L.A Cataloging Rules for Author and Title Entries.* Chicago: American Library Association, 1949.

American Library Association. *Catalog Rules: Author and Title Entries.* American Edition. Chicago: American Library Association, 1908.

American Library Association. *Catalog Rules: Author and Title Entries.* Chicago: American Library Association, 1941.

American National Standard Romanization of Hebrew. New York: American National Standards Institute, c1975.

Anglo-American Cataloging Rules, North American Text. Chicago: American Library Association, 1967.

Anglo-American Cataloguing Rules. 2d ed. Chicago: American Library Association, 1978.

Anglo-American Cataloguing Rules. 2d ed., 1988 revision. Ottawa: Canadian Library Association, 1988.

"ANSI Z39 Romanization Standards." *Bulletin of the American Society for Information Science* 3 (5) (June 1977), 35.

Baker, Zachary M. [Review of]: Brisman, Shimeon. *A History and Guide to Judaic Encyclopedias and Lexicons. Judaica Librarianship* 4 (2) (Spring 1988-Winter 1989), 140-43.

Bartolocci, Giulio. *Kiryat sefer. Bibliotheca magna rabbinica de scriptoribus, et scriptis hebraicis, ordine alphabetico Hebraice et Latine digestis.* Romae: ex typographia Sacrae congregationis de propaganda fide, 1675-1693. 4 vols.

Bass, Shabbetai. *Sifte yeshenim.* Amsterdam: David Tartas, 1680.

Ben-Yaakov, Jacob. *Otsar ha-sefarim.* Vilna: Romm, 1880.

Ben Yehuda, Meir. ["Transcription in the Hebrew Catalogue."] *Yad Lakore* 9 (July 1968): 85-92; in Hebrew.

Berger, Pearl, Sharona R. Wachs. "Catalog Department." *Judaica Librarianship* 1 (2) (Spring 1984), 67-69.

Bible. O.T. Apocrypha. 1958. [Apocrypha with commentary by E. S. Artom]. Tel-Aviv: Yavneh, 1958-1967. 9 vols.; in Hebrew.

Bibliography of the Hebrew Book 1473-1960 [CD-ROM]. Jerusalem: EPI/Electronic Pubs. Intl. and the Institute for Hebrew Bibliography, 1994.

Biella, Joan, and Rachel Simon. "Hayah noten ba-hem simanim: Hebrew Abbreviations, Chiefly Rabbinic, and their ALA/LC Romanization." *Judaica Librarianship* 9(1-2) (Spring 1994-Winter 1995), 75-82.

Bloch, Joshua. "The Classification of Jewish Literature in the New York Public Library." In *Studies in Jewish Bibliography and Related Subjects in Memory of Abraham Solomon Freidus.* New York: Alexander Kohut Memorial Foundation, 1929, 50-77.

Bourvine, Yehavi, and Hank Nussbacher (1993, May 3). *Hebrew Support Requirements for Use in TCP/IP Networks*, vol. 9, March 1993. *ILAN-H Discussion in and About Hebrew in the Network* [Online].

Brandhorst, Ted. "ANSI Z39 Romanization Standards and 'Reversibility': A Dialog to Arrive at a Policy." *Journal of the American Society for Information Science* 30 (1) (January 1979), 55-59.

Brisman, Shimeon. *A History and Guide to Judaic Bibliography.* New York: KTAV; Cincinnati: Hebrew Union College, 1977. (His Jewish Research Literature, 1).

British Museum. *Catalogue of the Hebrew Books in the Library of the British Museum,* [comp. Joseph Zedner]. London: British Museum, Dept. of Oriental Printed Books and Manuscripts, 1867.

Brunswick, Sheldon R. "Book Review" of Michael Yizhar, *Bibliography of Hebrew Publications on the Dead Sea Scrolls. Jewish Social Studies* 31 (July 1969), 220-21.

Brunswick, Sheldon. "Book Review" of Elazar, David H., and Elazar, Daniel J., *A Classification System for Libraries of Judaica. Jewish Social Studies* 32 (July 1970), 224-25.

Bunis, David. *The Historical Development of Judezmo Orthography.* Working Papers in Yiddish and East European Jewish Studies, 2. New York: Max Weinreich Center for Advanced Jewish Studies, 1974.

Buxtorf, Johannes. *Bibliotheca Rabbinica.* Basileae: Typis C. Waldkirchi, impensis L. Koenig, 1613.

Cataloging Service Bulletin 16 (Spring 1982), 39.

Central Cataloging Service Integrated Subject Headings List. Los Angeles, CA: Sinai Temple Library, July 1989.

Classification for Judaica. Jerusalem: Hebrew University, Jewish National and University Library, 1964.

Classification Schedules for Printed, Microcopy and Phonorecord Materials in the Reference Department. 2d ed. New York: The New York Public Library, 1955.

Clews, John. "Coded Character Sets in Hebrew Library Automation." In *Hebrew Studies: Papers Presented at a Colloquium on Resources for Hebraica in Europe* ... Edited by Diana Rowland Smith and Peter Shmuel Salinger. London: The British Library, 1991, 220-31.

Computerized Bibliographic Record Actions (CoBRA). *Research and Development for Libraries in Europe.* March 1995. (Its Fact Sheet 1).

Cutter, Charles A. *Rules for a Dictionary Catalog.* 4th ed., rewritten. Washington, D.C.: Government Printing Office, 1904.

Deinard, Ephraim. *Koheleth America: Catalogue of Hebrew Books Printed in America from 1735-1925.* St. Louis, MO: Moinester Printing, 1926.

Dewey, Melvil. *Abridged Dewey Decimal Classification and Relative Index.* 11th ed. Albany, Forest Press, 1979.

Dewey, Melvil. *Dewey Decimal Classification and Relative Index.* 19th ed. Albany: Forest Press, 1979.

Dewey, Melvil. *Dewey Decimal Classification.* 20th ed. Albany: Forest Press, 1989.

Dewey, Melvil. *Dewey Decimal Classification and Relative Index.* 21st ed. Albany: Forest Press, A Division of OCLC Computer Library Center, 1996.

Dewey, Melvil. *Taḳtsir ha-miyun ha-'esroni.* Ed. Issachaar Joel, trans. Lea Shalem and Hanan Wellisch. 3d rev. ed. Jerusalem: Histadrut, Jewish National and University Library, and Hebrew University Graduate Library School, 1965 (Hebrew).

Dewey, Melvil. *Taḳtsir ha-miyun ha-'esroni.* Trans. Lea Shalem from the English 10th ed. 4th rev. ed. Jerusalem: Center for Public Libraries in Israel, 1976. 2 vols. (Hebrew).

Dewey, Melvil. *Taḳtsir ha-miyun ha-'esroni.* 5th ed. Jerusalem: Center for Public Libraries in Israel, 1983 (Hebrew).

Dienstag, Claire. "Modifications Made by the New York Public Library to RLIN Hebraica Records," *Judaica Librarianship* 8 (1-2) (1993-1994), 27-30/.

Eilts, John. "Non-Roman Script Materials in North American Libraries: Automation and International Exchange." In *61st IFLA General Conference—Conference Proceedings—August 20-25,1995.* http://www.nlc-bnc.ca/ifla/IV/ifla61/61-eilj.htm. [figures taken from manuscript version provided by the author].

Elazar, David H., and Daniel J. Elazar. *A Classification Scheme for Libraries of Judaica.* Detroit: Wayne State University Libraries, 1968.

Elazar, David H., and Daniel J. Elazar. *A Classification Scheme for Libraries of Judaica.* 2d ed. Ramat Gan, Israel: Turtledove, 1979, c1978.

Encyclopedia Judaica, vols. 1-X. Berlin: 1928-34. Table, vol. I, xx.

Encyclopaedia Judaica. Jerusalem: Keter, 1971.

Etsel, I. ["The History of the Jews as Given in the Dewy (!) Decimal Classification"]. Yad Lakore 13 (March 1974), 201-207; in Hebrew.

Friedberg, Chaim D. *Bet 'eḳed sefarim.* Antwerp: 1928-1931.

Friedberg, Chaim D. *Bet 'eḳed sefarim.* 2d ed. Tel-Aviv: 1950-1956.

Frischer, Rita C. Cover letter of Central *Cataloging Service Bulletin* No. 18. Los Angeles: Sinai Temple [Library], July 28, 1989, Section D.

Fürst, Julius. *Bibliotheca Judaica: Bibliographisches Handbuch der gesammten Judischen Literatur.* Theil 1-3. Leipzig: Verlag von Wilhelm Engelmann,1849-1863.

Galron-Goldschlaeger, Joseph. *Library of Congress Subject Headings in Jewish Studies.* 1st ed. [s.l. :s.n.], 1989.

Galron-Goldschlaeger, Joseph. *Library of Congress Subject Headings in Jewish Studies.* 2d enlarged and updated ed. Bexley, Ohio: The author, 1991. 2 vols.

Galron-Goldschlaeger, Joseph. *Library of Congress Subject Headings in Jewish Studies.* 3d enlarged and updated ed. New York: Association of Jewish Libraries, 1992. 2 vols.

Galron-Goldschlaeger, Joseph. *Library of Congress Subject Headings in Jewish Studies.* 5th revised edition. New York: AJL, 1996. 2 vols.

Galron-Goldschlaeger, Joseph. *Library of Congress Subject Headings in Jewish Studies.* Available: http://aleph.lib.ohio-state.edu/www/lcsh.html.

Galron-Goldschlaeger, Joseph. *Library of Congress Subject Headings in Jewish Studies—1996.* Available: http://aleph.lib.ohio-state.edu/www/lcsh-new96.html.

"General Principles for the Conversion of One Written Language into Another (ISO/TC46 [Sec. 426] 697 [Rev.])." *Journal of Documentation* 21 (1) (March 1965), 15-16.

Goldman, E. A., et. al. "A 'Computer-Compatible' Semitic Alphabet." *Hebrew Union College Annual* 42 (1971), 251-78.

Hamdy, M. Nabil. *The Concept of Main Entry as Represented in the Anglo-American Cataloging Rules.* Littleton, CO, Libraries Unlimited, 1973.

Harvard University Library. *Catalogue of Hebrew Books.* Cambridge, MA: Harvard University Press, 1968. 6 vols.—Supplement I, 1972. 3 vols. *Appendix: Judaica in the Houghton Library* (in Supplement I, Vol. 1: Classified Listing).

Harvard University Library. *Judaica.* Cambridge, MA: Harvard University Press, 1971.

"Hebrew and Yiddish" [Romanization table]. *Cataloging Service,* Bulletin 118 (Summer 1976), 63.

Hebrew Subject Headings. Developed by the Hebrew Classification and Cataloging Department, Wurzweiler Central Library, Bar-Ilan University: Shlomo Rotenberg, Shifra Liebman, Gita Hoffman, Sara Schacham, David Wilk. Ramat Gan, Israel: June 1992. 2 vols.

Hebrew Subject Headings: Additions and Charges, July 1992-February 1993. Developed by the Hebrew Classification and Cataloging Department, Wurzweiler Central Library, Bar-IlanUniversity. Ramat Gan, Israel: February 1993.

Hebrew Union College—Jewish Institute of Religion. Library. *Dictionary Catalog of the Klau Library, Cincinnati.* Boston: G. K. Hall, 1964. 32 vols.

Hebrew University of Jerusalem. *Library of Congress Classification for Judaica.* Jerusalem: 1982.

Heilprin, Jehiel. *Seder meḥabrim ye-seder sefarim.* Karlsruhe: Johann Friedrich Cornelius Stern, 1769 (third part of his *Seder ha-dorot*).

Hoffman, Gita, et. al. "Hebrew Subject Headings: Development and Implementation at Bar-Ilan University." *Judaica Librarianship* 6 (1-2) (Spring 1991-Winter 1992), 24-37.

Hovne, Clara. "Indexing a Classified Catalog." *Library Resources and Technical Services* 14 (Fall 1970), 546-52.

Index to Hebrew Periodicals. Haifa: University of Haifa Library, 1977- ; in Hebrew.

International Federation for Documentation. *Miyun ʿesroni universali.* Added t.p. Universal Decimal Classification. Tel Aviv: ha-Merkaz la-meda tekhnologi u mada'i, 1969; (International Federation for Documentation [FID] #445).

ISBD (M): *International Standard Bibliographic Description for Monographic Publications.* London: International Federation of Library Associations and Institutions, Committee on Cataloguing, 1974.

International Organization for Standardization. *Information Processing—8-Bit Single-Byte Coded Graphic Character Sets, Part 8: Latin/Hebrew Alphabet.* ISO 8859-8, 1988.

International Organization for Standardization. *Recommendation R 259: Transliteration of Hebrew.* [Switzerland]: ISO, 1962.

Jewish Encyclopedia. New York: Funk & Wagnalls, 1901-1905. Table, vol. II (1902), ix.

Jewish Library Association of Greater Philadelphia. *Subject Headings for a Judaica Library.* 2d ed. Philadelphia: Division of Community Services of Gratz College, 1969.

Jewish Library Association of Greater Philadelphia. *Subject Headings for a Judaica Library.* 3d ed. [s.l.]: Distributed by Synagogue, School, and Center Division, Association of Jewish Libraries, 1972; Addenda 1975.

Jewish National and University Library. *Classification for Judaica, as Used in the Judaica Department of the Jewish National and University Library.* Jerusalem: JNUL, 1964.

Kaganoff, Nathan M. "LC Classification System." *AJL Convention 5, New York. Proceedings.* New York: AJL, 1970, 34-36.

Katchen, Rosalie. "Hebraica Authority Control at Brandeis." *Judaica Librarianship* 8 (1-2) (Spring 1993-Winter 1994), 56-60.

Katchen, Rosalie. "Hebrew Online: Current Issues and Future Concerns: A View from the Field." *Judaica Librarianship* 5 (Spring 1989-Winter 1990), 22-25.

Katchen, Rosalie (1994, October 31). Naco Hebraica Funnel. *Hasafran* [Online]. Available: e-mail: hasafran@lists.acs.ohio-state.edu.

Katchen, Rosalie. "Use or Non-Use of Parallel Linking Fields in RLIN for Hebrew-Script Access Points." *Judaica Librarianship* 8(1-2) (1993-1994), 31-32.

Kiryat Sefer. Jerusalem: Jewish National and University Library, 1924- .

Kuperman, Aaron Wolf. "Hebrew Word Processing." *Judaica Librarianship* 3 (1-2) (1986-1987), 17-21.

Kurland, Mildred, and Mae Weine. *Subject Headings for a Judaica Library.* 4th ed. [s.l.]: Distributed by Synagogue, School and Center Division of the Association of Jewish Libraries, 1982.

Lazinger, Susan. "ALEPH: Israel's Research Library Network: Background, Evolution, and Implications for Networking in a Small Country." *Information Technology & Libraries* 10 (4) (1991), 275-91.

Lazinger, Susan, and Judith Levi. "Multiple Non-Roman Scripts in ALEPH—Israel's Research Library Network." *Library Hi-Tech* 14 (1) (1996), 111-16.

Lehnus, Donald J. *A Comparison of Panizzi's 91 Rules and the AACR of 1967.* Urbana: University of Illinois at Urbana-Champaign, Graduate School of Library Science, 1972. (University of Illinois Graduate School of Library Science Occasional Papers, no. 105)

Leikind, Miriam. *Library Classification System.* [6th ed.]. Cleveland, OH: The Temple Library, [1967+].

Lepelstat, Sandy, "Weine Classification Scheme for Judaica Libraries: Pros and Cons." *AJL Bulletin* 16 (1) (Spring 1981), 7.

Lerner, Heidi G. "A Look at Hebraica Cataloging in the United States: Access Versus Cost." *Cataloging & Classification Quarterly* 17 (1/2) (1993), 115-31.

Lerner, Heidi G. "Current Practices and Standards of Cataloging in RLIN, "*Judaica Librarianship* 8(1-2) (1993-1994), 25-26.

Levi, Judith. "ALEPH: An Online Real-Time Integrated Library System." *Judaica Librarianship* 1 (2) (Spring 1984), 58-63.

Levi, Reuven. *'Iḳare ha-ḳitlug: sefer 'ezer la-safran.* Tel-Aviv: Mifale Tarbut ve-hinukh, 1958.

Library of Congress. *A Catalog of Books Represented by Library of Congress Printed Cards Issued to July 31, 1942.* Paterson, NJ: Rowman and Littlefield, 1963. 167 vols.

Library of Congress, *National Union Catalog, 1953-1957.* Paterson, NJ: Rowman and Littlefield, 1961.

Library of Congress. *National Union Catalog, 1963-1967.* Ann Arbor, MI: J. W. Edward, 1969.

Library of Congress. *Rules for Descriptive Cataloging in the Library of Congress (Adopted by the American Library Association).* Washington, D.C.: Library of Congress, Descriptive Cataloging Division, 1949.

Lipetz, Ben Ami. "Standards for Romanization of Languages of Languages That Use Non-Roman Alphabets." *Bulletin of the American Society for Information Science,* 35.

Maher, Paul. *Hebraica Cataloging: A Guide to ALA/LC Romanization and Descriptive Cataloging.* Washington, D.C.: Cataloging Distribution Service, Library of Congress, 1987.

Maimon, Zwi. ["General Catalog or Catalog by Language."] *Yad Lakore* 4 (September 1956-March 1957), 128-29; in Hebrew.

Malinconico, S. Michael, and Walter R. Grutchfield. "Vernacular Scripts in the NYPL Automated Bibliographic Control System." *Journal of Library Automation* 10 (September 1977), 205-255.

Maunsell, Andrew. *The First Part of the Catalogue of English Printed Bookes ...* London: 1595.

Merkaz ha-hadrakhah le-sifriyot be-yisra'el. *Otsar munhei miftuah,* experimental ed., Rochelle Kedar, ed. Jerusalem: ha-Merkaz, 1996.

Mif 'al ha-bibliyografyah ha-'ivrit. *Hoveret le-dugmah.* Jerusalem: 1963 (mimeographed).

Mif 'al ha-bibliyografyah ha-'ivrit. *Hoveret le-dugmah [Specimen Brochure].* Jerusalem: 1964.

"Modification of RLIN Hebraica Records: A Cataloging Workshop." *Judaica Librarianship* 8 (1-2) (1993-1994), 25-35.

Naveh, Peninah. ["In the Workshop of the Hebrew Encyclopedia."] *Yad Lakore* 4 (January-July 1956), 36-37; in Hebrew.

New York Public Library. Reference Department. *Dictionary Catalog of the Jewish Collection.* Boston: G. K. Hall, 1960.14 vols.—*First Supplement,* 1975. 8 vols.

New York Public Library. Research Libraries. *Classification Schedules for Printed, Microcopy and Phonorecord Materials in the Reference Department.* 2d ed. New York: NYPL, 1955.

New York Public Library. Research Libraries. *Dictionary Catalog of the Research Libraries.* New York: NYPL, 1972-1981.

New York Public Library. Research Libraries. *Hebrew-Character Title Catalog of the Jewish Collection.* Boston: G. K. Hall, 1981. 4 vols.

New York Public Library. Research Libraries. *Hebrew-Character Title Catalog of the Jewish Collection.* Boston: G. K. Hall, 1981. 4 vols.

["On the Order of Entries in the Encyclopedia and on Editorial Policy on Spelling and Transcription."] *ha-Entsiklopediyah ha-'ivrit*, vol. 1, Added t.p.: Encyclopaedia Hebraica. Tel Aviv: Encylopedia Publishing, 1949, col. 39-46; in Hebrew.

Oppenheimer, Hana. *Targilim be-kitlug.* Jerusalem: [s.n.], 1961.

Oppenheimer, Hana. *Targilim be-kitlug.* Jerusalem: [s.n.], 1963,

Oppenheimer, Hana. *Targilim be-kitlug.* Proofread ed. Jerusalem: [s.n.], 1966.

Oppenheimer, Hana. *Targilim be-kitlug.* New ed., adapted to the Anglo-American Cataloging Rules. Jerusalem: [s.n.], 1974.

Oxford University. Bodleian Library. *Catalogus Librorum Hebraeorum in Bibliotheca Bodleiana,* [ed.] M. Steinschneider. 1st ed., 1852-1860. Zweite (Faksimile) Auflage. Berlin: Welt-Verlag, 1931. 3 vols.

Oxford University. Bodleian Library. *A Concise Catalogue of the Hebrew Printed Books in the Bodleian Library,* by A. E. Cowley. Oxford: The Clarendon Press, 1929.

Palestine Government. *Transliteration for Arabic and Hebrew into English ...* Jerusalem: Goldberg's Press, 1931.

Panizzi, Antonio. "Rules for the Compilation of the Catalogue." In British Museum. *The Catalogue of Printed Books in the British Museum.* London: 1841.

Posner, Marcia. "At Last Elazar." *AJL Bulletin* 16 (1) (Spring 1981), 15-16.

Poulain, Jean. "The Transliteration of Hebrew Characters." *Unesco Bulletin for Libraries* XV (6) (November-December 1961), 329-33.

Proposal 96-10: USMARC Character Set Issues and Mapping to Unicode/UCS. Dated May 24, 1996, revised: July 22, 1996. Document and appendix are available from the Library of Congress server: URL: gopher://marvel.loc.gov: 70/00/.listarch/usmarc/96-10.doc and URL: gopher://marvel.loc.gov: 70/00/.listarch/usmarc/96-10.app.

Rabenstein, Bernard Hugo. "A Survey on the Use of Alphabetical Forms in Author and/or Title Headings in the Catalogs of Israeli Libraries." Master's Thesis, Catholic University of America, 1970.

Reardon-Anderson, J. *RLIN/CJK: The First Year.* New York: C. V. Starr East Asian Library, Columbia University, March 1985. (Unpublished paper, available from Distribution Services Center, RLG).

Relative Index to the Weine Classification Scheme for Judaica Libraries. 3d edition. Revised by Judith S. Greenblatt, Toby Rossner, and Edythe Wolf. New York: AJL, 1996.

Rosenthal, Avram. "Experiences at the Hebrew University Library in Jerusalem." *ALA Bulletin* 51 (February 15,1957), 111-15.

Royal Geographical Society. *Alphabets of Foreign Languages Transcribed English, According to the RGS II System,* by E. Gleichen and J. H. Reynolds. London: 1921, 67 f. "Hebrew," revised and printed as insert, 1925.

Rozental, Anna, and P. Rozental. *Vi azoy darf men funandershteln bikher in di bibliotekn.* Kiev: Melukhe-Farlag, Yidsektsye, 1921, (Kultur-Lige. Populer-Visnshaft-likhe bibliothek. Bibliotek-visn, 1).

Schmelzer, Menahem. "Book Review" of Elazar, David H., and Elazar, Daniel J., *A Classification System for Libraries of Judaica. Conservative Judaism* 23 (4) (Summer 1969), 87-88.

Schmelzer, Menahem. "Guides to the Perplexed in the Wilderness of Hebraica: From Historical to Contemporary Bibliographies and Catalogs of Hebraica." *Harvard Library Bulletin* 6 (2) (Spring 1995), 9-23.

Seder ha-miḳtso'ot be-mada'ei ha-yahadut. Jerusalem: Hebrew University, Jewish National and University Library, 1927.

Seder ha-miḳtso'ot be-mada'ei ha-yahadut. 3d ed. Jerusalem: Hebrew University, Jewish National and University Library, 1968.

Seder ha-miḳtso'ot be-mada'ei ha-yahadut. 4th ed. Jerusalem: Hebrew University, Jewish National and University Library, 1981.

Simon, Rachel. "Contributing Hebrew Name Headings to NACO: A Participant's View." *Judaica Librarianship* 8 (1-2) (Spring 1993-Winter 1994), 61-68.

Smith-Yoshimura, Karen. "Sidebar 9: RLIN'S JACKPHY-Plus Script Development." In: Michalko, James, and John Haeger. "The Research Libraries Group." *Library Hi-Tech* 12 (2) (1994), 25-29.

Spalding, C. Sumner. "Romanization Reexamined." *Library Resources & Technical Services* 21 (1) (Winter 1977), 3-12.

Strout, Ruth French. "The Development of the Catalog and Cataloging Codes." *Library Quarterly* 26 (October 1956), 254-75.

Stuhlman, Daniel D. *Library of Congress Subject Headings for Judaica.* Chicago: BYLS Press, 1982.

Stuhlman, Daniel D. *Library of Congress Subject Headings for Judaica.* 3rd ed. Chicago: BYLS Press, 1988.

Subject Headings for a Judaica Library. 4th edition. Revised by Mildred Kurland and Mae Weine. New York: AJL, 1982.

Suiter, David E. "Establishing Uniform Headings for the Sacred Scriptures: A Persistent Issue in Hebraica-Judaica Cataloging," *Judaica Librarianship* 9 (1-2) (1996), 83-85.

Tishbi, Peretz. ["Cutter Book Numbers Adapted to Hebrew Characters."] *Yad Lakore* 5 (January-March 1958), 20-36; in Hebrew.

Tseng, Sally C. *LC Romanization Tables and Cataloging Policies.* Metuchen, NJ: Scarecrow Press, 1990, 63-78.

U.S. Board of [on] Geographic Names. *Transliteration Guide.* Washington, D.C.: 1961.

Unicode Consortium, *The Unicode Standard, Version 2.0.* Reading, MA: Addison-Wesley, 1996.

Universal Jewish Encyclopedia. New York: Universal Jewish Encyclopedia, 1939-1943. Table, I.202.

"Ha-Universiṭah ha- ʻivrit bi-Yerushalayim." *The Hebrew University, Jerusalem, Its History and Development.* [Jerusalem: Haaretz Press, 1939], 108.

USMARC Specifications for Record Structure, Character Sets and Exchange Media. Prepared by Network Development and MARC Standards Office. 1994 ed. Washington, D.C.: Cataloging Distribution Service, Library of Congress, 1994.

"Vaʻad ha-lashon ha-ʻivrit be-erets yisra'el. [Rules For the Unpointed Script.] " *Leshonenu* 16 (1948); in Hebrew.

Vernon, Elizabeth. *Decision-Making for Automation: Hebrew and Arabic Script Materials in the Automated Library.* Urbana: University of Illinois, Graduate School of Library and Information Science, 1996. (Occasional Papers, no. 205).

Vernon, Elizabeth. "Hebrew and Arabic Script Materials in the Automated Library: the United States Scene." *Cataloging & Classification Quarterly* 14 (1) (1991), 49-67.

Walfish, Barry. "Hebrew and Yiddish Personal Name Authorities Under AACR2. *Cataloging & Classification Quarterly* 3(4) (Summer 1983), 51-64.

Weinberg, Bella Hass. "The Cataloging of Jewish Liturgy by the Library of Congress: A Critique." *Judaica Librarianship* 1 (2) (Spring 1984), 70-74.

Weinberg, Bella Hass. "Compilations of Library of Congress Subject Headings for Judaica: Comparison, Evaluation, and Recommendations. *Judaica Librarianship* 5 (1) (Spring 1989-Winter 1990), 36-40.

Weinberg, Bella Hass. "Cutter J4: Tampering with the Library of Congress Classification for Judaica." *Judaica Librarianship* 3 (1-2) (1986-1987), 45-48.

Weinberg, Bella Hass. "From Copy Cataloging to Derived Bibliographic Records: Cataloging and Its Automation in American Judaica Research Libraries from the Sixties Through the Eighties." *Judaica Librarianship* 4 (2) (Spring 1988-Winter 1989), 118-21.

Weinberg, Bella Hass. "Deweineazar: *Dewey Decimal Classification. 200 Religion Class: reprinted from Edition 20 of the Dewey Decimal Classification...with a revised and expanded index, and manual notes from Edition 20.* Albany, NY: Forest Press, a division of OCLC, 1989. viii, 191 p. ISBN 0-910608-43-1. $15. LCCN 89-27221." *Judaica Librarianship* 6 (1-2) (Spring 1991-Winter 1002), 120-21.

Weinberg, Bella Hass. "Hebraic Authorities: A Historical-Theoretical Perspective." *Judaica Librarianship* 8 (1-2) (Spring 1993-Winter 1994), 45-55.

Weinberg, Bella Hass. "Hebraica Cataloging and Classification." In *Cataloging and Classification of Non-Western Material: Concerns, Issues and Practices.* Edited by Mohammed M. Aman. Phoenix, AZ: Oryx Press, 1980. LCCN 89-27221." *Judaica Librarianship* 6 (1-2) (Spring 1991-Winter 1992), 120-21.

Weinberg, Bella Hass. "*Hebrew Subject Headings.* Developed by the Hebrew Classification and Cataloging Department, Wurzweiler Central Library, Bar-Ilan University: Shlomo Rotenberg, Shifra Liebman, Gita Hoffman, Sara Schacham, David Wil.Ramat Gan, Israel: June 1992. 2 vols. (798; 435 pp.) $400." *Judaica Librarianship* 7 (1-2) (Spring 1992-Winter 1993), 64-86.

Weinberg, Bella Hass. "The Hidden Classification in the Library of Congress Subject Headings for Judaica." *Library Resources and Technical Services* 37 (4) (October 1993), 369-79.

Weinberg, Bella Hass. "JEWS—DASH: Library of Congress Subject Headings for Judaica: A, Methodology for Analysis." *Judaica Librarianship* 2 (1-2) (Spring 1985), 20-25, 40.

Weinberg, Bella Hass. "Judaica Classification Schemes for Synagogue and School Libraries: A Structural Analysis." *Judaica Librarianship* 1(1) (Fall 1983), 26-30.

Weinberg, Bella Hass. "Judaica and Hebraica Cataloging: Anglo-American Traditions." *Judaica Librarianship* 6 (1-2) (Spring 1991-Winter 1992), 13-23.

Weinberg, Bella Hass. "Non-Roman Scripts in The Library of the the Future." Lecture given at Brandeis University, Waltham, Massachusetts, March 11, 1996.

Weinberg, Bella Hass. Proposed Hebraic Character Set for the Research Libraries Information Network. March 1985 (typescript).

Weinberg, Bella Hass. "Transliteration in Documentation." *Journal of Documentation* 21 (March 1974), 18-31.

Weinberg, Werner. "A History of Hebrew *Plene* Spelling," Part 1-6. *Hebrew Union College Annual* 46-50 (1975-1980).

Weinberg, Werner. "Transliteration and Transcription of Hebrew." *Hebrew Union College Annual* 40-41 (1969-1970), 31-32.

Weine, Mae. *Weine Classification Scheme for Judaica Libraries.* 5th ed. Camden, NJ: Synagogue, School and Center Division, Association of Jewish Libraries, 1969; relative index by Anita Loeb, Philadelphia, 1972.

Weine, Mae. *Weine Classification Scheme for Judaica Libraries.* 6th ed. Camden, NJ, Synagogue, School and Center Division, Association of Jewish Libraries, 1975.

Weine, Mae. *Weine Classification Scheme for Judaica Libraries.* 7th ed. [Oak Park]: Distributed by Synagogue, School and Center Division, Association of Jewish Libraries, 1982.

Weine, Mae. *Weine Classification Scheme for Judaica Libraries.* 8th ed. Revised by Judith S. Greenblatt, Rachel Glasser, Edythe Wolf, and Mae Weine. NewYork: AJL, 1995.

Weinreich, Uriel. *College Yiddish.* New York:YIVO, 1949, p. 26: *Romanization of Yiddish.* New York: American National Standards Institute, 1978. (BSR Z 39.38)

Weinreich, Uriel, ed. *The Field of Yiddish.* New York: Linguistic Circle of New York, 1954, vi-vii.

Weinreich, Uriel. *Modern English-Yiddish Yiddish-English Dictionary.* New York: YIVO and McGraw-Hill, 1968, xx-xxv.

Wellisch, Hans H.. *The Conversion of Scripts—Its Nature, History, and Utilization.* New York: John Wiley & Sons, 1978.

Wellisch, Hans H. "The Exchange of Bibliographic Data in Non-Roman Scripts." *UNESCO Journal of Information Science, Librarianship & Archives Administration* 2 (1) (Jan.-Mar. 1980), 13-21.

Wellisch, Hans H. *Kelale ha-sidur ha-alefbeti.* Added t.p.: Filing Rules. Jerusalem: Centre for Public Libraries, 1966, [v-vi].

Wellisch, Hans H. "Multiscript and Multilingual Bibliographic Control: Alternatives to Romanization." *Library Resources & Technical Services* 22 (2) (Spring 1978), 179-90.

Wellisch, Hans H. "Script Conversion and Bibliographic Control of Documents in Dissimilar Scripts: Problems and Alternatives." *International Library Review* 10 (3) (1978), 3-22.

Wellisch, Hans H. "Script Conversion Practices in the World's Libraries." *International Library Review* 8 (1976), 55-84.

Wolf, Johann Christophe. *Bibliotheca hebraea...* Hamburgi: Christian Liebezeit, 1715-33.

Wolfson. "Hebrew Card Production from RLIN Records at the Klau Library." *Judaica Librarianship* 8 (1-2) (1993-1994), 36-39.

Wunder, Meir. ["Religious Libraries and Their Problems"]. *Yad Lakore* 8 (March 1967), 73-79; in Hebrew.

YIVO. *Takones fun yidishn oysleyg.* Vilna: YIVO, 1937.

YIVO Institute for Jewish Research. *The Yiddish Catalog and Authority File of the YIVO Library*, edited by Zachary M. Baker and Bella Hass Weinberg. Boston: G. K. Hall, 1990. 5 vols.

Zafren, Herbert C. "Arranging Your Books." *Studies in Bibliography and Booklore* 4 (June 1959), 3-20.

Zafren, Herbert C. [Letter]. *AJL Bulletin* 4 (1) (Dec. 1969), 4.

Zipin, Amnon. "Romanized Hebrew Script in the Online Catalog at the Ohio State University Libraries." *Judaica Librarianship* 1 (2) (Spring 1984), 53-57.

INDEX